Responsive Web Design for Beginners

Learn HTML, CSS
Development Step by Step

By Laurence Lars Svekis

Dedicated to
Alexis and Sebastian
Thank you for your support

For more content and to learn more, visit

https://basescripts.com/

Source Code on GitHub

https://github.com/lsvekis/Responsive-Web-Design-for-Beginners

Introduction to Responsive Web Design

Welcome to your journey into modern web development! In this first chapter, we'll introduce you to the core concepts and tools behind Responsive Web Design (RWD), setting the stage for everything that follows. You'll gain an understanding of why designing for every device is essential, how the web has evolved to prioritize mobile-first approaches, and an overview of the HTML5 and CSS3 technologies that form the backbone of contemporary web design.

What is Responsive Web Design (RWD)?

Responsive Web Design is an approach to web development that ensures a website's layout, images, and user interface adapt fluidly to the screen size and orientation of the device on which it's viewed. Rather than designing separate websites for mobile, tablet, and desktop, RWD uses flexible grids, fluid images, and media queries to create a single, cohesive experience that works on all devices.

Key Points:

- **Flexible Layouts:** Utilize percentages, relative units, and CSS Grid/Flexbox for layouts that adjust dynamically.
- **Fluid Images:** Ensure that images scale within their containers, preventing overflow and distortion.
- **Media Queries:** Apply CSS rules conditionally based on device characteristics (e.g., screen width).

Why is Responsive Web Design Important?

In today's digital landscape, users access websites from a multitude of devices—smartphones, tablets, laptops, and desktops. Responsive Web Design is important because it:

- **Enhances User Experience:** A responsive site automatically adjusts to offer a comfortable viewing experience, reducing the need for zooming or horizontal scrolling.
- **Improves Accessibility:** With a consistent design across devices, content is easier to access for all users, including those with disabilities.
- **Boosts SEO:** Search engines favor websites that perform well on mobile devices. Responsive design is a key ranking factor in Google's algorithm.
- **Saves Time and Resources:** Instead of maintaining separate sites for different devices, you manage a single, unified codebase.

How the Web Has Evolved to Be Mobile-First

Over the past decade, the web has shifted from a desktop-centric medium to one dominated by mobile devices. This evolution has been driven by several factors:

- **Increased Mobile Usage:** The majority of users now access the internet via smartphones and tablets.
- **Faster Mobile Networks:** Advances in mobile technology have made it possible to deliver rich content quickly on the go.
- **User Expectations:** Modern users expect seamless, intuitive experiences regardless of the device.
- **Search Engine Prioritization:** Google and other search engines now index the mobile version of a website first, making mobile optimization critical for SEO.

This mobile-first mindset has reshaped web design, ensuring that the smallest, most constrained devices are considered from the outset.

Overview of HTML5 and CSS3

At the heart of modern web development are HTML5 and CSS3. These technologies provide the structure and styling for your website:

- **HTML5:**

- Provides semantic elements (e.g., `<header>`, `<nav>`, `<main>`, `<footer>`) that improve the clarity and accessibility of your content.
- Supports multimedia elements like `<video>` and `<audio>`, and interactive elements such as forms and APIs.

- **CSS3:**
  - Introduces powerful styling features such as Flexbox and Grid for responsive layouts.
  - Enables advanced visual effects with transitions, animations, and media queries.
  - Allows for the creation of scalable, dynamic designs that adjust to various screen sizes and devices.

Together, HTML5 and CSS3 form a solid foundation for building responsive, engaging, and accessible websites.

Tools Needed

Before you begin, here are the essential tools you'll need throughout this book:

- **Text Editor:**
  Choose a code editor that suits your workflow (e.g., Visual Studio Code, Sublime Text, or Atom). These editors offer features like syntax highlighting, auto-completion, and integrated terminal support.
- **Browser:**
  Modern browsers such as Google Chrome, Mozilla Firefox, or Microsoft Edge are essential. They not only render your website but also provide developer tools for debugging and performance testing.
- **Developer Tools:**
  Use browser developer tools (like Chrome DevTools) to inspect elements, simulate different screen sizes, debug CSS/JavaScript, and test responsive behavior in real time.

How to Use This Book

This book is designed to take you from the basics to advanced techniques in responsive web design. Here's how to make the most of it:

1. **Follow the Chapters Sequentially:**
   Each chapter builds upon the previous one. Start with foundational topics and progress to more complex concepts.

2. **Practice the Code Examples:**
   Every chapter includes practical code snippets and hands-on exercises. Experiment with the examples to reinforce your understanding.

3. **Complete the Exercises:**
   Coding exercises provide step-by-step instructions and complete code samples. They are designed to help you apply what you've learned in real-world scenarios.

4. **Test and Debug:**
   Use the recommended developer tools to test your designs on various devices and screen sizes. Debug any issues and iterate on your designs.

5. **Explore Additional Resources:**
   Each chapter includes tips and recommended resources. Don't hesitate to explore these further to deepen your knowledge.

6. **Apply Your Skills:**
   As you progress, you'll build a complete responsive website. Use this project as a portfolio piece and a practical application of your new skills.

Conclusion

In this introductory chapter, we've laid the groundwork for your journey into responsive web design. You now understand what Responsive Web Design is, why it's vital in today's mobile-first world, and how HTML5 and CSS3 enable you to create dynamic, adaptable websites. With the right tools and a clear roadmap provided in this book, you're ready to start building websites that look and perform beautifully on any device.

Chapter 1: Getting Started with HTML5

Detailed Outline

1. **Introduction to HTML5**
   - Overview of HTML5 and its evolution
   - Importance of HTML5 in modern web development
   - Learning objectives for the chapter

2. **The Structure of an HTML Document**
   - The DOCTYPE declaration and its purpose
   - The `<html>` element and language attributes
   - The `<head>` and `<body>` sections
   - Essential metadata and viewport configuration

3. **Basic HTML Elements**
   - **Headings and Paragraphs:** Understanding `<h1>` to `<h6>` and `<p>`
   - **Lists:** Differentiating between unordered (`<ul>`) and ordered (`<ol>`) lists, and using `<li>`
   - **Hyperlinks:** Creating clickable links with the `<a>` element

4. **Adding Images and Multimedia**
   - **Images:** Using `<img>` and the importance of the `alt` attribute
   - **Audio and Video:** Embedding audio with `<audio>` and video with `<video>`
   - **Media Alternatives:** Overview of `<figure>` and `<figcaption>` for contextual descriptions

5. **Forms and Input Fields**
   - **Basic Form Structure:** The `<form>` element and its attributes
   - **Input Types:** Text, email, number, date, and textarea fields

Chapter Content

1. Introduction to HTML5

HTML (HyperText Markup Language) is the foundation of web development. With the release of HTML5, web pages became more interactive and accessible, supporting modern multimedia, better semantic structure, and improved performance on mobile devices. In this chapter, you will learn the basics of HTML5 including how to structure a document, create content with various elements, embed multimedia, and build accessible forms. By the end of this chapter, you'll be ready to create your first responsive web page.

Learning Objectives:

- Understand what HTML5 is and why it's essential.
- Learn the standard structure of an HTML document.
- Get familiar with basic elements such as headings, paragraphs, lists, links, images, and multimedia.

- Build simple forms and learn best practices for writing semantic HTML.

2. The Structure of an HTML Document

Every HTML document follows a standard structure that includes several essential components:

The DOCTYPE Declaration

The document begins with a DOCTYPE declaration, which informs the browser that you are using HTML5:

```
<!DOCTYPE html>
```

This declaration ensures your page is rendered in standards mode.

The `<html>` Element and Language Attributes

The `<html>` tag encloses the entire HTML document. Specifying the language using the `lang` attribute improves accessibility:

```
<html lang="en">
  <!-- Content goes here -->
</html>
```

The `<head>` and `<body>` Sections

- **`<head>`:** Contains metadata such as the document title, character encoding, links to stylesheets, and other resources.
- **`<body>`:** Contains all the content that is displayed to the user (text, images, forms, etc.).

A basic HTML5 document structure looks like this:

```
<!DOCTYPE html>
<html lang="en">
<head>
  <meta charset="UTF-8">
  <meta name="viewport"
content="width=device-width, initial-
scale=1.0">
  <title>Basic HTML5 Document</title>
</head>
<body>
  <h1>Hello, HTML5!</h1>
```

```
<p>This is a basic HTML5 document
structure.</p>
</body>
</html>
```
This example demonstrates a complete, minimal HTML document.

3. Basic HTML Elements

Headings and Paragraphs

Headings (`<h1>` to `<h6>`) define the hierarchy of content, and paragraphs (`<p>`) are used for blocks of text.

```
<h1>Main Heading</h1>
<p>This is a paragraph under the main
heading.</p>
```

Lists: Unordered and Ordered

Unordered Lists (`<ul>`):

```
<ul>
  <li>Item One</li>
  <li>Item Two</li>
  <li>Item Three</li>
</ul>
```

Ordered Lists (`<ol>`):

```
<ol>
  <li>First Step</li>
  <li>Second Step</li>
  <li>Third Step</li>
</ol>
```

Lists help in organizing items clearly for the user.

Hyperlinks

Links are created using the `<a>` tag, which navigates users to different pages or sections.

```
<a href="https://www.example.com"
target="_blank">Visit Example.com</a>
```

The `target="_blank"` attribute ensures the link opens in a new tab.

4. Adding Images and Multimedia

Images

The `<img>` tag embeds images in your webpage. Always include the `alt` attribute for accessibility.

```
<img src="image.jpg" alt="A descriptive
text" width="300">
```

Embedding Audio and Video

Audio Example:

```
<audio controls>
  <source src="audio.mp3"
type="audio/mpeg">
  Your browser does not support the audio
element.
</audio>
```

Video Example:

```
<video width="320" height="240" controls>
  <source src="video.mp4" type="video/mp4">
  Your browser does not support the video
tag.
</video>
```

These elements provide built-in controls for playback.

Figures and Captions

For images that need context, use `<figure>` and `<figcaption>`:

```
<figure>
  <img src="landscape.jpg" alt="Beautiful
Landscape">
  <figcaption>A beautiful view of the
mountains during sunset.</figcaption>
</figure>
```

This grouping enhances accessibility and semantic clarity.

5. Forms and Input Fields

Forms allow users to send data to a server. HTML5 provides various input types to streamline user interaction.

Basic Form Structure

A simple form is created using the `<form>` element:

```
<form action="/submit" method="post">
  <label for="name">Name:</label>
```

```
  <input type="text" id="name"
name="user_name" required>
  <input type="submit" value="Submit">
</form>
```
This form includes a text input and a submit button. The `required` *attribute ensures the field is not left empty.*

Multiple Input Types

HTML5 introduces specific input types:

Email:
```
<input type="email" id="email"
name="user_email" required>
```
Number:
```
<input type="number" id="quantity"
name="quantity" min="1" max="10">
```
Date:
```
<input type="date" id="bday"
name="birthday">
```
Textarea for Multiline Text:
```
<textarea id="message"
name="message"></textarea>
```
These input types help with built-in validation and user experience.

Labeling for Accessibility

Using `<label>` tags binds text to the corresponding form element, enhancing usability:
```
<label for="email">Email:</label>
<input type="email" id="email"
name="user_email">
```
6. Best Practices for Semantic HTML

Semantic HTML uses elements that clearly describe their meaning in a human- and machine-readable way.

What is Semantic HTML?

Semantic elements not only define how the content looks but also describe its role. This is beneficial for:

- **Accessibility:** Screen readers rely on semantic elements to help visually impaired users.

16

- **SEO:** Search engines use semantic markup to better understand your content.
- **Maintainability:** Clear structure makes your code easier to read and update.

Key Semantic Elements

- **`<header>`:** Contains introductory content or navigation links.
- **`<nav>`:** Groups primary navigation links.
- **`<main>`:** Encloses the main content unique to the document.
- **`<section>` and `<article>`:** Organize content into thematic groups or standalone pieces.
- **`<aside>`:** Represents supplementary content or sidebars.
- **`<footer>`:** Contains footer information and related links.

Example of Semantic Markup:

```
<body>
  <header>
    <h1>My Website</h1>
    <nav>
      <a href="#home">Home</a>
      <a href="#about">About</a>
    </nav>
  </header>
  <main>
    <section>
      <article>
        <h2>Welcome to My Site</h2>
        <p>This is the main content of the
website.</p>
      </article>
    </section>
  </main>
  <aside>
```

```
  <p>Related information or
advertisements.</p>
  </aside>
  <footer>
    <p>&copy; 2025 My Website. All rights
reserved.</p>
  </footer>
</body>
```
This structure ensures that each part of your page is meaningful and accessible.

7. Conclusion and Next Steps

In this chapter, you have learned:

- The essential structure of an HTML5 document.
- How to use basic elements like headings, paragraphs, lists, and links.
- Methods for embedding images, audio, and video.
- How to build accessible forms with various input types.
- The importance of semantic HTML for SEO and accessibility.

Practice Exercises:

Work through the provided code snippets and exercises to reinforce your understanding. Test your skills by creating your own web page using the concepts learned in this chapter.

25 Code Snippets and Examples

Below are 25 individual HTML5 code snippets that introduce basic elements and concepts:

Basic HTML5 Document Structure

```
<!DOCTYPE html>
<html lang="en">
<head>
  <meta charset="UTF-8">
  <meta name="viewport"
content="width=device-width, initial-
scale=1.0">
  <title>Basic HTML5 Document</title>
```

```
</head>
<body>
  <h1>Hello, HTML5!</h1>
  <p>This is a basic HTML5 document
structure.</p>
</body>
</html>
```

1. *Explanation:* Demonstrates the minimum structure of an HTML5 document, including the DOCTYPE, `<html>`, `<head>`, and `<body>` tags.

HTML5 DOCTYPE Declaration

```
<!DOCTYPE html>
<html>
<!-- Content here -->
</html>
```

2. *Explanation:* The `<!DOCTYPE html>` declaration tells the browser to render the document in standards mode.

Defining the Language Attribute

```
<html lang="en">
  <!-- Content -->
</html>
```

3. *Explanation:* Setting `lang="en"` helps search engines and screen readers understand the primary language of your content.

Headings and Paragraphs

```
<h1>Main Heading</h1>
<p>This is a paragraph under the main
heading.</p>
```

4. *Explanation:* Illustrates use of `<h1>` for headings and `<p>` for paragraphs.

Unordered List Example

```
<ul>
  <li>Item One</li>
  <li>Item Two</li>
  <li>Item Three</li>
```

```
</ul>
```

5. *Explanation:* Uses an unordered list (`<ul>`) with list items (`<li>`) for bullet-point content.

Ordered List Example

```
<ol>
  <li>First Step</li>
  <li>Second Step</li>
  <li>Third Step</li>
</ol>
```

6. *Explanation:* Displays a numbered list using `<ol>`.

Creating a Hyperlink

```
<a href="https://www.example.com"
target="_blank">Visit Example.com</a>
```

7. *Explanation:* An anchor tag `<a>` creates a clickable link; `target="_blank"` opens it in a new tab.

Inserting an Image

```
<img src="image.jpg" alt="A descriptive
text" width="300">
```

8. *Explanation:* The `<img>` tag embeds an image; `alt` provides accessibility text.

Embedding Audio

```
<audio controls>
  <source src="audio.mp3"
type="audio/mpeg">
  Your browser does not support the audio
element.
</audio>
```

9. *Explanation:* Uses the `<audio>` element to include sound with built-in controls.

Embedding Video

```
<video width="320" height="240" controls>
  <source src="video.mp4" type="video/mp4">
  Your browser does not support the video
tag.
</video>
```

10. *Explanation:* The `<video>` element lets you embed video content with controls.

Basic HTML Form with a Text Input

```
<form action="/submit" method="post">
  <label for="name">Name:</label>
  <input type="text" id="name"
name="user_name">
  <input type="submit" value="Submit">
</form>
```

11. *Explanation:* This form contains a text input and a submit button. Labels improve accessibility.

Email Input Field

```
<form action="/subscribe" method="post">
  <label for="email">Email:</label>
  <input type="email" id="email"
name="user_email" required>
  <input type="submit" value="Subscribe">
</form>
```

12. *Explanation:* The `type="email"` input validates email addresses automatically.

Number Input Field

```
<form>
  <label for="quantity">Quantity:</label>
  <input type="number" id="quantity"
name="quantity" min="1" max="10">
</form>
```

13. *Explanation:* Allows users to input numbers within a specified range.

Date Input Field

```
<form>
  <label for="bday">Birthday:</label>
  <input type="date" id="bday"
name="birthday">
</form>
```

14. *Explanation:* Provides a date picker for selecting dates.

Semantic Header Element

```
<header>
  <h1>My Website</h1>
  <nav>
    <a href="#home">Home</a>
    <a href="#about">About</a>
  </nav>
</header>
```

    15. *Explanation:* Uses the `<header>` tag for top-of-page content including navigation.

Semantic Navigation Element

```
<nav>
  <ul>
    <li><a href="index.html">Home</a></li>
    <li><a href="services.html">Services</a></li>
    <li><a href="contact.html">Contact</a></li>
  </ul>
</nav>
```

    16. *Explanation:* The `<nav>` element defines a section of navigation links.

Semantic Main Content Element

```
<main>
  <article>
    <h2>Article Title</h2>
    <p>Article content goes here.</p>
  </article>
</main>
```

    17. *Explanation:* `<main>` wraps the primary content, and `<article>` represents an independent piece.

Semantic Footer Element

```
<footer>
  <p>&copy; 2025 My Website. All rights reserved.</p>
</footer>
```

18. *Explanation:* The `<footer>` tag is used for footer information at the bottom of the page.

Section Element for Grouping Content

```
<section>
  <h2>Section Title</h2>
  <p>Content within a section.</p>
</section>
```

19. *Explanation:* `<section>` is used to group related content under a common theme.

Article Element for Self-contained Content

```
<article>
  <h2>News Article</h2>
  <p>Details about a recent event.</p>
</article>
```

20. *Explanation:* The `<article>` tag is ideal for content that could stand alone, such as blog posts.

Aside Element for Sidebar Content

```
<aside>
  <h3>Related Links</h3>
  <ul>
    <li><a href="#">Link 1</a></li>
    <li><a href="#">Link 2</a></li>
  </ul>
</aside>
```

21. *Explanation:* `<aside>` is used for tangential content like sidebars or callouts.

Combining Semantic Elements

```
<body>
  <header>
    <h1>Website Title</h1>
  </header>
  <nav>
    <a href="#home">Home</a>
    <a href="#services">Services</a>
  </nav>
  <main>
```

```html
<section>
  <h2>Welcome</h2>
  <p>Introduction text here.</p>
</section>
  </main>
  <aside>
    <p>Side note or advertisement.</p>
  </aside>
  <footer>
    <p>Contact info and copyright.</p>
  </footer>
</body>
```

22. *Explanation:* Demonstrates how to structure an entire page with semantic elements.

Figure and Figcaption for Images with Description

```html
<figure>
  <img src="landscape.jpg" alt="Beautiful Landscape">
  <figcaption>A beautiful view of the mountains during sunset.</figcaption>
</figure>
```

23. *Explanation:* The `<figure>` and `<figcaption>` elements allow you to associate a caption with an image.

Multiple Input Types in One Form

```html
<form>
  <label for="username">Username:</label>
  <input type="text" id="username" name="username">
  <label for="age">Age:</label>
  <input type="number" id="age" name="age" min="1">
  <label for="dob">Date of Birth:</label>
  <input type="date" id="dob" name="dob">
  <input type="submit" value="Register">
</form>
```

24. *Explanation:* Combines various input types (text, number, date) to create a multi-field form.

Embedding External Content with an iframe

```
<iframe src="https://www.example.com"
width="600" height="400" title="Embedded
Website">
    Your browser does not support iframes.
</iframe>
```

25. *Explanation:* The `<iframe>` tag embeds another HTML page into your current document.

25 Coding Exercises with Full Code and Explanations

Each exercise below includes a task, complete sample code, and a detailed explanation.

Exercise 1: Create a Basic HTML Page

Task: Create an HTML page with a title, heading, and paragraph.

```
<!DOCTYPE html>
<html lang="en">
<head>
  <meta charset="UTF-8">
  <meta name="viewport"
content="width=device-width, initial-
scale=1.0">
  <title>My First Page</title>
</head>
<body>
  <h1>Welcome to My Website</h1>
  <p>This is my first HTML page. I am
learning HTML5!</p>
</body>
</html>
```

1. *Explanation:* This exercise reinforces the basic structure of an HTML document and the use of common tags.

Exercise 2: Create a Navigation Bar
Task: Build a simple navigation bar using semantic HTML.

```
<!DOCTYPE html>
<html lang="en">
<head>
  <meta charset="UTF-8">
  <meta name="viewport"
content="width=device-width, initial-
scale=1.0">
  <title>Navigation Example</title>
</head>
<body>
  <header>
    <h1>My Website</h1>
    <nav>
      <ul>
        <li><a href="#home">Home</a></li>
        <li><a href="#about">About</a></li>
        <li><a
href="#contact">Contact</a></li>
      </ul>
    </nav>
  </header>
</body>
</html>
```

2. *Explanation:* Uses <header> and <nav> to create a
semantically correct navigation section.

Exercise 3: Create an Image Gallery Section
Task: Display three images side by side with captions using
<figure> and <figcaption>.

```
<!DOCTYPE html>
<html lang="en">
<head>
  <meta charset="UTF-8">
```

```
  <meta name="viewport"
content="width=device-width, initial-
scale=1.0">
  <title>Image Gallery</title>
  <style>
    figure { display: inline-block; margin:
10px; }
    img { width: 200px; }
  </style>
</head>
<body>
  <figure>
    <img src="image1.jpg" alt="Image 1">
    <figcaption>Caption One</figcaption>
  </figure>
  <figure>
    <img src="image2.jpg" alt="Image 2">
    <figcaption>Caption Two</figcaption>
  </figure>
  <figure>
    <img src="image3.jpg" alt="Image 3">
    <figcaption>Caption Three</figcaption>
  </figure>
</body>
</html>
```

3. *Explanation:* Demonstrates how to group images
   with captions using semantic tags.

Exercise 4: Build a Simple Contact Form

Task: Create a form that asks for the user's name, email,
and a message.

```
<!DOCTYPE html>
<html lang="en">
<head>
  <meta charset="UTF-8">
```

```html
  <meta name="viewport"
content="width=device-width, initial-
scale=1.0">
  <title>Contact Form</title>
</head>
<body>
  <h1>Contact Us</h1>
  <form action="/contact" method="post">
    <label for="name">Name:</label>
    <input type="text" id="name"
name="name" required>
    <br>
    <label for="email">Email:</label>
    <input type="email" id="email"
name="email" required>
    <br>
    <label for="message">Message:</label>
    <textarea id="message"
name="message"></textarea>
    <br>
    <input type="submit" value="Send">
  </form>
</body>
</html>
```

4. *Explanation:* This form includes multiple input types
   and a `<textarea>`, reinforcing form-building
   fundamentals.

Exercise 5: Create a Page with Multiple Sections

Task: Build an HTML page that uses `<section>`,
`<article>`, and `<aside>`.

```html
<!DOCTYPE html>
<html lang="en">
<head>
  <meta charset="UTF-8">
```

```
  <meta name="viewport"
content="width=device-width, initial-
scale=1.0">
  <title>Structured Page</title>
</head>
<body>
  <header>
    <h1>My Blog</h1>
  </header>
  <main>
    <section>
      <article>
        <h2>Article Title</h2>
        <p>This is the main content of the
article.</p>
      </article>
    </section>
    <aside>
      <h3>Sidebar</h3>
      <p>Additional info or links.</p>
    </aside>
  </main>
  <footer>
    <p>&copy; 2025 My Blog</p>
  </footer>
</body>
</html>
```

5. *Explanation:* Combines semantic elements to create a well-structured web page.

Exercise 6: Add Multimedia to a Page

Task: Embed an audio clip and a video on a single page.

```
<!DOCTYPE html>
<html lang="en">
<head>
  <meta charset="UTF-8">
```

```html
  <meta name="viewport"
content="width=device-width, initial-
scale=1.0">
  <title>Multimedia Example</title>
</head>
<body>
  <h1>Multimedia Content</h1>
  <audio controls>
    <source src="audio.mp3"
type="audio/mpeg">
    Your browser does not support audio.
  </audio>
  <br>
  <video width="320" height="240" controls>
    <source src="video.mp4"
type="video/mp4">
    Your browser does not support video.
  </video>
</body>
</html>
```

6. *Explanation:* This exercise shows how to include both audio and video using the `<audio>` and `<video>` tags.

Exercise 7: Create a List of Favorite Websites

Task: Use an unordered list to display three favorite websites with links.

```html
<!DOCTYPE html>
<html lang="en">
<head>
  <meta charset="UTF-8">
  <meta name="viewport"
content="width=device-width, initial-
scale=1.0">
  <title>Favorite Websites</title>
</head>
<body>
```

```
<h1>My Favorite Websites</h1>
<ul>
    <li><a
href="https://www.example1.com">Example
1</a></li>
    <li><a
href="https://www.example2.com">Example
2</a></li>
    <li><a
href="https://www.example3.com">Example
3</a></li>
    </ul>
</body>
</html>
```

7. *Explanation:* Reinforces the use of lists and
   hyperlinks together.

**Exercise 8: Create a Page with a Headline and
Subheadings**

Task: Use different heading levels to create a hierarchy on
the page.

```
<!DOCTYPE html>
<html lang="en">
<head>
  <meta charset="UTF-8">
  <meta name="viewport"
content="width=device-width, initial-
scale=1.0">
  <title>Heading Hierarchy</title>
</head>
<body>
  <h1>Main Title</h1>
  <h2>Section Title</h2>
  <h3>Subsection Title</h3>
  <p>Some text under the subheading.</p>
</body>
</html>
```

8. *Explanation:* Teaches the importance of proper heading structure for content hierarchy and SEO.

Exercise 9: Create a Form with Different Input Types

Task: Build a form that includes text, number, date, and email inputs.

```html
<!DOCTYPE html>
<html lang="en">
<head>
  <meta charset="UTF-8">
  <meta name="viewport"
content="width=device-width, initial-
scale=1.0">
  <title>Multi-input Form</title>
</head>
<body>
  <h1>Register</h1>
  <form>
    <label for="username">Username:</label>
    <input type="text" id="username"
name="username" required>
    <br>
    <label for="age">Age:</label>
    <input type="number" id="age"
name="age" min="1">
    <br>
    <label for="dob">Date of Birth:</label>
    <input type="date" id="dob" name="dob">
    <br>
    <label for="email">Email:</label>
    <input type="email" id="email"
name="email" required>
    <br>
    <input type="submit" value="Register">
  </form>
</body>
</html>
```

9. *Explanation:* This exercise helps practice using various input types and enforcing basic validation.

Exercise 10: Create a Simple Blog Post Layout

Task: Use semantic elements to create a blog post with a header, article, and footer.

```
<!DOCTYPE html>
<html lang="en">
<head>
  <meta charset="UTF-8">
  <meta name="viewport"
content="width=device-width, initial-
scale=1.0">
  <title>Blog Post</title>
</head>
<body>
  <header>
    <h1>My Blog</h1>
  </header>
  <article>
    <h2>Blog Post Title</h2>
    <p>Blog post content goes here.</p>
  </article>
  <footer>
    <p>Published on January 1, 2025</p>
  </footer>
</body>
</html>
```

10. *Explanation:* Shows how to use `<article>` for a blog post and structure the page semantically.

Exercise 11: Create a Page with a Sidebar

Task: Build a page with a main content area and an `<aside>` for additional information.

```
<!DOCTYPE html>
<html lang="en">
<head>
  <meta charset="UTF-8">
```

```html
  <meta name="viewport"
content="width=device-width, initial-
scale=1.0">
  <title>Page with Sidebar</title>
  <style>
    main { width: 70%; float: left; }
    aside { width: 25%; float: right;
background: #f4f4f4; padding: 10px; }
  </style>
</head>
<body>
  <main>
    <h1>Main Content</h1>
    <p>This is the main area of the
page.</p>
  </main>
  <aside>
    <h2>Sidebar</h2>
    <p>This is additional info.</p>
  </aside>
</body>
</html>
```

11. *Explanation:* Combines HTML structure with simple
CSS for layout, emphasizing the `<aside>` element.

Exercise 12: Create a Page with Embedded YouTube Video

Task: Embed a YouTube video using an `<iframe>`.

```html
<!DOCTYPE html>
<html lang="en">
<head>
  <meta charset="UTF-8">
  <meta name="viewport"
content="width=device-width, initial-
scale=1.0">
  <title>Embedded Video</title>
</head>
```

```
<body>
  <h1>Watch this Video</h1>
  <iframe width="560" height="315"
src="https://www.youtube.com/embed/dQw4w9Wg
XcQ"
          title="YouTube video player"
frameborder="0"
          allow="accelerometer; autoplay;
clipboard-write; encrypted-media;
gyroscope; picture-in-picture"
          allowfullscreen>
  </iframe>
</body>
</html>
```

12. *Explanation:* Demonstrates how to embed external video content with an iframe.

Exercise 13: Create a Page Demonstrating HTML Comments

Task: Add HTML comments to document your code.

```
<!DOCTYPE html>
<html lang="en">
<head>
  <meta charset="UTF-8">
  <meta name="viewport"
content="width=device-width, initial-
scale=1.0">
  <title>Comments Example</title>
</head>
<body>
  <!-- This is a main heading -->
  <h1>Main Heading</h1>
  <!-- Paragraph explaining the heading -->
  <p>This paragraph explains the main
heading.</p>
</body>
</html>
```

13. *Explanation:* Shows how to use comments (`<!-- -->`) to annotate HTML code.

Exercise 14: Create a Semantic Footer with Contact Information

Task: Build a footer that includes contact details.

```
<!DOCTYPE html>
<html lang="en">
<head>
  <meta charset="UTF-8">
  <meta name="viewport"
content="width=device-width, initial-
scale=1.0">
  <title>Footer Example</title>
</head>
<body>
  <footer>
    <p>Contact us at: <a
href="mailto:info@example.com">info@example
.com</a></p>
    <p>&copy; 2025 Example Inc.</p>
  </footer>
</body>
</html>
```

14. *Explanation:* Emphasizes the use of `<footer>` for concluding page content and includes a mailto link.

Exercise 15: Create a Page with a Responsive Meta Tag

Task: Include a viewport meta tag for mobile responsiveness.

```
<!DOCTYPE html>
<html lang="en">
<head>
  <meta charset="UTF-8">
  <!-- Responsive meta tag -->
  <meta name="viewport"
content="width=device-width, initial-
scale=1.0">
```

```html
    <title>Responsive Meta Tag</title>
</head>
<body>
    <h1>Responsive Design Example</h1>
    <p>This page is optimized for mobile
devices.</p>
</body>
</html>
```

15. *Explanation:* The meta viewport tag is crucial for ensuring proper scaling on mobile devices.

Exercise 16: Create a Page with a Favicon

Task: Add a favicon to your HTML page.

```html
<!DOCTYPE html>
<html lang="en">
<head>
    <meta charset="UTF-8">
    <meta name="viewport"
content="width=device-width, initial-
scale=1.0">
    <title>Favicon Example</title>
    <link rel="icon" href="favicon.ico"
type="image/x-icon">
</head>
<body>
    <h1>Welcome</h1>
    <p>Notice the favicon in the browser
tab.</p>
</body>
</html>
```

16. *Explanation:* The <link rel="icon"> tag specifies an icon for the webpage.

Exercise 17: Create a Page with an External CSS Link

Task: Link an external CSS file to style your HTML page.

```html
<!DOCTYPE html>
<html lang="en">
<head>
```

```
  <meta charset="UTF-8">
  <meta name="viewport"
content="width=device-width, initial-
scale=1.0">
  <title>External CSS Example</title>
  <link rel="stylesheet" href="styles.css">
</head>
<body>
  <h1>Styled with External CSS</h1>
  <p>This page uses an external
stylesheet.</p>
</body>
</html>
```

17. *Explanation:* Demonstrates how to include an external stylesheet using `<link>`.

Exercise 18: Create a Page with Inline Styles

Task: Apply styles directly to HTML elements using the `style` attribute.

```
<!DOCTYPE html>
<html lang="en">
<head>
  <meta charset="UTF-8">
  <meta name="viewport"
content="width=device-width, initial-
scale=1.0">
  <title>Inline Styles Example</title>
</head>
<body>
  <h1 style="color: blue; text-align:
center;">Hello, World!</h1>
  <p style="font-size: 18px;">This
paragraph is styled with inline CSS.</p>
</body>
</html>
```

18. *Explanation:* Shows how inline styling works, though external CSS is preferred for larger projects.

Exercise 19: Create a Page with a Local Navigation Menu
Task: Build a navigation menu that links to different sections within the same page.

```
<!DOCTYPE html>
<html lang="en">
<head>
  <meta charset="UTF-8">
  <meta name="viewport"
content="width=device-width, initial-
scale=1.0">
  <title>Local Navigation</title>
</head>
<body>
  <nav>
    <a href="#section1">Section 1</a> |
    <a href="#section2">Section 2</a>
  </nav>
  <section id="section1">
    <h2>Section 1</h2>
    <p>Content for section one.</p>
  </section>
  <section id="section2">
    <h2>Section 2</h2>
    <p>Content for section two.</p>
  </section>
</body>
</html>
```

19. *Explanation:* Demonstrates linking to internal page anchors using IDs.

Exercise 20: Create a Page with a Simple Table
Task: Build an HTML table that lists a few items with headers.

```
<!DOCTYPE html>
<html lang="en">
<head>
  <meta charset="UTF-8">
```

```html
  <meta name="viewport"
content="width=device-width, initial-
scale=1.0">
  <title>Simple Table</title>
</head>
<body>
  <h1>Simple Table Example</h1>
  <table border="1">
    <thead>
      <tr>
        <th>Name</th>
        <th>Age</th>
      </tr>
    </thead>
    <tbody>
      <tr>
        <td>Alice</td>
        <td>30</td>
      </tr>
      <tr>
        <td>Bob</td>
        <td>25</td>
      </tr>
    </tbody>
  </table>
</body>
</html>
```

20. *Explanation:* Introduces basic table structure with
    `<table>`, `<thead>`, `<tbody>`, and
    `<tr>`/`<th>`/`<td>` elements.

Exercise 21: Create a Page with Embedded Google Maps (iframe)

Task: Embed a Google Map into your webpage.

```html
<!DOCTYPE html>
<html lang="en">
<head>
```

```
  <meta charset="UTF-8">
  <meta name="viewport"
content="width=device-width, initial-
scale=1.0">
  <title>Google Maps Embed</title>
</head>
<body>
  <h1>Our Location</h1>
  <iframe

src="https://www.google.com/maps/embed?pb=!
1m18..."
    width="600" height="450"
style="border:0;" allowfullscreen=""
loading="lazy">
  </iframe>
</body>
</html>
```

21. *Explanation:* Uses an `<iframe>` to embed a Google Map. (Replace the `src` URL with a valid embed link.)

Exercise 22: Create a Page Using HTML Entities

Task: Use HTML entities to display special characters.

```
<!DOCTYPE html>
<html lang="en">
<head>
  <meta charset="UTF-8">
  <meta name="viewport"
content="width=device-width, initial-
scale=1.0">
  <title>HTML Entities</title>
</head>
<body>
  <p>5 &lt; 10 and 10 &gt; 5</p>
  <p>Copyright &copy; 2025</p>
</body>
```

```
</html>
```
22. *Explanation:* Demonstrates how to use HTML entities (e.g., <, >, ©) for special characters.

Exercise 23: Create a Page that Uses the <mark> Tag

Task: Highlight a portion of text using the <mark> tag.

```
<!DOCTYPE html>
<html lang="en">
<head>
  <meta charset="UTF-8">
  <meta name="viewport"
content="width=device-width, initial-
scale=1.0">
  <title>Text Highlight</title>
</head>
<body>
  <p>This is a <mark>highlighted</mark>
text example.</p>
</body>
</html>
```
23. *Explanation:* The <mark> tag is used for marking text that is of special relevance.

Exercise 24: Create a Page with a Simple HTML Comment Block

Task: Add a multi-line comment to explain a section of your code.

```
<!DOCTYPE html>
<html lang="en">
<head>
  <meta charset="UTF-8">
  <meta name="viewport"
content="width=device-width, initial-
scale=1.0">
  <title>Comment Block</title>
</head>
<body>
```

```
<!--
    This section is dedicated to displaying
user testimonials.
    More testimonials will be added later.
-->
<h1>Testimonials</h1>
<p>"This website is fantastic!" - User
A</p>
</body>
</html>
```

24. *Explanation:* Shows how multi-line comments can be used to document sections of HTML code.

Exercise 25: Create a Page with Semantic Grouping of Content

Task: Organize your content using `<header>`, `<nav>`, `<main>`, `<aside>`, and `<footer>`.

```
<!DOCTYPE html>
<html lang="en">
<head>
  <meta charset="UTF-8">
  <meta name="viewport"
content="width=device-width, initial-
scale=1.0">
  <title>Fully Structured Page</title>
</head>
<body>
  <header>
    <h1>My Website</h1>
  </header>
  <nav>
    <a href="#home">Home</a> |
    <a href="#services">Services</a> |
    <a href="#contact">Contact</a>
  </nav>
  <main>
    <section id="home">
```

```
      <h2>Welcome</h2>
      <p>Main content goes here.</p>
    </section>
  </main>
  <aside>
    <p>Side notes or additional links.</p>
  </aside>
  <footer>
    <p>&copy; 2025 My Website</p>
  </footer>
</body>
</html>
```

25. *Explanation:* This final exercise integrates all semantic elements to create a complete, accessible webpage.

25 Multiple Choice Questions with Explanations

Each question below tests your understanding of HTML5 basics. The correct answer is indicated with a full explanation.

Question 1: What is the purpose of the `<!DOCTYPE html>` declaration?

    A) It links to an external stylesheet.

    B) It indicates the document is an HTML5 document.

    C) It sets the language of the document.

    D) It creates a comment.

    Correct Answer: B

    Explanation: `<!DOCTYPE html>` tells the browser that the document follows HTML5 standards.

Question 2: Which tag is used to define the main content of an HTML document?

    A) `<section>`

    B) `<div>`

    C) `<main>`

D) `<article>`

Correct Answer: C

Explanation: The `<main>` element is designed to enclose the dominant content of the document.

Question 3: How do you set the character encoding to UTF-8 in an HTML document?

A) `<meta charset="UTF-8">`

B) `<meta encoding="utf-8">`

C) `<charset="UTF-8">`

D) `<script charset="UTF-8"></script>`

Correct Answer: A

Explanation: `<meta charset="UTF-8">` correctly sets the document's character encoding.

Question 4: Which HTML element is used for creating a hyperlink?

A) `<link>`

B) `<a>`

C) `<href>`

D) `<nav>`

Correct Answer: B

Explanation: The `<a>` element creates hyperlinks in HTML.

Question 5: What attribute should always be used with `<img>` for accessibility?

A) `src`

B) `alt`

C) `title`

D) `width`

Correct Answer: B

Explanation: The `alt` attribute provides alternative text for screen readers.

Question 6: Which element is used to embed audio content?

A) `<sound>`

B) `<audio>`

C) `<music>`

D) `<media>`

Correct Answer: B

Explanation: The `<audio>` element is used to embed sound content.

Question 7: In which section of an HTML document should the viewport meta tag be placed?

A) `<body>`
B) `<header>`
C) `<head>`
D) `<footer>`

Correct Answer: C

Explanation: The viewport meta tag is placed in the `<head>` section.

Question 8: Which of the following is a semantic element?

A) `<div>`
B) `<span>`
C) `<main>`
D) `<font>`

Correct Answer: C

Explanation: `<main>` is semantic because it conveys meaning about the content it contains.

Question 9: What is the purpose of the `<figure>` element?

A) To group inline elements.
B) To create a form container.
C) To encapsulate media along with a caption.
D) To style text.

Correct Answer: C

Explanation: `<figure>` is used to group media elements with an optional `<figcaption>`.

Question 10: Which input type is used for email addresses?

A) `type="text"`
B) `type="email"`
C) `type="number"`

D) `type="password"`

Correct Answer: B

Explanation: `type="email"` provides built-in validation for email addresses.

Question 11: What is the benefit of using semantic HTML elements?

A) They automatically style your page.

B) They improve SEO and accessibility.

C) They reduce page load time.

D) They enable advanced animations.

Correct Answer: B

Explanation: Semantic elements help search engines and screen readers understand the content better.

Question 12: Which tag is used to add a comment in HTML?

A) `<comment>`

B) `<!-- comment -->`

C) `<!-- comment -->`

D) `// comment`

Correct Answer: B

Explanation: HTML comments are added using `<!-- comment -->`.

Question 13: Which element is used to embed a video?

A) `<video>`

B) `<movie>`

C) `<media>`

D) `<embed>`

Correct Answer: A

Explanation: The `<video>` element is designed for embedding video content.

Question 14: What does the `<meta name="viewport">` tag do?

A) Links the document to a stylesheet.

B) Sets the browser viewport for responsive design.

C) Specifies the document language.

D) Embeds multimedia content.

Correct Answer: B

Explanation: It instructs the browser on how to control the page's dimensions and scaling on different devices.

Question 15: Which element should you use to group related navigation links?

A) `<group>`
B) `<nav>`
C) `<ul>`
D) `<div>`

Correct Answer: B

Explanation: The `<nav>` element semantically groups navigation links.

Question 16: Which attribute of the `<a>` tag opens the link in a new tab?

A) `rel="new"`
B) `target="_blank"`
C) `href="_blank"`
D) `newtab="true"`

Correct Answer: B

Explanation: The attribute `target="_blank"` tells the browser to open the link in a new tab.

Question 17: What is the purpose of the `<label>` element in a form?

A) To style the form.
B) To bind text to a specific form control for accessibility.
C) To add placeholders.
D) To submit the form.

Correct Answer: B

Explanation: `<label>` tags improve form accessibility by associating text with form elements.

Question 18: Which element is used for multi-line text input in a form?

A) `<input type="textarea">`
B) `<multiline>`

C) `<textarea>`
D) `<input type="text">`
Correct Answer: C

Explanation: `<textarea>` is designed for multi-line text input.

Question 19: Which tag would you use to mark up a self-contained piece of content, such as a blog post?

A) `<section>`
B) `<div>`
C) `<article>`
D) `<aside>`
Correct Answer: C

Explanation: `<article>` is used for independent, self-contained content.

Question 20: Which attribute is essential for making images accessible?

A) `src`
B) `alt`
C) `title`
D) `class`
Correct Answer: B

Explanation: The `alt` attribute describes the image for users who rely on screen readers.

Question 21: How do you specify the language of an HTML document?

A) `<html lang="en">`
B) `<meta lang="en">`
C) `<language en>`
D) `<doc lang="en">`
Correct Answer: A

Explanation: The language is set using the `lang` attribute in the `<html>` tag.

Question 22: Which element should be used to group content that is tangentially related to the main content?

A) `<footer>`
B) `<aside>`

C) `<section>`
D) `<article>`

Correct Answer: B

Explanation: `<aside>` is best used for content related to the main content but not part of it.

Question 23: What is the purpose of the `<head>` section in an HTML document?

A) To display content to the user.
B) To contain metadata and links to scripts or stylesheets.
C) To add comments.
D) To create navigation links.

Correct Answer: B

Explanation: The `<head>` element holds metadata, links, and other resources that are not directly displayed.

Question 24: Which HTML element is used to create a numbered list?

A) `<ul>`
B) `<ol>`
C) `<li>`
D) `<list>`

Correct Answer: B

Explanation: `<ol>` creates an ordered (numbered) list.

Question 25: Why is it important to use semantic HTML elements?

A) They automatically optimize your code.
B) They make your code harder to read.
C) They improve accessibility, SEO, and code clarity.
D) They are required for browser compatibility.

Correct Answer: C

Explanation: Semantic HTML elements add meaning to the content, improving accessibility and SEO while making the code easier to understand.

Chapter 2: Introduction to CSS3

Detailed Outline

1. **Introduction to CSS and Its Role in Web Development**
   - What is CSS?
   - How CSS works in conjunction with HTML
   - Benefits of using CSS (separation of content and presentation)
2. **Applying CSS: Inline, Internal, and External Styles**
   - Inline styling: pros and cons
   - Internal style sheets: using the `<style>` tag
   - External style sheets: linking with `<link>`
   - When and why to choose each method
3. **CSS Syntax and Selectors**
   - Basic CSS rule structure: selector, property, and value
   - Type, class, and ID selectors
   - Grouping and nesting selectors
   - Descendant and child selectors
4. **Colors, Backgrounds, and Text Styling**
   - Color values (named, HEX, RGB, RGBA, HSL)
   - Styling text: font properties, text alignment, and decoration
   - Background properties: background-color, background-image, background-size
5. **The CSS Box Model**
   - Understanding content, padding, border, and margin
   - Visualizing and debugging the box model
   - Using developer tools to inspect box properties
6. **CSS Units**
   - Absolute units (px, pt, cm, etc.)
   - Relative units (em, rem, %, vh, vw)

  o When to use each type for responsive design
7. **Conclusion and Next Steps**
  o Recap of key concepts
  o Practical tips for writing clean and maintainable CSS
  o Preview of upcoming chapters (e.g., advanced selectors and responsive layouts)

Chapter Content

1. Introduction to CSS and Its Role in Web Development

CSS (Cascading Style Sheets) is the language used to describe the presentation of an HTML document. It enables you to separate content (HTML) from design (CSS), making it easier to maintain and update your website's look and feel. In this chapter, you'll learn how CSS works with HTML and explore the various methods of adding styles to your web pages.

2. Applying CSS: Inline, Internal, and External Styles

There are three primary ways to add CSS to your web page:

Inline Styles:

Applied directly on an HTML element using the `style` attribute.

Example:

```
<p style="color: blue;">This text is blue.</p>
```

Internal Styles:

Defined within a `<style>` element in the `<head>` section of your HTML document.

Example:

```
<head>
  <style>
    p { color: green; }
  </style>
</head>
```

External Styles:
Placed in a separate CSS file and linked to the HTML document via a `<link>` tag.
Example:

```
<head>
  <link rel="stylesheet" href="styles.css">
</head>
```

3. CSS Syntax and Selectors

A CSS rule consists of a selector and a declaration block. The selector targets the HTML element(s), while the declaration block (inside curly braces) contains one or more declarations separated by semicolons. Each declaration includes a property and a value.
Example of a rule:

```
h1 {
  color: red;
  font-size: 2em;
}
```

Selectors Overview:

- **Type Selector:** Targets all elements of a given type (e.g., `p`, `h1`).
- **Class Selector:** Targets elements with a specific class. (e.g., `.highlight`)
- **ID Selector:** Targets an element with a specific ID. (e.g., `#header`)
- **Descendant Selector:** Targets elements within another element (e.g., `nav a`).

4. Colors, Backgrounds, and Text Styling

CSS gives you many ways to style text and backgrounds:
Colors:
Use named colors, HEX, RGB, or HSL values.
Example:

```
p { color: #333; }
```

Backgrounds:
Set solid colors or images for element backgrounds.
Example:

```
body { background-color: #f9f9f9; }
```

Text Styling:

Customize font family, size, weight, and alignment.

Example:

```
h1 { font-family: Arial, sans-serif; text-align: center; }
```

5. The CSS Box Model

Every HTML element is considered a box, which consists of:

- **Content:** The text or image inside the element.
- **Padding:** The space between the content and the border.
- **Border:** The edge around the padding (if any).
- **Margin:** The space outside the border.

Understanding the box model is key to creating well-designed layouts.

Example Visualization:

```
div {
    width: 200px;
    padding: 10px;
    border: 2px solid black;
    margin: 20px;
}
```

6. CSS Units

CSS units control how sizes are measured:

- **Absolute Units:**
  px (pixels) – Fixed size regardless of other factors.
- **Relative Units:**
  em and rem – Relative to the font-size of the element or root element.
  % – Relative to the parent element's dimensions.
  vh and vw – Relative to the viewport height and width.

Example:

```
p { font-size: 1.2rem; }
```

7. Conclusion and Next Steps

In this chapter, you have learned:

- The role of CSS in web development and its relationship with HTML.
- The different methods of adding CSS (inline, internal, external).
- CSS syntax, selectors, and how to style colors, backgrounds, and text.
- The box model and how margins, borders, padding, and content work.
- Various CSS units and when to use them.

Practice these concepts with the code snippets and exercises provided below. In the next chapter, we will build upon these fundamentals to explore more advanced CSS techniques and responsive layouts.

25 Code Snippets and Examples

Below are 25 focused code snippets that demonstrate key CSS3 concepts:

Inline Style Example

```
<p style="color: blue; font-size:
16px;">This text is blue and 16px in
size.</p>
```

1. *Explanation:* Applies CSS directly to a single element using the `style` attribute.

Internal Style Example

```
<head>
  <style>
    p { color: green; font-size: 18px; }
  </style>
</head>
<body>
  <p>This text is green and 18px in
size.</p>
</body>
```

2. *Explanation:* Defines styles within the document's head that affect all `<p>` elements.

External Style Example

```
<head>
  <link rel="stylesheet" href="styles.css">
```

```
</head>
<!-- In styles.css -->
p { color: purple; font-size: 20px; }
```
3. *Explanation:* Uses an external stylesheet to separate content from design.

Type Selector Example
```
h1 { color: red; }
```
4. *Explanation:* Targets all <h1> elements and sets their color to red.

Class Selector Example
```
.highlight { background-color: yellow; }
```
HTML:
```
<p class="highlight">This paragraph is highlighted.</p>
```
5. *Explanation:* Applies styles to elements with the class "highlight."

ID Selector Example
```
#main-title { font-size: 2.5em; }
```
HTML:

```
<h1 id="main-title">Big Heading</h1>
```
6. *Explanation:* Styles a single element with the ID "main-title."

Grouped Selector Example

```
h1, h2, h3 { font-family: 'Arial', sans-serif; }
```
7. *Explanation:* Applies the same font to multiple heading levels.

Descendant Selector Example

```
nav a { color: darkblue; text-decoration: none; }
```
8. *Explanation:* Targets all <a> elements that are descendants of a <nav> element.

Pseudo-class Example: Hover

```
a:hover { color: orange; }
```
    9. *Explanation:* Changes the link color to orange when hovered over.

Color Using HEX Value

```
p { color: #333333; }
```
    10. *Explanation:* Uses a HEX color value to style text.

Background Color Example

```
body { background-color: #f0f0f0; }
```
    11. *Explanation:* Sets a light grey background for the entire page.

Text Alignment Example

```
h1 { text-align: center; }
```
    12. *Explanation:* Centers the text within an <h1> element.

Font Family and Weight Example

```
p { font-family: 'Verdana', sans-serif;
font-weight: bold; }
```
    13. *Explanation:* Applies the Verdana font with bold text style.

Setting a Background Image

```
.banner {
  background-image: url('banner.jpg');
  background-size: cover;
}
```
    14. *Explanation:* Uses a background image that covers the entire element.

Simple CSS Transition

```
button {
  background-color: blue;
```

```css
  transition: background-color 0.3s;
}
button:hover {
  background-color: darkblue;
}
```

15. *Explanation:* Adds a smooth color transition effect to a button on hover.

Box Model Visualization: Padding

```css
.box {
  background-color: #ccc;
  padding: 20px;
}
```

16. *Explanation:* Adds 20 pixels of padding inside the element.

Box Model Visualization: Border

```css
.box {
  border: 2px solid #000;
}
```

17. *Explanation:* Applies a solid border around the element.

Box Model Visualization: Margin

```css
.box {
  margin: 30px;
}
```

18. *Explanation:* Creates 30 pixels of space outside the element.

Combined Box Model Example

```css
.container {
  width: 300px;
  padding: 10px;
  border: 1px solid #333;
  margin: 20px;
}
```

19. *Explanation:* Demonstrates the complete box model on a container element.

Using px Unit

```
p { font-size: 16px; }
```
20. *Explanation:* Sets the font size in pixels, which is an absolute unit.

Using em and rem Units

```
p { font-size: 1.2em; }
h1 { font-size: 2rem; }
```
21. *Explanation:* Uses relative units based on the current and root font sizes.

Using Percent Units

```
.progress {
  width: 75%;
  background-color: green;
}
```
22. *Explanation:* Sets the width of an element to 75% of its parent container.

Viewport Units Example (vh, vw)

```
.full-screen {
  height: 100vh;
  width: 100vw;
}
```
23. *Explanation:* Makes an element full-screen using viewport height and width.

CSS Comment Example

```
/* This is a CSS comment explaining the
following rule */
p { line-height: 1.5; }
```
24. *Explanation:* Uses comments to document CSS code.

Advanced Selector: Attribute Selector

```css
a[target="_blank"] {
  color: red;
}
```

25. *Explanation:* Styles only links that open in a new tab.

25 Coding Exercises with Full Code and Explanations

Each exercise below reinforces a key CSS3 concept.

Exercise 1: Create a Simple Webpage with External CSS

Task: Build an HTML page that links to an external stylesheet.

HTML:

```html
<!DOCTYPE html>
<html lang="en">
<head>
  <meta charset="UTF-8">
  <meta name="viewport"
content="width=device-width, initial-
scale=1.0">
  <title>External CSS Exercise</title>
  <link rel="stylesheet" href="styles.css">
</head>
<body>
  <h1>Welcome to My Site</h1>
  <p>This page is styled with external
CSS.</p>
</body>
</html>
```

styles.css:

```css
body {
  background-color: #eef;
  font-family: sans-serif;
}
h1 {
```

```
  color: navy;
}
p {
  font-size: 18px;
}
```

1. *Explanation:* This exercise demonstrates linking an external CSS file and applying basic styles.

Exercise 2: Apply Inline Styles

Task: Modify an HTML element with inline CSS to change its text color and font size.

```
<p style="color: darkgreen; font-size:
20px;">This paragraph is styled inline.</p>
```

2. *Explanation:* The `style` attribute directly applies styles to the element.

Exercise 3: Use an Internal Style Sheet

Task: Create an HTML document with a `<style>` block that styles headings and paragraphs.

```
<!DOCTYPE html>
<html lang="en">
<head>
  <meta charset="UTF-8">
  <meta name="viewport"
content="width=device-width, initial-
scale=1.0">
  <title>Internal Styles</title>
  <style>
    h1 { color: maroon; }
    p { font-size: 16px; line-height: 1.6;
}
  </style>
</head>
<body>
  <h1>Internal CSS Example</h1>
  <p>This paragraph is styled using
internal CSS.</p>
</body>
```

```
</html>
```

3. *Explanation:* Shows how to include CSS within the `<head>` using the `<style>` tag.

Exercise 4: Create a Navigation Bar Using Class Selectors

Task: Build a navigation bar and style it using a class selector.

```
<!DOCTYPE html>
<html lang="en">
<head>
  <meta charset="UTF-8">
  <meta name="viewport"
content="width=device-width, initial-
scale=1.0">
  <title>Navigation Bar</title>
  <style>
    .nav-bar {
      background-color: #333;
      padding: 10px;
      text-align: center;
    }
    .nav-bar a {
      color: white;
      margin: 0 10px;
      text-decoration: none;
    }
  </style>
</head>
<body>
  <div class="nav-bar">
    <a href="#">Home</a>
    <a href="#">About</a>
    <a href="#">Contact</a>
  </div>
</body>
</html>
```

4. *Explanation:* Uses a class selector to style a simple navigation bar.

Exercise 5: Style Text with Different Font Properties

Task: Change the font family, size, and weight for headings and paragraphs.

```
<!DOCTYPE html>
<html lang="en">
<head>
  <meta charset="UTF-8">
  <meta name="viewport"
content="width=device-width, initial-
scale=1.0">
  <title>Text Styling</title>
  <style>
    h1 { font-family: 'Georgia', serif;
font-size: 2.5em; font-weight: bold; }
    p { font-family: 'Arial', sans-serif;
font-size: 1em; }
  </style>
</head>
<body>
  <h1>Styled Heading</h1>
  <p>This paragraph is styled with
different font properties.</p>
</body>
</html>
```

5. *Explanation:* Demonstrates text styling with various font properties.

Exercise 6: Set a Background Image with Cover

Task: Apply a background image that covers the entire element.

```
<!DOCTYPE html>
<html lang="en">
<head>
  <meta charset="UTF-8">
```

```html
    <meta name="viewport"
content="width=device-width, initial-
scale=1.0">
    <title>Background Image</title>
    <style>
      .hero {
        background-image: url('hero.jpg');
        background-size: cover;
        height: 400px;
      }
    </style>
  </head>
  <body>
    <div class="hero"></div>
  </body>
</html>
```

6. *Explanation:* Uses `background-size: cover` to ensure the image fills the element.

Exercise 7: Demonstrate a CSS Transition on Hover

Task: Create a button that changes its background color smoothly when hovered.

```html
<!DOCTYPE html>
<html lang="en">
<head>
  <meta charset="UTF-8">
  <meta name="viewport"
content="width=device-width, initial-
scale=1.0">
  <title>Button Transition</title>
  <style>
    button {
      background-color: #0055aa;
      color: #fff;
      padding: 10px 20px;
      border: none;
      transition: background-color 0.3s;
```

```
      }
      button:hover {
        background-color: #003377;
      }
    </style>
  </head>
  <body>
    <button>Hover Me</button>
  </body>
</html>
```

7. *Explanation:* Applies a CSS transition to animate the background color change on hover.

Exercise 8: Visualize the Box Model with Padding

Task: Create a div with padding and a visible background color to show spacing.

```
<!DOCTYPE html>
<html lang="en">
<head>
  <meta charset="UTF-8">
  <meta name="viewport"
content="width=device-width, initial-
scale=1.0">
  <title>Padding Example</title>
  <style>
    .box {
      background-color: #ddd;
      padding: 20px;
    }
  </style>
</head>
<body>
  <div class="box">This box has
padding.</div>
</body>
</html>
```

8. *Explanation:* Visualizes the padding area inside an element.

Exercise 9: Demonstrate Borders with the Box Model

Task: Add a border to an element and observe how it affects the layout.

```
<!DOCTYPE html>
<html lang="en">
<head>
  <meta charset="UTF-8">
  <meta name="viewport"
content="width=device-width, initial-
scale=1.0">
  <title>Border Example</title>
  <style>
    .box {
      padding: 20px;
      border: 3px solid #333;
    }
  </style>
</head>
<body>
  <div class="box">This box has a
border.</div>
</body>
</html>
```

9. *Explanation:* Adds a border to show the box model's border area.

Exercise 10: Add Margin to an Element

Task: Create an element with a margin to separate it from other content.

```
<!DOCTYPE html>
<html lang="en">
<head>
  <meta charset="UTF-8">
```

```html
    <meta name="viewport"
content="width=device-width, initial-
scale=1.0">
    <title>Margin Example</title>
    <style>
      .box {
        background-color: #eef;
        margin: 30px;
        padding: 10px;
      }
    </style>
</head>
<body>
    <div class="box">This box has a margin
around it.</div>
</body>
</html>
```

10. *Explanation:* Demonstrates adding margin space outside an element.

Exercise 11: Combine Box Model Properties

Task: Create a container that uses padding, border, and margin together.

```html
<!DOCTYPE html>
<html lang="en">
<head>
    <meta charset="UTF-8">
    <meta name="viewport"
content="width=device-width, initial-
scale=1.0">
    <title>Combined Box Model</title>
    <style>
      .container {
        width: 300px;
        padding: 15px;
        border: 2px solid #555;
        margin: 25px auto;
```

```
    background-color: #fafafa;
    }
  </style>
</head>
<body>
  <div class="container">This container
combines padding, border, and margin.</div>
</body>
</html>
```

11. *Explanation:* Integrates multiple box model
    properties to demonstrate spacing.

Exercise 12: Use px, em, and rem Units

Task: Create elements with different sizing units to
compare their behavior.

```
<!DOCTYPE html>
<html lang="en">
<head>
  <meta charset="UTF-8">
  <meta name="viewport"
content="width=device-width, initial-
scale=1.0">
  <title>CSS Units</title>
  <style>
    .pixel { font-size: 16px; }
    .em { font-size: 1.5em; }
    .rem { font-size: 1.5rem; }
  </style>
</head>
<body>
  <p class="pixel">This text is sized in
pixels.</p>
  <p class="em">This text is sized in em
units.</p>
  <p class="rem">This text is sized in rem
units.</p>
</body>
```

```
</html>
```

12. *Explanation:* Compares absolute and relative sizing
    units.

Exercise 13: Create a Responsive Element Using Percentages

Task: Build a container whose width is defined by a
percentage.

```
<!DOCTYPE html>
<html lang="en">
<head>
  <meta charset="UTF-8">
  <meta name="viewport"
content="width=device-width, initial-
scale=1.0">
  <title>Responsive Container</title>
  <style>
    .responsive {
      width: 80%;
      background-color: #cce;
      margin: 0 auto;
      padding: 10px;
    }
  </style>
</head>
<body>
  <div class="responsive">This container is
80% wide relative to its parent.</div>
</body>
</html>
```

13. *Explanation:* Uses percentage-based width for a
    responsive layout.

Exercise 14: Create a Full-Screen Section with Viewport Units

Task: Design an element that covers the full viewport
height.

```
<!DOCTYPE html>
```

```
<html lang="en">
<head>
  <meta charset="UTF-8">
  <meta name="viewport"
content="width=device-width, initial-
scale=1.0">
  <title>Full-Screen Section</title>
  <style>
    .full-screen {
      height: 100vh;
      background-color: #ddd;
      display: flex;
      justify-content: center;
      align-items: center;
    }
  </style>
</head>
<body>
  <div class="full-screen">
    <h1>Full Viewport Height</h1>
  </div>
</body>
</html>
```
14. *Explanation:* Uses viewport height units (vh) to create a full-screen element.

Exercise 15: Create a CSS Rule Using a Descendant Selector

Task: Style only the links inside a specific navigation area.

```
<!DOCTYPE html>
<html lang="en">
<head>
  <meta charset="UTF-8">
  <meta name="viewport"
content="width=device-width, initial-
scale=1.0">
  <title>Descendant Selector</title>
```

```
<style>
  nav a {
    color: #0066cc;
    text-decoration: none;
  }
</style>
</head>
<body>
  <nav>
    <a href="#">Home</a>
    <a href="#">Services</a>
  </nav>
</body>
</html>
```

15. *Explanation:* Applies styles only to `<a>` tags inside a
    `<nav>` element.

Exercise 16: Use an Attribute Selector to Style Links

Task: Change the color of links that open in a new tab.

```
<!DOCTYPE html>
<html lang="en">
<head>
  <meta charset="UTF-8">
  <meta name="viewport"
content="width=device-width, initial-
scale=1.0">
  <title>Attribute Selector</title>
  <style>
    a[target="_blank"] {
      color: crimson;
    }
  </style>
</head>
<body>
  <a href="https://www.example.com"
target="_blank">External Link</a>
</body>
```

```
</html>
```

16. *Explanation:* The attribute selector targets links with `target="_blank"`.

Exercise 17: Create a Hover Effect Using Pseudo-classes

Task: Build a navigation link that changes style when hovered.

```
<!DOCTYPE html>
<html lang="en">
<head>
  <meta charset="UTF-8">
  <meta name="viewport"
content="width=device-width, initial-
scale=1.0">
  <title>Hover Effect</title>
  <style>
    a {
      color: blue;
      transition: color 0.3s;
    }
    a:hover {
      color: darkblue;
    }
  </style>
</head>
<body>
  <a href="#">Hover Over Me</a>
</body>
</html>
```

17. *Explanation:* Demonstrates the use of pseudo-class `:hover` and CSS transitions.

Exercise 18: Create a Styled Button Using External CSS

Task: Style a button with padding, border, and a background color from an external stylesheet.

HTML:

```
<!DOCTYPE html>
<html lang="en">
```

```html
<head>
  <meta charset="UTF-8">
  <meta name="viewport"
content="width=device-width, initial-
scale=1.0">
  <title>Styled Button</title>
  <link rel="stylesheet" href="button.css">
</head>
<body>
  <button>Click Me</button>
</body>
</html>
```

button.css:

```css
button {
  background-color: #28a745;
  border: none;
  color: #fff;
  padding: 12px 24px;
  font-size: 16px;
  cursor: pointer;
}
button:hover {
  background-color: #218838;
}
```

18. *Explanation:* Separates button styling into an external CSS file for clarity and reusability.

Exercise 19: Use a Class Selector to Style Multiple Elements

Task: Apply the same styling to several paragraphs using a shared class.

```html
<!DOCTYPE html>
<html lang="en">
<head>
  <meta charset="UTF-8">
```

```html
  <meta name="viewport"
content="width=device-width, initial-
scale=1.0">
  <title>Shared Class Styling</title>
  <style>
    .styled-text { color: teal; font-size:
18px; }
  </style>
</head>
<body>
  <p class="styled-text">This is the first
styled paragraph.</p>
  <p class="styled-text">This is the second
styled paragraph.</p>
</body>
</html>
```

19. *Explanation:* Uses a class to apply identical styling to multiple elements.

Exercise 20: Create a Page with a CSS Reset

Task: Include a simple CSS reset to remove default browser styles.

```html
<!DOCTYPE html>
<html lang="en">
<head>
  <meta charset="UTF-8">
  <meta name="viewport"
content="width=device-width, initial-
scale=1.0">
  <title>CSS Reset Example</title>
  <style>
    /* Simple CSS Reset */
    * {
      margin: 0;
      padding: 0;
      box-sizing: border-box;
    }
```

```
  body {
    font-family: sans-serif;
  }
  </style>
</head>
<body>
  <h1>CSS Reset in Action</h1>
  <p>Default margins and paddings are
removed.</p>
</body>
</html>
```
20. *Explanation:* Resets default styling to create a consistent baseline.

Exercise 21: Style a Form Using CSS

Task: Build a simple form and apply styling to its elements.

```
<!DOCTYPE html>
<html lang="en">
<head>
  <meta charset="UTF-8">
  <meta name="viewport"
content="width=device-width, initial-
scale=1.0">
  <title>Styled Form</title>
  <style>
    form {
      width: 300px;
      margin: 20px auto;
      padding: 15px;
      border: 1px solid #ccc;
    }
    label {
      display: block;
      margin-bottom: 5px;
    }
    input, textarea {
      width: 100%;
```

```
      margin-bottom: 10px;
      padding: 8px;
    }
  </style>
</head>
<body>
  <form>
    <label for="name">Name:</label>
    <input type="text" id="name"
name="name">
    <label for="message">Message:</label>
    <textarea id="message"
name="message"></textarea>
    <input type="submit" value="Submit">
  </form>
</body>
</html>
```

21. *Explanation:* Styles a form for a cleaner and more organized appearance.

Exercise 22: Use CSS to Create a Two-Column Layout

Task: Build a simple two-column layout using CSS floats.

```
<!DOCTYPE html>
<html lang="en">
<head>
  <meta charset="UTF-8">
  <meta name="viewport"
content="width=device-width, initial-
scale=1.0">
  <title>Two-Column Layout</title>
  <style>
    .column {
      float: left;
      width: 48%;
      margin: 1%;
      background-color: #eef;
      padding: 10px;
```

```
      }
    .clearfix::after {
      content: "";
      clear: both;
      display: table;
    }
  </style>
</head>
<body>
  <div class="clearfix">
    <div class="column">Column 1</div>
    <div class="column">Column 2</div>
  </div>
</body>
</html>
```

22. *Explanation:* Demonstrates a basic two-column layout using CSS float and clearfix techniques.

Exercise 23: Create a Styled Table

Task: Design an HTML table with custom CSS styles for borders and background colors.

```
<!DOCTYPE html>
<html lang="en">
<head>
  <meta charset="UTF-8">
  <meta name="viewport"
content="width=device-width, initial-
scale=1.0">
  <title>Styled Table</title>
  <style>
    table {
      width: 100%;
      border-collapse: collapse;
    }
    th, td {
      border: 1px solid #999;
      padding: 8px;
```

```
        text-align: left;
      }
      th {
        background-color: #f2f2f2;
      }
    </style>
  </head>
  <body>
    <table>
      <thead>
        <tr>
          <th>Name</th>
          <th>Age</th>
        </tr>
      </thead>
      <tbody>
        <tr>
          <td>Alice</td>
          <td>30</td>
        </tr>
        <tr>
          <td>Bob</td>
          <td>25</td>
        </tr>
      </tbody>
    </table>
  </body>
</html>
```

23. *Explanation:* Applies custom styles to an HTML table for improved readability.

Exercise 24: Create a CSS-Animated Element

Task: Animate a box moving from left to right using keyframes.

```
<!DOCTYPE html>
<html lang="en">
<head>
```

```html
    <meta charset="UTF-8">
    <meta name="viewport"
content="width=device-width, initial-
scale=1.0">
    <title>CSS Animation</title>
    <style>
      .animate {
        width: 50px;
        height: 50px;
        background-color: coral;
        position: relative;
        animation: slide 2s infinite
alternate;
      }
      @keyframes slide {
        from { left: 0; }
        to { left: 200px; }
      }
    </style>
</head>
<body>
    <div class="animate"></div>
</body>
</html>
```

24. *Explanation:* Uses keyframes to animate an element's horizontal movement.

Exercise 25: Create a Custom CSS Class for Reusable Button Styles

Task: Define a CSS class for buttons and apply it to multiple buttons.

```html
<!DOCTYPE html>
<html lang="en">
<head>
    <meta charset="UTF-8">
```

```
  <meta name="viewport"
content="width=device-width, initial-
scale=1.0">
  <title>Reusable Button Class</title>
  <style>
    .btn {
      background-color: #007bff;
      border: none;
      color: white;
      padding: 10px 15px;
      cursor: pointer;
      font-size: 16px;
      margin: 5px;
    }
    .btn:hover {
      background-color: #0056b3;
    }
  </style>
</head>
<body>
  <button class="btn">Button 1</button>
  <button class="btn">Button 2</button>
</body>
</html>
```

25. *Explanation:* Creates a reusable CSS class that can be applied to any button element for consistent styling.

25 Multiple Choice Questions with Full Explanations

Each question below tests your understanding of CSS3 fundamentals.

Question 1: What does CSS stand for?

    A) Creative Style Sheets

    B) Cascading Style Sheets

    C) Computer Style Syntax

D) Colorful Style Sheets

Correct Answer: B

Explanation: CSS stands for Cascading Style Sheets, which describes how HTML elements are presented.

Question 2: Which method of applying CSS is recommended for large projects?

A) Inline styles

B) Internal styles

C) External stylesheets

D) JavaScript styling

Correct Answer: C

Explanation: External stylesheets help separate content from design and are easier to maintain for large projects.

Question 3: What is the correct syntax for a CSS rule?

A) `selector { property: value; }`

B) `{ selector: property value }`

C) `property: value; selector`

D) `selector ( property: value; )`

Correct Answer: A

Explanation: The correct syntax is a selector followed by a declaration block enclosed in curly braces.

Question 4: Which selector is used to target all `<p>` elements?

A) `.p`

B) `#p`

C) `p`

D) `*p`

Correct Answer: C

Explanation: The type selector `p` selects all paragraph elements.

Question 5: How do you apply a background color of blue to the entire body?

A) `body { background-color: blue; }`

B) `* { background: blue; }`

C) `<body style="background:blue;">`

D) Both A and C

Correct Answer: D

Explanation: You can use an external/internal stylesheet (A) or inline style (C), though using CSS rules is preferred.

Question 6: Which CSS property is used to change the text color?

A) font-color

B) color

C) text-color

D) background-color

Correct Answer: B

Explanation: The `color` property changes the text color.

Question 7: What unit is considered an absolute unit in CSS?

A) em

B) rem

C) px

D) %

Correct Answer: C

Explanation: Pixels (`px`) are absolute units, while others are relative.

Question 8: Which property controls the spacing inside an element's border?

A) margin

B) padding

C) border-width

D) spacing

Correct Answer: B

Explanation: Padding adds space between the content and the border.

Question 9: How can you select an element with the class "menu"?

A) `menu`

B) `.menu`

C) `#menu`

D) *menu

Correct Answer: B

Explanation: The period (.) is used to select a class in CSS.

Question 10: Which pseudo-class is used to style an element when the mouse hovers over it?

A) :active

B) :hover

C) :focus

D) :visited

Correct Answer: B

Explanation: The `:hover` pseudo-class applies when a user hovers over an element.

Question 11: What does the property `box-sizing: border-box;` do?

A) Includes padding and border in the element's total width and height

B) Excludes padding and border from the element's total width and height

C) Adds a box shadow around the element

D) Resets all box model properties

Correct Answer: A

Explanation: This setting makes the width and height properties include padding and border.

Question 12: Which CSS property adds a shadow effect to text?

A) text-shadow

B) box-shadow

C) font-shadow

D) shadow

Correct Answer: A

Explanation: `text-shadow` adds shadows to text content.

Question 13: How do you select all <a> elements that have a `target` attribute with the value `_blank`?

A) `a[target="_blank"]`

B) `a#target="_blank"`

C) a[target]
D) a._blank
Correct Answer: A
Explanation: The attribute selector
a[target="_blank"] targets links that open in a new tab.

Question 14: Which property is used to adjust the space between lines of text?
A) letter-spacing
B) line-height
C) word-spacing
D) text-spacing
Correct Answer: B
Explanation: The line-height property adjusts the vertical spacing between lines.

Question 15: Which of the following is a valid way to write a comment in CSS?
A) // This is a comment
B) /* This is a comment */
C) <!-- This is a comment -->
D) # This is a comment
Correct Answer: B
Explanation: CSS comments are enclosed within /* */.

Question 16: What does the CSS property background-size: cover; do?
A) Tiles the background image
B) Scales the background image to cover the element
C) Centers the background image
D) Repeats the background image
Correct Answer: B
Explanation: cover scales the background image so that it completely covers the element.

Question 17: Which CSS unit is relative to the viewport's width?
A) em
B) rem

C) vw

D) vh

Correct Answer: C

Explanation: The vw unit is relative to the viewport's width.

Question 18: Which selector targets only direct child elements?

A) Descendant selector (space)

B) Child selector (>)

C) Sibling selector (+)

D) Universal selector (*)

Correct Answer: B

Explanation: The child selector (>) targets only direct children.

Question 19: What is the purpose of using an external CSS file?

A) To improve website performance by caching the file

B) To separate content from presentation

C) To allow multiple pages to share the same styles

D) All of the above

Correct Answer: D

Explanation: External CSS files offer all these benefits.

Question 20: Which of the following CSS units is best for responsive font sizing?

A) px

B) em

C) pt

D) cm

Correct Answer: B

Explanation: Relative units like em adjust according to the parent's font size, aiding responsiveness.

Question 21: How do you group multiple selectors to share the same declaration block?

A) Separate them with a comma

B) Separate them with a space

C) Use a semicolon between selectors

D) Enclose them in parentheses
Correct Answer: A
Explanation: Group selectors with commas so they share the same CSS rules.

Question 22: What is the default unit for the CSS property `line-height` if no unit is specified?

A) px
B) em
C) Unitless (number multiplier)
D) %

Correct Answer: C
Explanation: A unitless value for `line-height` acts as a multiplier of the element's font size.

Question 23: Which of the following best describes the CSS cascade?

A) The order in which styles are applied based on specificity and source order
B) The process of downloading CSS files
C) A method for compressing CSS code
D) A property used to display block elements

Correct Answer: A
Explanation: The cascade defines how conflicting CSS rules are applied based on specificity and order.

Question 24: What does the term "responsive design" refer to in CSS?

A) Designs that respond to user interactions
B) Layouts that adapt to different screen sizes and devices
C) Designs that change color on hover
D) Code that responds to media queries

Correct Answer: B
Explanation: Responsive design ensures layouts adapt fluidly to various screen sizes.

Question 25: Which of the following CSS properties is NOT part of the box model?

A) Margin
B) Padding
C) Border

D) Font-size

Correct Answer: D

Explanation: Font-size affects text appearance and is not part of the box model structure.

Chapter 3: Responsive Design Fundamentals

Detailed Outline

1. **Introduction to Responsive Design**
   - **What makes a website responsive?**
     - Explanation of responsive design: fluidity, flexible images, and media queries.
     - Why responsiveness is crucial in today's multi-device world.
   - **Goals of Responsive Design:**
     - Enhanced user experience on mobile, tablet, and desktop.
     - Improved accessibility and search engine optimization (SEO).
2. **Fluid Grids vs. Fixed Layouts**
   - **Fixed Layouts:**
     - Description and limitations: static widths in pixels.
   - **Fluid Grids:**
     - Use of percentages and relative units to create flexible layouts.
     - Advantages of fluid grids in adapting to different screen sizes.
   - **Comparison and when to use each approach.**
3. **Understanding Breakpoints**
   - **What are breakpoints?**
     - Specific screen widths at which the design adapts.
   - **Choosing Breakpoints:**
     - Common breakpoints for mobile, tablet, and desktop.
     - Tips on designing breakpoints based on content rather than devices.

- Practical examples of breakpoint implementations.
4. **Introduction to Media Queries**
   - **What are Media Queries?**
     - Syntax and purpose.
     - How they enable conditional styling based on device characteristics.
   - **Basic Media Query Syntax:**
     - Using `@media` rules.
     - Examples targeting screen widths.
   - **Combining media queries with fluid layouts for a fully responsive design.**
5. **How to Test for Responsiveness**
   - **Tools and Techniques:**
     - Browser developer tools (responsive design mode).
     - Online emulators and device simulators.
   - **Best practices for testing:**
     - Testing on real devices.
     - Using breakpoints and verifying content flow.
6. **Conclusion and Next Steps**
   - **Recap of Key Concepts:**
     - Responsive design basics, fluid grids, breakpoints, media queries, and testing.
   - **Further Reading and Practice:**
     - Encouragement to experiment with code and use developer tools.
   - **Preview of Upcoming Topics:**
     - How these fundamentals integrate with CSS frameworks and advanced layout techniques.

Chapter Content
1. Introduction to Responsive Design

Responsive design ensures that websites look and work well on any device—from smartphones and tablets to desktops. By using flexible grids, fluid images, and media queries, developers can craft layouts that adjust to varying screen sizes and orientations. This chapter explains what makes a website responsive and why it is critical in today's digital landscape. You'll learn how to implement fluid grids, set appropriate breakpoints, and use media queries to create a design that automatically adapts to the viewer's device.

2. Fluid Grids vs. Fixed Layouts

In the past, web layouts were built with fixed widths (often defined in pixels), which could break on smaller screens. Responsive design favors fluid grids—layouts based on relative units (like percentages) that adjust with the screen size.

- **Fixed Layouts:** Provide consistency on desktop screens but do not adapt to different devices.
- **Fluid Grids:** Allow content to scale and reflow; for example, a container set to 80% width will occupy 80% of any screen.

  This section discusses when to use fluid grids and the advantages they bring to responsive web design.

3. Understanding Breakpoints

Breakpoints are the key points in the design where the layout changes to suit the device's screen size. For example, you might adjust the layout for screens under 768px (tablets) or under 480px (mobile phones).

- **Choosing Breakpoints:**
  - Look at your content and design requirements rather than sticking strictly to device sizes.
  - Common breakpoints include 320px, 480px, 768px, 1024px, etc. Breakpoints help you tailor the design so that users get an optimal experience regardless of device.

4. Introduction to Media Queries

Media queries are CSS techniques that apply styles based on conditions such as viewport width, height, orientation, and resolution.

Basic Syntax:

```
@media (max-width: 768px) {
   /* Styles for devices with a maximum
width of 768px */
}
```

- **Usage:**
  They are used to override or modify CSS rules when a device meets certain conditions. Media queries work hand in hand with fluid grids to make your website responsive.

5. How to Test for Responsiveness

Testing responsiveness is a critical part of web development. Use browser developer tools (like Chrome's device toolbar) to simulate different screen sizes and orientations. Additionally, test on actual devices when possible. Emulators and online tools can help catch issues that might not be visible in desktop browsers. This section provides practical advice and tips for ensuring your responsive design works as intended on every device.

6. Conclusion and Next Steps

By now, you should understand the fundamentals of responsive design:

- **What makes a website responsive?**
- **Fluid grids vs. fixed layouts:** How using percentages instead of pixels can enhance adaptability.
- **Breakpoints and Media Queries:** How to change your design based on screen size.
- **Testing for responsiveness:** The tools and techniques necessary to validate your design.

Practice these techniques with the provided examples and exercises. In upcoming chapters, you'll learn to integrate these principles with more advanced CSS techniques and frameworks for even more robust responsive designs.

25 Code Snippets and Examples

Below are 25 focused code snippets that demonstrate responsive design techniques.

Responsive HTML Boilerplate with Meta Tag

```html
<!DOCTYPE html>
<html lang="en">
<head>
  <meta charset="UTF-8">
  <meta name="viewport"
content="width=device-width, initial-
scale=1.0">
  <title>Responsive Example</title>
</head>
<body>
  <h1>Responsive Design</h1>
</body>
</html>
```

   1. *Explanation:* Ensures proper scaling on mobile devices with the viewport meta tag.

Fluid Container Using Percentage Width

```html
<style>
  .container {
    width: 80%;
    margin: 0 auto;
    background-color: #f0f0f0;
  }
</style>
<div class="container">Fluid container (80%
width)</div>
```

   2. *Explanation:* The container's width adjusts with the viewport.

Fixed vs. Fluid Layout Comparison

```html
<style>
  .fixed { width: 960px; background-color:
#ddd; }
```

```
.fluid { width: 90%; background-color:
#ccc; }
</style>
<div class="fixed">Fixed layout
(960px)</div>
<div class="fluid">Fluid layout (90%
width)</div>
```
3. *Explanation:* Demonstrates the difference between fixed and fluid widths.

Simple Media Query for Mobile Devices

```
@media (max-width: 480px) {
  body {
    background-color: #fafafa;
    font-size: 14px;
  }
}
```
4. *Explanation:* Applies specific styles for screens smaller than 480px.

Media Query Adjusting Container Padding

```
@media (max-width: 768px) {
  .container {
    padding: 10px;
  }
}
```
5. *Explanation:* Reduces padding on smaller screens for better fit.

Using Flexbox for a Responsive Layout

```
<style>
  .flex-container {
    display: flex;
    flex-wrap: wrap;
  }
  .flex-item {
    flex: 1 1 200px;
    margin: 10px;
    background-color: #eee;
```

```
      padding: 20px;
   }
</style>
<div class="flex-container">
   <div class="flex-item">Item 1</div>
   <div class="flex-item">Item 2</div>
   <div class="flex-item">Item 3</div>
</div>
```

6. *Explanation:* Flexbox allows items to wrap and adjust based on available space.

Fluid Grid Example Using CSS Grid

```
<style>
   .grid-container {
      display: grid;
      grid-template-columns: repeat(auto-fit,
minmax(200px, 1fr));
      gap: 10px;
   }
</style>
<div class="grid-container">
   <div style="background:#ccc;
padding:20px;">Grid Item 1</div>
   <div style="background:#bbb;
padding:20px;">Grid Item 2</div>
   <div style="background:#aaa;
padding:20px;">Grid Item 3</div>
</div>
```

7. *Explanation:* The grid adapts to the viewport, automatically fitting as many 200px columns as possible.

Image with Fluid Width

```
<style>
   img {
      max-width: 100%;
      height: auto;
   }
```

```
</style>
<img src="example.jpg" alt="Responsive
Image">
```

8. *Explanation:* Ensures images scale down with the container.

Navigation Bar Adjusting with Media Query

```
<style>
  .nav { background: #333; padding: 10px;
text-align: center; }
  .nav a { color: #fff; margin: 0 10px;
text-decoration: none; }
  @media (max-width: 600px) {
    .nav { font-size: 14px; }
  }
</style>
<div class="nav">
  <a href="#">Home</a>
  <a href="#">About</a>
  <a href="#">Contact</a>
</div>
```

9. *Explanation:* Adjusts text size in the navigation for smaller screens.

Responsive Typography with Media Queries

```
h1 {
  font-size: 2.5em;
}
@media (max-width: 600px) {
  h1 {
    font-size: 2em;
  }
}
```

10. *Explanation:* Changes heading size based on viewport width.

Fluid Sidebar Layout with Flexbox

```
<style>
  .layout {
```

```css
    display: flex;
    flex-wrap: wrap;
  }
  .main {
    flex: 3;
    background: #e0e0e0;
    padding: 20px;
  }
  .sidebar {
    flex: 1;
    background: #c0c0c0;
    padding: 20px;
  }
</style>
<div class="layout">
  <div class="main">Main Content</div>
  <div class="sidebar">Sidebar</div>
</div>
```

11. *Explanation:* A responsive two-column layout that adapts using flexbox.

Breakpoint for Tablet Devices

```css
@media (max-width: 768px) {
  .container {
    width: 95%;
  }
}
```

12. *Explanation:* Adjusts container width for tablet-sized screens.

Breakpoint for Large Desktop Screens

```css
@media (min-width: 1200px) {
  .container {
    max-width: 1140px;
    margin: 0 auto;
  }
}
```

13. *Explanation:* Sets a maximum width for large desktop screens.

Responsive Table Using Overflow Scroll

```
<style>
  .table-responsive {
    overflow-x: auto;
  }
  table {
    width: 100%;
    border-collapse: collapse;
  }
</style>
<div class="table-responsive">
  <table border="1">
    <tr>
      <th>Header 1</th>
      <th>Header 2</th>
      <th>Header 3</th>
    </tr>
    <tr>
      <td>Data 1</td>
      <td>Data 2</td>
      <td>Data 3</td>
    </tr>
  </table>
</div>
```

14. *Explanation:* Allows horizontal scrolling for wide tables on small screens.

Fluid Video Embed Using CSS

```
<style>
  .video-container {
    position: relative;
    padding-bottom: 56.25%; /* 16:9 ratio
*/
    height: 0;
    overflow: hidden;
```

```css
    }
    .video-container iframe {
      position: absolute;
      top: 0;
      left: 0;
      width: 100%;
      height: 100%;
    }
</style>
<div class="video-container">
  <iframe
src="https://www.youtube.com/embed/dQw4w9Wg
XcQ" frameborder="0"
allowfullscreen></iframe>
</div>
```

15. *Explanation:* Maintains video aspect ratio and scales with its container.

Responsive Card Layout Using Grid

```css
<style>
  .card-grid {
    display: grid;
    grid-template-columns: repeat(auto-fit,
minmax(250px, 1fr));
    gap: 20px;
  }
  .card {
    background: #fff;
    padding: 15px;
    border: 1px solid #ddd;
  }
</style>
<div class="card-grid">
  <div class="card">Card 1</div>
  <div class="card">Card 2</div>
  <div class="card">Card 3</div>
  <div class="card">Card 4</div>
```

```
</div>
```

16. *Explanation:* A grid of cards that adjusts automatically to screen width.

Media Query for Landscape Orientation

```
@media (orientation: landscape) {
  body {
    background-color: #f5f5f5;
  }
}
```

17. *Explanation:* Applies styles when the device is in landscape mode.

Responsive Footer with Centered Content

```
<style>
  footer {
    text-align: center;
    padding: 20px;
    background: #222;
    color: #fff;
  }
  @media (max-width: 600px) {
    footer { font-size: 14px; }
  }
</style>
<footer>
  &copy; 2025 Responsive Web Design
</footer>
```

18. *Explanation:* Ensures the footer adapts in font size for small screens.

Using Rem Units for Consistent Scaling

```
html { font-size: 16px; }
p { font-size: 1rem; }
@media (max-width: 600px) {
  html { font-size: 14px; }
}
```

19. *Explanation:* Adjusts base font size with rem for consistent scaling across breakpoints.

Container with Max-Width and Fluid Behavior

```
<style>
  .container {
    max-width: 1200px;
    width: 90%;
    margin: 0 auto;
  }
</style>
<div class="container">Responsive container
with max-width</div>
```

20. *Explanation:* Combines fluid and fixed design by limiting maximum width.

Media Query for High-Resolution Devices

```
@media only screen and (min-resolution:
2dppx) {
  .logo {
    background-image: url('logo@2x.png');
  }
}
```

21. *Explanation:* Uses high-resolution images for devices with high pixel density.

Responsive Navigation Toggle (CSS Only)

```
<style>
  .nav-toggle {
    display: none;
  }
  @media (max-width: 768px) {
    .nav-toggle {
      display: block;
      background: #333;
      color: #fff;
      padding: 10px;
      text-align: center;
      cursor: pointer;
    }
    .nav-menu {
```

```
      display: none;
    }
  }
</style>
<div class="nav-toggle">Menu</div>
<ul class="nav-menu">
  <li><a href="#">Home</a></li>
  <li><a href="#">About</a></li>
</ul>
```
  22. *Explanation:* Displays a toggle for navigation on
    small screens.

Responsive Image Gallery with Flex Wrap
```
<style>
  .gallery {
    display: flex;
    flex-wrap: wrap;
  }
  .gallery img {
    flex: 1 1 200px;
    margin: 5px;
  }
</style>
<div class="gallery">
  <img src="img1.jpg" alt="Image 1">
  <img src="img2.jpg" alt="Image 2">
  <img src="img3.jpg" alt="Image 3">
</div>
```
  23. *Explanation:* Images wrap as needed to maintain a
    responsive gallery.

Fluid Form Layout Using Flexbox
```
<style>
  .form-row {
    display: flex;
    flex-wrap: wrap;
  }
  .form-row label, .form-row input {
```

```
    flex: 1 1 45%;
    margin: 5px;
  }
</style>
<form>
  <div class="form-row">
    <label for="name">Name:</label>
    <input type="text" id="name">
  </div>
</form>
```
24. *Explanation:* Arranges form elements responsively with flexbox.

Responsive Embedded Map with Full-Width
```
<style>
  .map-container {
    width: 100%;
    height: 400px;
  }
  .map-container iframe {
    width: 100%;
    height: 100%;
  }
</style>
<div class="map-container">
  <iframe
src="https://www.google.com/maps/embed?..."
></iframe>
</div>
```
25. *Explanation:* Ensures an embedded map scales to the full width of its container.

25 Coding Exercises with Full Code and Explanations

Each exercise below helps you apply responsive design fundamentals step by step.

Exercise 1: Create a Responsive HTML Template
Task: Build a basic HTML page with the responsive viewport meta tag and a fluid container.
HTML:

```html
<!DOCTYPE html>
<html lang="en">
<head>
  <meta charset="UTF-8">
  <meta name="viewport"
content="width=device-width, initial-
scale=1.0">
  <title>Responsive Template</title>
  <style>
    .container {
      width: 90%;
      max-width: 1200px;
      margin: 0 auto;
      background: #fafafa;
      padding: 20px;
    }
  </style>
</head>
<body>
  <div class="container">
    <h1>Responsive Template</h1>
    <p>This layout adjusts to the screen
size.</p>
  </div>
</body>
</html>
```

1. *Explanation:* A fluid container adapts to various screen sizes while respecting a maximum width.

Exercise 2: Convert a Fixed Layout to a Fluid Grid

Task: Modify a fixed-width container to use percentage-based widths.

Before:

```
<div style="width:960px; margin: 0
auto;">Fixed Layout</div>
```

After:

```
<div style="width:90%; max-width:960px;
margin: 0 auto;">Fluid Layout</div>
```

2. *Explanation:* Using percentages makes the layout flexible while retaining a max-width.

Exercise 3: Implement a Basic Media Query

Task: Create a media query that changes the background color on screens smaller than 600px.

```
<style>
  body { background-color: #fff; }
  @media (max-width: 600px) {
    body { background-color: #eef; }
  }
</style>
<body>
  <p>Resize the browser window to see the
background color change.</p>
</body>
```

3. *Explanation:* Demonstrates how media queries can conditionally apply CSS rules.

Exercise 4: Responsive Typography

Task: Adjust the font size of a heading for devices under 600px.

```
<style>
  h1 { font-size: 2.5em; }
  @media (max-width: 600px) {
    h1 { font-size: 2em; }
  }
</style>
<h1>Responsive Heading</h1>
```

4. *Explanation:* Changes the heading size to maintain readability on smaller devices.

Exercise 5: Create a Fluid Navigation Bar

Task: Build a navigation bar that adjusts its font size based on the screen width.

```html
<!DOCTYPE html>
<html lang="en">
<head>
  <meta charset="UTF-8">
  <meta name="viewport"
content="width=device-width, initial-
scale=1.0">
  <title>Fluid Nav Bar</title>
  <style>
    .nav {
      background: #333;
      padding: 10px;
      text-align: center;
    }
    .nav a { color: #fff; margin: 0 10px;
text-decoration: none; }
    @media (max-width: 600px) {
      .nav a { font-size: 14px; }
    }
  </style>
</head>
<body>
  <div class="nav">
    <a href="#">Home</a>
    <a href="#">Services</a>
    <a href="#">Contact</a>
  </div>
</body>
</html>
```

5. *Explanation:* The navigation bar's link size adapts to the device width.

Exercise 6: Build a Responsive Image Gallery

Task: Create a gallery where images adjust their size based on the screen.

```
<!DOCTYPE html>
<html lang="en">
<head>
  <meta charset="UTF-8">
  <meta name="viewport"
content="width=device-width, initial-
scale=1.0">
  <title>Image Gallery</title>
  <style>
    .gallery {
      display: flex;
      flex-wrap: wrap;
      gap: 10px;
    }
    .gallery img {
      flex: 1 1 200px;
      max-width: 100%;
    }
  </style>
</head>
<body>
  <div class="gallery">
    <img src="img1.jpg" alt="Gallery Image
1">
    <img src="img2.jpg" alt="Gallery Image
2">
    <img src="img3.jpg" alt="Gallery Image
3">
  </div>
</body>
</html>
```

6. *Explanation:* Uses flexbox for a responsive image gallery layout.

Exercise 7: Create a Responsive Sidebar Layout
Task: Design a page with a main content area and a sidebar that stacks on small screens.

```
<!DOCTYPE html>
<html lang="en">
<head>
  <meta charset="UTF-8">
  <meta name="viewport"
content="width=device-width, initial-
scale=1.0">
  <title>Sidebar Layout</title>
  <style>
    .layout {
      display: flex;
      flex-wrap: wrap;
    }
    .main { flex: 3; padding: 20px;
background: #e0e0e0; }
    .sidebar { flex: 1; padding: 20px;
background: #c0c0c0; }
    @media (max-width: 768px) {
      .layout { flex-direction: column; }
    }
  </style>
</head>
<body>
  <div class="layout">
    <div class="main">Main Content</div>
    <div class="sidebar">Sidebar</div>
  </div>
</body>
</html>
```

7. *Explanation:* Adjusts the layout for smaller screens by stacking the sidebar under the main content.

Exercise 8: Implement a Responsive Card Grid with CSS Grid

Task: Build a card layout that adapts to the screen using CSS Grid.

```html
<!DOCTYPE html>
<html lang="en">
<head>
  <meta charset="UTF-8">
  <meta name="viewport"
content="width=device-width, initial-
scale=1.0">
  <title>Card Grid</title>
  <style>
    .card-grid {
      display: grid;
      grid-template-columns: repeat(auto-
fit, minmax(250px, 1fr));
      gap: 20px;
    }
    .card {
      background: #fff;
      padding: 15px;
      border: 1px solid #ddd;
    }
  </style>
</head>
<body>
  <div class="card-grid">
    <div class="card">Card 1</div>
    <div class="card">Card 2</div>
    <div class="card">Card 3</div>
  </div>
</body>
</html>
```

8. *Explanation:* CSS Grid automatically adjusts the number of columns based on available space.

Exercise 9: Responsive Video Embed

Task: Embed a video that scales with the viewport.

```
<!DOCTYPE html>
<html lang="en">
<head>
  <meta charset="UTF-8">
  <meta name="viewport"
content="width=device-width, initial-
scale=1.0">
  <title>Responsive Video</title>
  <style>
    .video-container {
      position: relative;
      padding-bottom: 56.25%;
      height: 0;
      overflow: hidden;
    }
    .video-container iframe {
      position: absolute;
      top: 0;
      left: 0;
      width: 100%;
      height: 100%;
    }
  </style>
</head>
<body>
  <div class="video-container">
    <iframe
src="https://www.youtube.com/embed/dQw4w9Wg
XcQ" frameborder="0"
allowfullscreen></iframe>
  </div>
</body>
</html>
```

9. *Explanation:* Maintains the video aspect ratio while scaling with the container.

Exercise 10: Create a Responsive Table

Task: Design a table that can be scrolled horizontally on small screens.

```html
<!DOCTYPE html>
<html lang="en">
<head>
  <meta charset="UTF-8">
  <meta name="viewport"
content="width=device-width, initial-
scale=1.0">
  <title>Responsive Table</title>
  <style>
    .table-responsive {
      overflow-x: auto;
    }
    table {
      width: 100%;
      border-collapse: collapse;
    }
    th, td {
      border: 1px solid #999;
      padding: 8px;
      text-align: left;
    }
  </style>
</head>
<body>
  <div class="table-responsive">
    <table>
      <thead>
        <tr>
          <th>Header 1</th>
          <th>Header 2</th>
          <th>Header 3</th>
```

```
        </tr>
      </thead>
      <tbody>
        <tr>
          <td>Data 1</td>
          <td>Data 2</td>
          <td>Data 3</td>
        </tr>
      </tbody>
    </table>
  </div>
</body>
</html>
```

10. *Explanation:* Uses a wrapper to allow horizontal scrolling on narrow viewports.

Exercise 11: Implement a Responsive Footer

Task: Create a footer that adapts to the screen size.

```
<!DOCTYPE html>
<html lang="en">
<head>
  <meta charset="UTF-8">
  <meta name="viewport"
content="width=device-width, initial-
scale=1.0">
  <title>Responsive Footer</title>
  <style>
    footer {
      text-align: center;
      padding: 20px;
      background: #222;
      color: #fff;
    }
    @media (max-width: 600px) {
      footer { font-size: 14px; }
    }
  </style>
```

```
  </head>
  <body>
    <footer>&copy; 2025 Responsive
Design</footer>
  </body>
</html>
```

11. *Explanation:* Ensures that footer text remains legible on smaller screens.

Exercise 12: Fluid Form Layout

Task: Build a form that uses a fluid layout and adjusts its width based on the viewport.

```
<!DOCTYPE html>
<html lang="en">
<head>
  <meta charset="UTF-8">
  <meta name="viewport"
content="width=device-width, initial-
scale=1.0">
  <title>Responsive Form</title>
  <style>
    form {
      width: 90%;
      max-width: 500px;
      margin: 20px auto;
      padding: 20px;
      border: 1px solid #ccc;
    }
    input, textarea {
      width: 100%;
      margin-bottom: 10px;
      padding: 8px;
    }
  </style>
</head>
<body>
  <form>
```

```
    <label for="name">Name:</label>
    <input type="text" id="name"
name="name">
    <label for="msg">Message:</label>
    <textarea id="msg"
name="msg"></textarea>
    <input type="submit" value="Send">
  </form>
</body>
</html>
```

12. *Explanation:* The form scales to the viewport and remains centered.

Exercise 13: Responsive Breakpoints with Multiple Media Queries

Task: Write CSS that applies different background colors at three breakpoints.

```
<style>
  body { background-color: #fff; }
  @media (max-width: 1024px) {
    body { background-color: #e0e0e0; }
  }
  @media (max-width: 768px) {
    body { background-color: #c0c0c0; }
  }
  @media (max-width: 480px) {
    body { background-color: #a0a0a0; }
  }
</style>
<p>Resize your browser window to see the
background color change.</p>
```

13. *Explanation:* Uses multiple breakpoints to change the page's background color.

Exercise 14: Responsive Logo Scaling

Task: Make a logo image scale down on smaller screens.

```
<style>
  .logo {
```

```css
    width: 300px;
    height: auto;
  }
  @media (max-width: 600px) {
    .logo { width: 200px; }
  }
</style>
```
```html
<img src="logo.png" alt="Logo"
class="logo">
```

    14. *Explanation:* Adjusts the logo size with a media
       query.

Exercise 15: Responsive Navigation Menu Toggle (CSS Only)

Task: Create a menu that shows a "Menu" button on small screens and hides the full navigation.

```css
<style>
  .nav-menu { display: block; }
  .menu-button { display: none; }
  @media (max-width: 768px) {
    .nav-menu { display: none; }
    .menu-button { display: block;
background: #333; color: #fff; padding:
10px; text-align: center; cursor: pointer;
}
  }
</style>
```
```html
<div class="menu-button">Menu</div>
<ul class="nav-menu">
  <li><a href="#">Home</a></li>
  <li><a href="#">Services</a></li>
</ul>
```

    15. *Explanation:* Uses media queries to switch between
       full navigation and a menu button.

Exercise 16: Responsive Content Columns with CSS Grid

Task: Create a layout with three columns that collapse to one column on small screens.

```
<style>
  .grid-layout {
    display: grid;
    grid-template-columns: repeat(3, 1fr);
    gap: 10px;
  }
  @media (max-width: 600px) {
    .grid-layout {
      grid-template-columns: 1fr;
    }
  }
</style>
<div class="grid-layout">
  <div style="background:#ccc;
padding:20px;">Column 1</div>
  <div style="background:#bbb;
padding:20px;">Column 2</div>
  <div style="background:#aaa;
padding:20px;">Column 3</div>
</div>
```

16. *Explanation:* CSS Grid rearranges the columns based on viewport width.

Exercise 17: Responsive Pricing Table

Task: Build a pricing table that stacks on smaller screens.

```
<style>
  .pricing-table {
    display: flex;
    flex-wrap: wrap;
  }
  .price-card {
    flex: 1 1 300px;
    border: 1px solid #ddd;
    margin: 10px;
```

```
    padding: 20px;
  }
</style>
<div class="pricing-table">
  <div class="price-card">Plan A</div>
  <div class="price-card">Plan B</div>
  <div class="price-card">Plan C</div>
</div>
```

17. *Explanation:* Flexbox ensures the cards stack on narrow screens.

Exercise 18: Responsive Hero Section with Background Image

Task: Create a hero section that adjusts its height based on the viewport.

```
<style>
  .hero {
    background-image: url('hero.jpg');
    background-size: cover;
    background-position: center;
    height: 60vh;
    display: flex;
    justify-content: center;
    align-items: center;
    color: #fff;
  }
</style>
<div class="hero">
  <h1>Welcome to Our Site</h1>
</div>
```

18. *Explanation:* Uses viewport height (vh) to set a dynamic hero section.

Exercise 19: Responsive Form Elements Using Rem Units

Task: Build a form that uses rem units for padding and margins to scale with font size.

```
<style>
  form {
```

```css
      width: 90%;
      max-width: 400px;
      margin: 2rem auto;
      padding: 1rem;
      border: 1px solid #ccc;
    }
    input, textarea {
      width: 100%;
      padding: 0.5rem;
      margin-bottom: 1rem;
    }
```
```html
</style>
<form>
  <label for="email">Email:</label>
  <input type="email" id="email"
name="email">
  <input type="submit" value="Subscribe">
</form>
```
    19. *Explanation:* Rem units make spacing consistent relative to the base font size.

Exercise 20: Create a Responsive Blog Post Layout
Task: Use semantic HTML and responsive CSS to create a blog post layout that adapts to different screens.
```html
<!DOCTYPE html>
<html lang="en">
<head>
  <meta charset="UTF-8">
  <meta name="viewport"
content="width=device-width, initial-
scale=1.0">
  <title>Responsive Blog Post</title>
  <style>
    body { font-family: sans-serif; line-
height: 1.6; }
```

```
header, footer { background: #333;
color: #fff; text-align: center; padding:
1rem; }
    article { padding: 1rem; }
    @media (max-width: 600px) {
      article { padding: 0.5rem; }
    }
  </style>
</head>
<body>
  <header><h1>My Blog</h1></header>
  <article>
    <h2>Post Title</h2>
    <p>This is the blog post content. It
adjusts its padding based on screen
size.</p>
  </article>
  <footer>&copy; 2025 My Blog</footer>
</body>
</html>
```

20. *Explanation:* A complete layout that uses media
    queries for spacing adjustments.

Exercise 21: Use a Media Query to Hide an Element on Small Screens

Task: Create a banner that disappears when the screen is below 480px wide.

```
<style>
  .banner { background: #ffcc00; padding:
20px; text-align: center; }
  @media (max-width: 480px) {
    .banner { display: none; }
  }
</style>
<div class="banner">This banner hides on
small screens.</div>
```

21. *Explanation:* Uses a media query to hide content based on viewport width.

Exercise 22: Responsive Modal Window

Task: Design a modal window that adjusts its width according to the screen size.

```
<style>
  .modal {
    width: 80%;
    max-width: 500px;
    margin: 50px auto;
    background: #fff;
    padding: 20px;
    border: 1px solid #ccc;
  }
</style>
<div class="modal">
  <p>This is a responsive modal.</p>
</div>
```

22. *Explanation:* The modal uses percentage width and max-width for responsiveness.

Exercise 23: Create a Responsive Breadcrumb Navigation

Task: Build breadcrumb navigation that wraps on small screens.

```
<style>
  .breadcrumbs {
    display: flex;
    flex-wrap: wrap;
    list-style: none;
    padding: 10px;
    background: #f5f5f5;
  }
  .breadcrumbs li {
    margin-right: 5px;
  }
</style>
<ul class="breadcrumbs">
```

```
  <li>Home</li>
  <li>&gt;</li>
  <li>Blog</li>
  <li>&gt;</li>
  <li>Post</li>
</ul>
```
23. *Explanation:* Flex-wrap allows breadcrumb items to flow to the next line on small screens.

Exercise 24: Responsive Pricing Table with a Toggle

Task: Create a pricing table where a toggle can switch between monthly and yearly pricing (CSS-only layout demonstration).

```
<style>
  .pricing {
    display: flex;
    flex-wrap: wrap;
    gap: 20px;
  }
  .price {
    flex: 1 1 250px;
    border: 1px solid #ddd;
    padding: 20px;
  }
  @media (max-width: 600px) {
    .pricing { flex-direction: column; }
  }
</style>
<div class="pricing">
  <div class="price">Plan A:
$10/month</div>
  <div class="price">Plan B:
$20/month</div>
  <div class="price">Plan C:
$30/month</div>
</div>
```

24. *Explanation:* The pricing table adapts its layout based on available width.

Exercise 25: Test Responsiveness Using CSS Outline for Debugging

Task: Add outlines to all elements to visualize the responsive layout during development.

```
<style>
  * {
    outline: 1px dashed red;
  }
</style>
<p>This technique is useful to debug layout
issues during responsive design
development.</p>
```

25. *Explanation:* Outlines help visualize element boundaries when testing responsiveness.

25 Multiple Choice Questions with Full Explanations

Question 1: What is the primary goal of responsive design?

A) To create fixed layouts

B) To ensure websites work well on any device

C) To use JavaScript for animations

D) To limit website functionality

Correct Answer: B

Explanation: Responsive design aims to create websites that adapt to various screen sizes and devices.

Question 2: Which of the following is a key component of responsive design?

A) Fixed-width containers

B) Fluid grids

C) Inline styles

D) Static images

Correct Answer: B

Explanation: Fluid grids allow layouts to scale proportionally with the viewport.

Question 3: What are breakpoints in responsive design?

A) Points where JavaScript is executed
B) Specific screen widths where layout changes occur
C) Fixed pixel values for images
D) Browser cache settings
Correct Answer: B
Explanation: Breakpoints are defined screen widths where the design adapts to better fit the device.

Question 4: Which CSS feature is most commonly used to implement breakpoints?
A) CSS animations
B) Media queries
C) Flexbox
D) CSS variables
Correct Answer: B
Explanation: Media queries are used to apply CSS rules based on conditions like screen width.

Question 5: What does the viewport meta tag do in an HTML document?
A) Sets the document language
B) Controls layout scaling on mobile devices
C) Specifies CSS file location
D) Adds animation effects
Correct Answer: B
Explanation: The viewport meta tag instructs the browser on how to scale the page on different devices.

Question 6: How does a fluid grid differ from a fixed layout?
A) A fluid grid uses relative units, while fixed layouts use absolute units
B) A fluid grid is less flexible than a fixed layout
C) A fixed layout uses percentages
D) Both use the same units
Correct Answer: A
Explanation: Fluid grids use relative measurements (percentages) that adapt to screen size, whereas fixed layouts use fixed pixel values.

Question 7: Which CSS unit is commonly used in fluid grids?

A) px
B) em
C) %
D) pt

Correct Answer: C

Explanation: Percentages allow elements to scale relative to their parent container.

Question 8: What is a common breakpoint for mobile devices?

A) 1200px
B) 768px
C) 480px
D) 320px

Correct Answer: C

Explanation: Many designs use 480px as a breakpoint for mobile devices, although breakpoints can vary based on design needs.

Question 9: Which of the following best describes a media query?

A) A query to load images from a server
B) A CSS rule that applies styles based on device characteristics
C) A JavaScript function for responsive animations
D) A server-side script

Correct Answer: B

Explanation: Media queries allow conditional application of CSS based on factors like screen width, orientation, or resolution.

Question 10: How can you test a website's responsiveness in a browser?

A) By resizing the browser window or using developer tools
B) By clearing the browser cache
C) By running a JavaScript debugger

D) By using a fixed-width layout

Correct Answer: A

Explanation: Browser developer tools provide responsive design mode and resizing capabilities for testing.

Question 11: Which of these properties is often modified inside a media query?

A) margin

B) padding

C) font-size

D) All of the above

Correct Answer: D

Explanation: Media queries can modify any CSS property to adjust layout for different screen sizes.

Question 12: What does the following media query target?

`@media (max-width: 768px) { ... }`

A) Devices with a width greater than 768px

B) Devices with a width less than or equal to 768px

C) Devices with a width equal to 768px only

D) All devices

Correct Answer: B

Explanation: It applies styles to viewports with a maximum width of 768px.

Question 13: Why is it important to test responsive designs on actual devices?

A) Emulators can miss real-world performance issues

B) It is not important

C) Because only mobile devices support CSS

D) To speed up loading times

Correct Answer: A

Explanation: Real devices can reveal performance and usability issues that emulators may not catch.

Question 14: Which CSS layout method is especially helpful for responsive design?

A) Floats

B) Flexbox

C) Tables

D) Inline styles

Correct Answer: B

Explanation: Flexbox is designed for flexible layouts and helps create responsive designs with minimal code.

Question 15: What is the benefit of using relative units like percentages in responsive design?

A) They ensure that elements have a fixed size

B) They allow elements to scale relative to their container

C) They are only used for fonts

D) They have no benefits

Correct Answer: B

Explanation: Relative units let elements adjust their size according to the size of the parent container or viewport.

Question 16: Which HTML element is essential for ensuring a responsive layout on mobile devices?

A) `<meta name="viewport">`

B) `<link rel="stylesheet">`

C) `<script>`

D) `<header>`

Correct Answer: A

Explanation: The viewport meta tag is crucial for mobile responsiveness.

Question 17: In a fluid grid, if a container is set to 80% width, what happens on larger screens?

A) It always remains 80% of the viewport

B) It becomes fixed at 80 pixels

C) It may become too small

D) It will break the layout

Correct Answer: A

Explanation: A fluid container remains 80% of its parent element, scaling with the viewport size.

Question 18: Which of the following is NOT a typical tool for testing responsiveness?

A) Browser developer tools

B) Online device emulators

C) Real devices
D) Word processors
Correct Answer: D
Explanation: Word processors are not used for testing website responsiveness.

Question 19: What does the CSS property `max-width` help achieve in responsive design?
A) It fixes the width to an exact number
B) It prevents an element from growing too large
C) It sets the element to 100% width
D) It only works on images
Correct Answer: B
Explanation: `max-width` restricts an element from exceeding a specified width, which is useful for maintaining readability on large screens.

Question 20: How can media queries improve the user experience on mobile devices?
A) By forcing fixed layouts
B) By enabling custom styles that enhance usability on smaller screens
C) By disabling images
D) By reducing page content
Correct Answer: B
Explanation: Media queries tailor the design for smaller screens, making the interface more user-friendly.

Question 21: Which of the following best describes a fluid layout?
A) A layout that uses fixed pixel values
B) A layout that adapts using relative units and percentages
C) A layout that does not change with screen size
D) A layout that requires JavaScript for adjustment
Correct Answer: B
Explanation: Fluid layouts adjust naturally by using relative units such as percentages.

Question 22: What does the term "breakpoint" refer to in responsive design?

A) The moment when a website crashes

B) The point at which a layout changes based on screen width

C) A specific pixel value for font size

D) A CSS function

Correct Answer: B

Explanation: Breakpoints define the screen widths at which the design adapts.

Question 23: Which CSS technique can be used to create a responsive image?

A) Using a fixed width in pixels

B) Setting `max-width: 100%;` and `height: auto;`

C) Using inline styles exclusively

D) Removing the `alt` attribute

Correct Answer: B

Explanation: These properties ensure the image scales down with its container while maintaining aspect ratio.

Question 24: Why are media queries important for responsive design?

A) They allow conditional CSS rules based on device features

B) They only work on desktop browsers

C) They replace HTML entirely

D) They are used to add animations

Correct Answer: A

Explanation: Media queries apply different styles based on conditions like screen size, orientation, or resolution.

Question 25: What is one of the best practices when developing responsive websites?

A) Designing for the desktop first only

B) Testing on a variety of devices and using developer tools

C) Using only fixed layouts

D) Avoiding media queries

Correct Answer: B

Explanation: Testing across multiple devices and using developer tools ensures a consistent and user-friendly experience.

This comprehensive package for **Chapter 3: Responsive Design Fundamentals** provides a detailed outline and thorough content introduction, 25 code snippets and examples, 25 coding exercises with full code and explanations, and 25 multiple-choice questions with detailed explanations. Use these resources to build a strong foundation in responsive design, ensuring your websites look great on every device.

Chapter 4: CSS Layout Techniques for Responsive Design

Detailed Outline

1. **Introduction to CSS Layout Techniques**
   - The importance of layout in responsive design.
   - Overview of display properties, Flexbox, and CSS Grid.
2. **Understanding Display Properties**
   - **Block:**
     - Elements that take up the full width, starting on a new line.
   - **Inline:**
     - Elements that flow within a line without breaking it.
   - **Inline-block:**
     - Elements that flow inline but allow width/height adjustments.
   - Examples and common use cases.
3. **Flexbox Layout**
   - **Defining a Flexible Container:**
     - Setting `display: flex;` on a container.
   - **Aligning Items Horizontally:**
     - Using properties like `justify-content` (center, space-between, etc.).
   - **Aligning Items Vertically:**
     - Using `align-items` and `align-content`.
   - **Responsive Navigation Bars:**
     - Creating navigation bars that adjust gracefully on different screen sizes.
   - Practical examples with code.
4. **CSS Grid Layout**

Chapter Content

1. Introduction to CSS Layout Techniques

Modern responsive design depends on creating layouts that adapt seamlessly across devices. In this chapter, you will learn how to use CSS display properties, Flexbox, and CSS Grid to construct complex, responsive layouts. Understanding these techniques allows you to control how elements are arranged on the page, making your designs both flexible and visually appealing on any device.

2. Understanding Display Properties

CSS offers three primary display types:

- **Block Elements:**
  These elements (e.g., `<div>`, `<p>`, `<h1>`) automatically begin on a new line and extend to the full width available.
- **Inline Elements:**
  Inline elements (e.g., `<span>`, `<a>`) flow along with text and do not force line breaks.

- **Inline-block Elements:**
  These combine characteristics of both block and inline elements. They flow inline but can have defined widths and heights.

Example Explanation:
Understanding these properties is essential because they form the foundation for building any layout. You will use them to structure content before moving on to advanced techniques like Flexbox and Grid.

3. Flexbox Layout

Flexbox is designed to provide a more efficient way to lay out, align, and distribute space among items in a container — even when their size is unknown or dynamic.

- **Defining a Flexible Container:**
  Simply add `display: flex;` to a container.
- **Horizontal Alignment:**
  The `justify-content` property helps align items along the main axis (left, center, space-between, etc.).
- **Vertical Alignment:**
  The `align-items` property aligns items along the cross axis (top, center, bottom).
- **Responsive Navigation Bars:**
  Flexbox is ideal for building navigation bars that rearrange themselves on different screen sizes.

Example Explanation:
By mastering Flexbox, you can create layouts that adjust automatically to the available space, making it a key tool in responsive design.

4. CSS Grid Layout

CSS Grid Layout provides a two-dimensional grid-based layout system that is optimized for building complex responsive layouts.

- **Setting Up a Grid Container:**
  Apply `display: grid;` to the container.

- **Defining Columns and Rows:**
  Use `grid-template-columns` and `grid-template-rows` to set up your grid.
- **Grid Template Areas:**
  This feature allows you to name areas of your grid and then place items into those areas for a more semantic approach.

Example Explanation:

CSS Grid is extremely powerful for creating layouts where both rows and columns need to be controlled. It works beautifully in tandem with media queries to build responsive designs that adapt to different screen sizes.

5. Conclusion and Next Steps

In this chapter, you have learned:

- How display properties control the basic layout of elements.
- How Flexbox provides dynamic, one-dimensional layout control for aligning items.
- How CSS Grid offers a robust two-dimensional layout system.
- Techniques for building responsive navigation bars and grid layouts.

Practice these techniques using the code snippets, exercises, and quiz questions below. As you build your understanding, you'll be able to choose the right layout tool for any design challenge and create responsive designs that work beautifully on any device.

25 Code Snippets and Examples

Below are 25 code snippets that illustrate key concepts in CSS layout techniques for responsive design.

Block Element Example

```
<div style="background: lightblue; padding:
10px;">
   <p>This is a block element. It starts on
a new line and stretches full width.</p>
</div>
```

1. *Explanation:* Demonstrates a block-level element taking full available width.

Inline Element Example

```
<p>This is an <span style="color:
red;">inline element</span> inside a
paragraph.</p>
```

2. *Explanation:* Shows an inline element (`<span>`) within text that does not force a line break.

Inline-block Element Example

```
<span style="display: inline-block;
background: yellow; padding: 5px;">Inline-
block element</span>
```

3. *Explanation:* Combines inline flow with the ability to set dimensions.

Defining a Flex Container

```
<style>
  .flex-container {
    display: flex;
    background: #f2f2f2;
    padding: 10px;
  }
</style>
<div class="flex-container">
  <div>Item 1</div>
  <div>Item 2</div>
  <div>Item 3</div>
</div>
```

4. *Explanation:* Creates a basic Flexbox container.

Horizontal Alignment with Flexbox

```
<style>
  .flex-container {
    display: flex;
    justify-content: center;
    background: #e0e0e0;
  }
</style>
```

```
<div class="flex-container">
  <div>Centered Item</div>
</div>
```
5. *Explanation:* Centers items horizontally using
   `justify-content: center;`.

Vertical Alignment with Flexbox
```
<style>
  .flex-container {
    display: flex;
    align-items: center;
    height: 200px;
    background: #d0d0d0;
  }
</style>
<div class="flex-container">
  <div>Vertically Centered Item</div>
</div>
```
6. *Explanation:* Uses `align-items: center;` to
   center items vertically.

Flexbox with Wrap
```
<style>
  .flex-container {
    display: flex;
    flex-wrap: wrap;
    gap: 10px;
  }
  .flex-item {
    flex: 1 1 150px;
    background: #ccc;
    padding: 10px;
  }
</style>
<div class="flex-container">
  <div class="flex-item">Item 1</div>
  <div class="flex-item">Item 2</div>
  <div class="flex-item">Item 3</div>
```

```
  <div class="flex-item">Item 4</div>
</div>
```

7. *Explanation:* Demonstrates wrapping of flex items when space is limited.

Responsive Navigation Bar with Flexbox

```
<style>
  .nav {
    display: flex;
    justify-content: space-around;
    background: #333;
    padding: 10px;
  }
  .nav a {
    color: white;
    text-decoration: none;
  }
</style>
<div class="nav">
  <a href="#">Home</a>
  <a href="#">About</a>
  <a href="#">Contact</a>
</div>
```

8. *Explanation:* A simple responsive navigation bar using Flexbox.

Defining a Grid Container

```
<style>
  .grid-container {
    display: grid;
    gap: 10px;
    background: #f9f9f9;
    padding: 10px;
  }
</style>
<div class="grid-container">
  <div style="background: #ccc; padding:
10px;">Grid Item 1</div>
```

```html
  <div style="background: #bbb; padding:
10px;">Grid Item 2</div>
  <div style="background: #aaa; padding:
10px;">Grid Item 3</div>
</div>
```

9. *Explanation:* Sets up a basic grid container with a gap between items.

Defining Grid Columns

```html
<style>
  .grid-container {
    display: grid;
    grid-template-columns: repeat(3, 1fr);
    gap: 10px;
  }
</style>
<div class="grid-container">
  <div style="background: #ccc; padding:
10px;">Column 1</div>
  <div style="background: #bbb; padding:
10px;">Column 2</div>
  <div style="background: #aaa; padding:
10px;">Column 3</div>
</div>
```

10. *Explanation:* Creates three equal-width columns using 1fr units.

Defining Grid Rows

```html
<style>
  .grid-container {
    display: grid;
    grid-template-rows: 100px 200px;
    gap: 10px;
  }
</style>
<div class="grid-container">
  <div style="background: #ccc;">Row
1</div>
```

```
  <div style="background: #bbb;">Row
2</div>
</div>
```

11. *Explanation:* Sets up two rows with fixed heights.

Using Grid Template Areas

```
<style>
  .grid-container {
    display: grid;
    grid-template-columns: 1fr 2fr;
    grid-template-rows: auto;
    grid-template-areas:
      "header header"
      "sidebar content"
      "footer footer";
    gap: 10px;
  }
  .header { grid-area: header; background:
#888; padding: 10px; }
  .sidebar { grid-area: sidebar;
background: #bbb; padding: 10px; }
  .content { grid-area: content;
background: #ddd; padding: 10px; }
  .footer { grid-area: footer; background:
#999; padding: 10px; }
</style>
<div class="grid-container">
  <div class="header">Header</div>
  <div class="sidebar">Sidebar</div>
  <div class="content">Content</div>
  <div class="footer">Footer</div>
</div>
```

12. *Explanation:* Uses named grid areas to lay out a
    common webpage structure.

Inline-flex Example

```
<style>
  .inline-flex-container {
```

138

```css
    display: inline-flex;
    background: #eef;
    padding: 10px;
  }
  .inline-flex-item {
    margin: 5px;
    padding: 10px;
    background: #ddd;
  }
</style>
<div class="inline-flex-container">
  <div class="inline-flex-item">Item
1</div>
  <div class="inline-flex-item">Item
2</div>
</div>
```

13. *Explanation:* Demonstrates an inline-flex container that behaves like inline content but supports flex properties.

Combining Display and Flexbox for Responsive Layout

```css
<style>
  .responsive-container {
    display: block;
    margin: 0 auto;
  }
  .responsive-flex {
    display: flex;
    justify-content: space-between;
  }
</style>
<div class="responsive-container">
  <div class="responsive-flex">
    <div>Left</div>
    <div>Right</div>
  </div>
</div>
```

14. *Explanation:* Shows how block and flex layouts can be combined in a responsive context.

Flexbox: Vertical Column Layout

```
<style>
  .column-flex {
    display: flex;
    flex-direction: column;
    align-items: center;
    gap: 10px;
  }
</style>
<div class="column-flex">
  <div>Top</div>
  <div>Middle</div>
  <div>Bottom</div>
</div>
```

15. *Explanation:* Arranges items vertically with center alignment.

Responsive Flex Navigation with Wrap

```
<style>
  .nav-flex {
    display: flex;
    flex-wrap: wrap;
    background: #444;
    padding: 10px;
  }
  .nav-flex a {
    color: #fff;
    padding: 5px 10px;
    text-decoration: none;
    margin: 5px;
  }
</style>
<div class="nav-flex">
  <a href="#">Home</a>
  <a href="#">About</a>
```

```
<a href="#">Services</a>
<a href="#">Contact</a>
</div>
```

16. *Explanation:* Uses flex-wrap so navigation links flow to new lines on small screens.

Grid: Implicit vs. Explicit Grids

```
<style>
  .explicit-grid {
    display: grid;
    grid-template-columns: repeat(3, 1fr);
    grid-auto-rows: 100px;
    gap: 10px;
  }
</style>
<div class="explicit-grid">
  <div style="background: #ccc;">1</div>
  <div style="background: #bbb;">2</div>
  <div style="background: #aaa;">3</div>
  <div style="background: #ccc;">4</div>
</div>
```

17. *Explanation:* Demonstrates explicit column definitions with implicit rows.

Using Minmax() in Grid Layout

```
<style>
  .minmax-grid {
    display: grid;
    grid-template-columns: repeat(auto-fit,
minmax(150px, 1fr));
    gap: 10px;
  }
</style>
<div class="minmax-grid">
  <div style="background: #ccc; padding:
10px;">Item 1</div>
  <div style="background: #bbb; padding:
10px;">Item 2</div>
```

```
  <div style="background: #aaa; padding:
10px;">Item 3</div>
</div>
```
18. *Explanation:* Ensures columns never shrink below
   150px but grow equally.

Grid with Auto-fit for Responsive Behavior

```
<style>
  .auto-fit-grid {
    display: grid;
    grid-template-columns: repeat(auto-fit,
minmax(200px, 1fr));
    gap: 15px;
  }
</style>
<div class="auto-fit-grid">
  <div style="background: #ccc; padding:
20px;">Box 1</div>
  <div style="background: #bbb; padding:
20px;">Box 2</div>
  <div style="background: #aaa; padding:
20px;">Box 3</div>
  <div style="background: #ccc; padding:
20px;">Box 4</div>
</div>
```
19. *Explanation:* Automatically adjusts the number of
   columns based on available width.

Inline-Grid Example

```
<style>
  .inline-grid {
    display: inline-grid;
    grid-template-columns: 1fr 1fr;
    gap: 10px;
  }
</style>
<div class="inline-grid">
```

```html
  <div style="background: #ddd; padding:
10px;">A</div>
  <div style="background: #eee; padding:
10px;">B</div>
</div>
```

20. *Explanation:* An inline-grid behaves like an inline
    element while using grid layout.

Flexbox: Aligning Items with Baseline

```html
<style>
  .baseline-flex {
    display: flex;
    align-items: baseline;
    gap: 10px;
  }
</style>
<div class="baseline-flex">
  <h1>Heading</h1>
  <p>Some text aligned on baseline.</p>
</div>
```

21. *Explanation:* Uses `align-items: baseline;` for
    aligning text elements by their baseline.

Using Order Property in Flexbox

```html
<style>
  .order-flex {
    display: flex;
  }
  .item1 { order: 2; background: #ccc;
padding: 10px; }
  .item2 { order: 1; background: #bbb;
padding: 10px; }
</style>
<div class="order-flex">
  <div class="item1">Second in order
visually</div>
  <div class="item2">First in order
visually</div>
```

```
</div>
```

22. *Explanation:* The order property rearranges items without changing the HTML structure.

Grid: Overlapping Items Using Grid Area

```
<style>
  .overlap-grid {
    display: grid;
    grid-template-columns: 1fr 1fr;
    grid-template-rows: 100px;
  }
  .item1 { grid-column: 1 / span 2;
background: #ccc; }
  .item2 { grid-column: 1; background:
#bbb; }
  .item3 { grid-column: 2; background:
#aaa; }
</style>
<div class="overlap-grid">
  <div class="item1">Overlapping
Header</div>
  <div class="item2">Left Content</div>
  <div class="item3">Right Content</div>
</div>
```

23. *Explanation:* Shows how grid items can span multiple columns for overlapping effects.

Flexbox: Responsive Wrap with Centered Items

```
<style>
  .wrap-center {
    display: flex;
    flex-wrap: wrap;
    justify-content: center;
    gap: 10px;
  }
  .wrap-center div {
    background: #ddd;
    padding: 10px;
```

```css
    flex: 1 1 100px;
  }
</style>
<div class="wrap-center">
  <div>Box 1</div>
  <div>Box 2</div>
  <div>Box 3</div>
</div>
```

24. *Explanation:* Centers items that wrap on smaller screens.

Grid: Creating a Complex Layout with Template Areas

```css
<style>
  .complex-grid {
    display: grid;
    grid-template-columns: 200px 1fr;
    grid-template-rows: auto 1fr auto;
    grid-template-areas:
      "sidebar header"
      "sidebar content"
      "sidebar footer";
    gap: 10px;
  }
  .header { grid-area: header; background:
#888; padding: 10px; }
  .sidebar { grid-area: sidebar;
background: #bbb; padding: 10px; }
  .content { grid-area: content;
background: #ddd; padding: 10px; }
  .footer { grid-area: footer; background:
#999; padding: 10px; }
</style>
<div class="complex-grid">
  <div class="header">Header</div>
  <div class="sidebar">Sidebar</div>
  <div class="content">Content</div>
  <div class="footer">Footer</div>
```

```
</div>
```
25. *Explanation:* A complex, semantic layout using grid template areas.

25 Coding Exercises with Full Code and Explanations

Each exercise below reinforces key concepts from this chapter.

Exercise 1: Create a Simple Block Layout

Task: Build an HTML page with block-level elements that stack vertically.

HTML:

```
<!DOCTYPE html>
<html lang="en">
<head>
  <meta charset="UTF-8">
  <meta name="viewport"
content="width=device-width, initial-
scale=1.0">
  <title>Block Layout</title>
</head>
<body>
  <div style="background: lightblue;
padding: 10px;">Block Element 1</div>
  <div style="background: lightgreen;
padding: 10px;">Block Element 2</div>
</body>
</html>
```

1. *Explanation:* Demonstrates that block elements stack vertically and occupy full width.

Exercise 2: Inline vs. Inline-Block Comparison

Task: Create examples showing the difference between inline and inline-block elements.

HTML:

```
<!DOCTYPE html>
<html lang="en">
<head>
```

```
  <meta charset="UTF-8">
  <meta name="viewport"
content="width=device-width, initial-
scale=1.0">
  <title>Inline Comparison</title>
  <style>
    .inline { display: inline; background:
#fdd; padding: 5px; }
    .inline-block { display: inline-block;
background: #dfd; padding: 5px; width:
100px; }
  </style>
</head>
<body>
  <span class="inline">Inline 1</span>
  <span class="inline">Inline 2</span>
  <br>
  <span class="inline-block">Inline-block
1</span>
  <span class="inline-block">Inline-block
2</span>
</body>
</html>
```

2. *Explanation:* Shows how inline elements do not
   accept width, whereas inline-block elements do.

Exercise 3: Build a Flex Container with Horizontal Alignment

Task: Create a Flexbox container that centers its items horizontally.

HTML:

```
<!DOCTYPE html>
<html lang="en">
<head>
  <meta charset="UTF-8">
```

```
  <meta name="viewport"
content="width=device-width, initial-
scale=1.0">
  <title>Flex Horizontal</title>
  <style>
    .flex-container {
      display: flex;
      justify-content: center;
      background: #f0f0f0;
      padding: 20px;
    }
    .flex-item {
      background: #ccc;
      padding: 10px;
      margin: 5px;
    }
  </style>
</head>
<body>
  <div class="flex-container">
    <div class="flex-item">Item A</div>
    <div class="flex-item">Item B</div>
    <div class="flex-item">Item C</div>
  </div>
</body>
</html>
```
3. *Explanation:* Centers flex items along the horizontal axis.

Exercise 4: Build a Flex Container with Vertical Alignment

Task: Create a Flexbox container that centers items vertically within a fixed height.

HTML:
```
<!DOCTYPE html>
<html lang="en">
<head>
```

```
    <meta charset="UTF-8">
    <meta name="viewport"
content="width=device-width, initial-
scale=1.0">
    <title>Flex Vertical</title>
    <style>
      .flex-container {
        display: flex;
        align-items: center;
        height: 200px;
        background: #e0e0e0;
      }
      .flex-item {
        background: #ccc;
        padding: 10px;
      }
    </style>
</head>
<body>
    <div class="flex-container">
      <div class="flex-item">Centered
Item</div>
    </div>
</body>
</html>
```

4. *Explanation:* Centers a single flex item vertically.

Exercise 5: Create a Responsive Navigation Bar with Flexbox

Task: Build a navigation bar that distributes links evenly.

HTML:

```
<!DOCTYPE html>
<html lang="en">
<head>
    <meta charset="UTF-8">
```

```html
    <meta name="viewport"
content="width=device-width, initial-
scale=1.0">
    <title>Flex Nav Bar</title>
    <style>
      .nav {
        display: flex;
        justify-content: space-around;
        background: #333;
        padding: 10px;
      }
      .nav a {
        color: #fff;
        text-decoration: none;
      }
    </style>
</head>
<body>
    <div class="nav">
      <a href="#">Home</a>
      <a href="#">Services</a>
      <a href="#">About</a>
      <a href="#">Contact</a>
    </div>
</body>
</html>
```

5. *Explanation:* Uses Flexbox to evenly space navigation links.

Exercise 6: Create a Responsive Grid Container
Task: Build a grid container with three equal columns.
HTML:

```html
<!DOCTYPE html>
<html lang="en">
<head>
  <meta charset="UTF-8">
```

```html
    <meta name="viewport"
content="width=device-width, initial-
scale=1.0">
    <title>Simple Grid</title>
    <style>
      .grid-container {
        display: grid;
        grid-template-columns: repeat(3,
1fr);
        gap: 10px;
        padding: 10px;
        background: #f9f9f9;
      }
      .grid-item {
        background: #ccc;
        padding: 20px;
      }
    </style>
</head>
<body>
  <div class="grid-container">
    <div class="grid-item">Column 1</div>
    <div class="grid-item">Column 2</div>
    <div class="grid-item">Column 3</div>
  </div>
</body>
</html>
```

6. *Explanation:* Creates a simple three-column grid layout.

Exercise 7: Create a Grid with Template Areas

Task: Use grid template areas to define a header, sidebar, content, and footer.

HTML:

```html
<!DOCTYPE html>
<html lang="en">
<head>
```

```html
  <meta charset="UTF-8">
  <meta name="viewport"
content="width=device-width, initial-
scale=1.0">
  <title>Grid Template Areas</title>
  <style>
    .grid-container {
      display: grid;
      grid-template-columns: 200px 1fr;
      grid-template-rows: auto 1fr auto;
      grid-template-areas:
        "header header"
        "sidebar content"
        "footer footer";
      gap: 10px;
      padding: 10px;
      background: #f1f1f1;
    }
    .header { grid-area: header;
background: #888; padding: 10px; }
    .sidebar { grid-area: sidebar;
background: #bbb; padding: 10px; }
    .content { grid-area: content;
background: #ddd; padding: 10px; }
    .footer { grid-area: footer;
background: #999; padding: 10px; }
  </style>
</head>
<body>
  <div class="grid-container">
    <div class="header">Header</div>
    <div class="sidebar">Sidebar</div>
    <div class="content">Content</div>
    <div class="footer">Footer</div>
  </div>
</body>
```

```
</html>
```

7. *Explanation:* Uses named areas to semantically structure a page.

Exercise 8: Implement Inline-flex for Navigation

Task: Create an inline-flex container to display navigation items inline with flex features.

HTML:

```
<!DOCTYPE html>
<html lang="en">
<head>
  <meta charset="UTF-8">
  <meta name="viewport"
content="width=device-width, initial-
scale=1.0">
  <title>Inline-Flex Nav</title>
  <style>
    .nav {
      display: inline-flex;
      gap: 15px;
      background: #333;
      padding: 10px;
    }
    .nav a { color: #fff; text-decoration:
none; }
  </style>
</head>
<body>
  <div class="nav">
    <a href="#">Home</a>
    <a href="#">Portfolio</a>
    <a href="#">Contact</a>
  </div>
</body>
</html>
```

8. *Explanation:* Inline-flex allows the nav container to behave inline while applying flex layout.

Exercise 9: Create a Responsive Grid with Auto-fit
Task: Build a grid layout that automatically adjusts the number of columns based on available space.
HTML:

```html
<!DOCTYPE html>
<html lang="en">
<head>
  <meta charset="UTF-8">
  <meta name="viewport"
content="width=device-width, initial-
scale=1.0">
  <title>Auto-fit Grid</title>
  <style>
    .auto-fit-grid {
      display: grid;
      grid-template-columns: repeat(auto-
fit, minmax(200px, 1fr));
      gap: 15px;
      padding: 10px;
    }
    .auto-fit-grid div {
      background: #ccc;
      padding: 20px;
    }
  </style>
</head>
<body>
  <div class="auto-fit-grid">
    <div>Item 1</div>
    <div>Item 2</div>
    <div>Item 3</div>
    <div>Item 4</div>
  </div>
</body>
</html>
```

9. *Explanation:* Automatically adjusts columns with a minimum width of 200px.

Exercise 10: Create a Responsive Footer Using Flexbox

Task: Build a footer that centers its content and adjusts for smaller screens.

HTML:

```html
<!DOCTYPE html>
<html lang="en">
<head>
  <meta charset="UTF-8">
  <meta name="viewport"
content="width=device-width, initial-
scale=1.0">
  <title>Flex Footer</title>
  <style>
    footer {
      display: flex;
      justify-content: center;
      align-items: center;
      background: #222;
      color: #fff;
      padding: 20px;
    }
    @media (max-width: 600px) {
      footer { font-size: 14px; }
    }
  </style>
</head>
<body>
  <footer>&copy; 2025 Responsive
Layouts</footer>
</body>
</html>
```

10. *Explanation:* Centers footer content and adjusts text size with media queries.

Exercise 11: Create a Two-Column Layout Using Flexbox
Task: Design a layout with a main content area and sidebar that stacks on narrow screens.
HTML:

```
<!DOCTYPE html>
<html lang="en">
<head>
  <meta charset="UTF-8">
  <meta name="viewport"
content="width=device-width, initial-
scale=1.0">
  <title>Flex Two-Column</title>
  <style>
    .container {
      display: flex;
      gap: 20px;
    }
    .main { flex: 3; background: #e0e0e0;
padding: 20px; }
    .sidebar { flex: 1; background:
#c0c0c0; padding: 20px; }
    @media (max-width: 768px) {
      .container { flex-direction: column;
}
    }
  </style>
</head>
<body>
  <div class="container">
    <div class="main">Main Content</div>
    <div class="sidebar">Sidebar</div>
  </div>
</body>
</html>
```

11. *Explanation:* Uses Flexbox to create a two-column layout that stacks on small screens.

Exercise 12: Create a Responsive Card Layout Using Grid

Task: Build a card layout that adjusts automatically using CSS Grid.

HTML:

```html
<!DOCTYPE html>
<html lang="en">
<head>
  <meta charset="UTF-8">
  <meta name="viewport"
content="width=device-width, initial-
scale=1.0">
  <title>Responsive Cards</title>
  <style>
    .card-grid {
      display: grid;
      grid-template-columns: repeat(auto-
fit, minmax(250px, 1fr));
      gap: 20px;
      padding: 10px;
    }
    .card {
      background: #fff;
      border: 1px solid #ddd;
      padding: 15px;
    }
  </style>
</head>
<body>
  <div class="card-grid">
    <div class="card">Card 1</div>
    <div class="card">Card 2</div>
    <div class="card">Card 3</div>
    <div class="card">Card 4</div>
  </div>
</body>
</html>
```

12. *Explanation:* A responsive grid of cards that adjusts based on screen width.

Exercise 13: Create a Layout with Mixed Flexbox and Grid

Task: Combine Flexbox for the header and Grid for the content area.

HTML:

```html
<!DOCTYPE html>
<html lang="en">
<head>
  <meta charset="UTF-8">
  <meta name="viewport"
content="width=device-width, initial-
scale=1.0">
  <title>Mixed Layout</title>
  <style>
    header {
      display: flex;
      justify-content: center;
      background: #333;
      color: #fff;
      padding: 15px;
    }
    .content {
      display: grid;
      grid-template-columns: 1fr 2fr;
      gap: 20px;
      padding: 20px;
    }
  </style>
</head>
<body>
  <header>My Mixed Layout</header>
  <div class="content">
    <div style="background:#ccc;
padding:10px;">Sidebar</div>
```

```
    <div style="background:#eee;
padding:10px;">Main Content</div>
  </div>
</body>
</html>
```

13. *Explanation:* Integrates Flexbox and Grid for different page sections.

Exercise 14: Responsive Image with Flexbox Container

Task: Place an image inside a flex container and ensure it scales.

HTML:

```
<!DOCTYPE html>
<html lang="en">
<head>
  <meta charset="UTF-8">
  <meta name="viewport"
content="width=device-width, initial-
scale=1.0">
  <title>Flex Image</title>
  <style>
    .flex-container {
      display: flex;
      justify-content: center;
      align-items: center;
      height: 300px;
      background: #f5f5f5;
    }
    img {
      max-width: 100%;
      height: auto;
    }
  </style>
</head>
<body>
  <div class="flex-container">
```

```
      <img src="responsive.jpg"
alt="Responsive">
  </div>
</body>
</html>
```

14. *Explanation:* Ensures the image scales with the flex
    container.

Exercise 15: Create a Modal with Grid Layout

Task: Build a simple modal window that uses CSS Grid for
layout.

HTML:

```
<!DOCTYPE html>
<html lang="en">
<head>
  <meta charset="UTF-8">
  <meta name="viewport"
content="width=device-width, initial-
scale=1.0">
  <title>Grid Modal</title>
  <style>
    .modal {
      display: grid;
      grid-template-rows: auto 1fr auto;
      width: 80%;
      max-width: 500px;
      margin: 50px auto;
      background: #fff;
      border: 1px solid #ccc;
      padding: 20px;
    }
    .modal header, .modal footer {
      background: #f0f0f0;
      padding: 10px;
      text-align: center;
    }
  </style>
```

```
</head>
<body>
  <div class="modal">
    <header>Modal Header</header>
    <div>Modal Content goes here.</div>
    <footer>Modal Footer</footer>
  </div>
</body>
</html>
```

15. *Explanation:* Uses grid rows to structure a modal dialog.

Exercise 16: Create a Responsive Layout Using Grid and Media Queries

Task: Build a grid layout that changes column count on small screens.

HTML:

```
<!DOCTYPE html>
<html lang="en">
<head>
  <meta charset="UTF-8">
  <meta name="viewport"
content="width=device-width, initial-
scale=1.0">
  <title>Responsive Grid with Media
Queries</title>
  <style>
    .grid-container {
      display: grid;
      grid-template-columns: repeat(4,
1fr);
      gap: 10px;
      padding: 10px;
    }
    @media (max-width: 768px) {
      .grid-container {
```

```
      grid-template-columns: repeat(2,
1fr);
      }
    }
  </style>
</head>
<body>
  <div class="grid-container">
    <div style="background:#ccc;
padding:10px;">1</div>
    <div style="background:#bbb;
padding:10px;">2</div>
    <div style="background:#aaa;
padding:10px;">3</div>
    <div style="background:#ccc;
padding:10px;">4</div>
  </div>
</body>
</html>
```

16. *Explanation:* Adjusts the number of grid columns based on screen width.

Exercise 17: Use Order Property in Flexbox for Responsive Reordering

Task: Create a flex container where items change order on smaller screens.

HTML:

```
<!DOCTYPE html>
<html lang="en">
<head>
  <meta charset="UTF-8">
  <meta name="viewport"
content="width=device-width, initial-
scale=1.0">
  <title>Flex Order</title>
  <style>
    .flex-container {
```

```
      display: flex;
      gap: 10px;
    }
    .item1 { order: 1; background: #ccc;
padding: 10px; }
    .item2 { order: 2; background: #bbb;
padding: 10px; }
    @media (max-width: 600px) {
      .item1 { order: 2; }
      .item2 { order: 1; }
    }
  </style>
</head>
<body>
  <div class="flex-container">
    <div class="item1">Item 1</div>
    <div class="item2">Item 2</div>
  </div>
</body>
</html>
```

17. *Explanation:* Reorders flex items for improved layout on smaller devices.

Exercise 18: Create a Layout Using Inline-Grid for a Button Group

Task: Design a button group that uses inline-grid for layout.

HTML:

```
<!DOCTYPE html>
<html lang="en">
<head>
  <meta charset="UTF-8">
  <meta name="viewport"
content="width=device-width, initial-
scale=1.0">
  <title>Inline-Grid Buttons</title>
  <style>
```

```css
.button-group {
  display: inline-grid;
  grid-template-columns: repeat(3, auto);
  gap: 10px;
}
.button-group button {
  padding: 10px 15px;
  background: #007bff;
  color: #fff;
  border: none;
  cursor: pointer;
}
</style>
</head>
<body>
  <div class="button-group">
    <button>One</button>
    <button>Two</button>
    <button>Three</button>
  </div>
</body>
</html>
```

18. *Explanation:* Uses inline-grid to arrange buttons in a compact group.

Exercise 19: Create a Responsive Sidebar Using Grid Template Areas

Task: Build a sidebar layout using grid template areas that adapts for mobile devices.

HTML:

```html
<!DOCTYPE html>
<html lang="en">
<head>
  <meta charset="UTF-8">
```

```html
    <meta name="viewport"
content="width=device-width, initial-
scale=1.0">
    <title>Sidebar with Grid Areas</title>
    <style>
      .layout {
        display: grid;
        grid-template-columns: 250px 1fr;
        grid-template-areas: "sidebar
content";
        gap: 10px;
        padding: 10px;
      }
      .sidebar { grid-area: sidebar;
background: #bbb; padding: 10px; }
      .content { grid-area: content;
background: #ddd; padding: 10px; }
        @media (max-width: 768px) {
        .layout { grid-template-columns: 1fr;
grid-template-areas: "sidebar" "content"; }
      }
    </style>
</head>
<body>
    <div class="layout">
      <div class="sidebar">Sidebar</div>
      <div class="content">Main Content</div>
    </div>
</body>
</html>
```

19. *Explanation:* Uses grid template areas and a media query to stack the sidebar on smaller screens.

Exercise 20: Create a Responsive Header with Flexbox and Media Queries

Task: Build a header that changes its layout (logo and nav) on smaller screens.

HTML:

```html
<!DOCTYPE html>
<html lang="en">
<head>
  <meta charset="UTF-8">
  <meta name="viewport"
content="width=device-width, initial-
scale=1.0">
  <title>Responsive Header</title>
  <style>
    header {
      display: flex;
      justify-content: space-between;
      align-items: center;
      background: #444;
      padding: 10px;
      color: #fff;
    }
    nav a { color: #fff; margin-left: 15px;
text-decoration: none; }
    @media (max-width: 600px) {
      header { flex-direction: column; }
      nav { margin-top: 10px; }
    }
  </style>
</head>
<body>
  <header>
    <div class="logo">MyLogo</div>
    <nav>
      <a href="#">Home</a>
      <a href="#">Products</a>
```

```
    <a href="#">Contact</a>
  </nav>
 </header>
</body>
</html>
```

20. *Explanation:* Changes header layout for mobile by stacking elements.

Exercise 21: Create a Responsive Grid-Based Portfolio Layout

Task: Build a portfolio grid layout that adapts to different screen sizes using CSS Grid.

HTML:

```
<!DOCTYPE html>
<html lang="en">
<head>
  <meta charset="UTF-8">
  <meta name="viewport"
content="width=device-width, initial-
scale=1.0">
  <title>Portfolio Grid</title>
  <style>
    .portfolio {
      display: grid;
      grid-template-columns: repeat(auto-
fit, minmax(200px, 1fr));
      gap: 20px;
      padding: 10px;
    }
    .portfolio-item {
      background: #eee;
      padding: 20px;
      border: 1px solid #ddd;
    }
  </style>
</head>
<body>
```

```html
<div class="portfolio">
    <div class="portfolio-item">Project
1</div>
    <div class="portfolio-item">Project
2</div>
    <div class="portfolio-item">Project
3</div>
    <div class="portfolio-item">Project
4</div>
  </div>
</body>
</html>
```

21. *Explanation:* A grid portfolio layout that automatically adjusts the number of columns.

Exercise 22: Create a Responsive Banner with Overlapping Elements

Task: Use grid to create a banner with overlapping text over an image.

HTML:

```html
<!DOCTYPE html>
<html lang="en">
<head>
  <meta charset="UTF-8">
  <meta name="viewport"
content="width=device-width, initial-
scale=1.0">
  <title>Overlapping Banner</title>
  <style>
    .banner {
      display: grid;
      position: relative;
      background: url('banner.jpg') no-
repeat center/cover;
      height: 300px;
    }
    .banner-text {
```

```
      grid-area: 1 / 1;
      place-self: center;
      background: rgba(0, 0, 0, 0.5);
      color: #fff;
      padding: 20px;
    }
  </style>
</head>
<body>
  <div class="banner">
    <div class="banner-text">Welcome to Our
Site</div>
  </div>
</body>
</html>
```

22. *Explanation:* Uses grid layering to overlay text on a background image.

Exercise 23: Create a Responsive Testimonial Section with Flexbox

Task: Build a testimonial section where quotes align and wrap responsively.

HTML:

```
<!DOCTYPE html>
<html lang="en">
<head>
  <meta charset="UTF-8">
  <meta name="viewport"
content="width=device-width, initial-
scale=1.0">
  <title>Testimonials</title>
  <style>
    .testimonials {
      display: flex;
      flex-wrap: wrap;
      gap: 20px;
      padding: 20px;
```

```
      }
      .testimonial {
        flex: 1 1 300px;
        background: #f9f9f9;
        border: 1px solid #ddd;
        padding: 20px;
      }
  </style>
</head>
<body>
  <div class="testimonials">
    <div class="testimonial">"Great
service!" - Customer A</div>
    <div class="testimonial">"Amazing
quality!" - Customer B</div>
  </div>
</body>
</html>
```

23. *Explanation:* Flexbox layout ensures testimonials wrap and align nicely.

Exercise 24: Create a Responsive Call-to-Action Section Using Flexbox

Task: Design a section with a call-to-action button that centers on the screen.

HTML:

```
<!DOCTYPE html>
<html lang="en">
<head>
  <meta charset="UTF-8">
  <meta name="viewport"
content="width=device-width, initial-
scale=1.0">
  <title>Call-to-Action</title>
  <style>
    .cta {
      display: flex;
```

170

```
      justify-content: center;
      align-items: center;
      height: 200px;
      background: #007bff;
      color: #fff;
      font-size: 1.5em;
    }
    .cta button {
      padding: 10px 20px;
      font-size: 1em;
      border: none;
      background: #fff;
      color: #007bff;
      cursor: pointer;
    }
  </style>
</head>
<body>
  <div class="cta">
    <button>Get Started</button>
  </div>
</body>
</html>
```

24. *Explanation:* Centers a call-to-action within a full-width section.

Exercise 25: Debug Layout with CSS Outline

Task: Add outlines to all elements to visualize spacing and layout boundaries.

HTML:

```
<!DOCTYPE html>
<html lang="en">
<head>
  <meta charset="UTF-8">
  <meta name="viewport"
content="width=device-width, initial-
scale=1.0">
```

```
<title>Debug Layout</title>
<style>
  * { outline: 1px dashed red; }
</style>
</head>
<body>
  <div>Check the outlines to see layout
boundaries.</div>
</body>
</html>
```
25. *Explanation:* Outlines help in visualizing element boundaries for debugging responsive layouts.

25 Multiple Choice Questions with Full Explanations

Question 1: What is the default display property of a `<div>` element?

A) inline

B) block

C) inline-block

D) none

Correct Answer: B

Explanation: A `<div>` is a block-level element by default, taking up the full width available.

Question 2: Which display value allows an element to flow inline but accept width and height properties?

A) block

B) inline

C) inline-block

D) flex

Correct Answer: C

Explanation: Inline-block combines characteristics of inline and block elements.

Question 3: How do you define a flex container in CSS?

A) `display: block;`

B) `display: grid;`

C) `display: flex;`

D) `display: inline;`

Correct Answer: C

Explanation: The property `display: flex;` creates a flex container.

Question 4: Which property aligns flex items horizontally along the main axis?

A) align-items

B) justify-content

C) flex-direction

D) order

Correct Answer: B

Explanation: `justify-content` distributes space along the main axis.

Question 5: What property would you use to align flex items vertically along the cross axis?

A) align-content

B) justify-items

C) align-items

D) text-align

Correct Answer: C

Explanation: `align-items` aligns items along the cross axis in a flex container.

Question 6: Which of the following is NOT a valid value for the `display` property?

A) block

B) inline

C) inline-block

D) float

Correct Answer: D

Explanation: `float` is a separate property, not a value of `display`.

Question 7: How do you create a grid container in CSS?

A) `display: grid;`

B) `display: flex;`

C) `grid-layout: true;`

D) `display: block;`

Correct Answer: A

Explanation: Use `display: grid;` to establish a grid container.

Question 8: Which property is used to define columns in a grid layout?

A) grid-template-areas
B) grid-template-rows
C) grid-template-columns
D) grid-gap

Correct Answer: C

Explanation: `grid-template-columns` sets the columns in a grid.

Question 9: What does the CSS property `grid-template-areas` do?

A) Defines fixed widths for grid columns
B) Names regions of the grid for semantic placement
C) Specifies the gap between grid items
D) Automatically places grid items

Correct Answer: B

Explanation: It allows you to assign names to areas of the grid.

Question 10: Which property in Flexbox controls the order in which items appear?

A) order
B) flex-direction
C) justify-content
D) align-items

Correct Answer: A

Explanation: The `order` property specifies the order of flex items.

Question 11: What does `flex-wrap: wrap;` do in a flex container?

A) Prevents items from wrapping
B) Allows items to wrap onto multiple lines
C) Changes the flex direction to column

D) Aligns items vertically

Correct Answer: B

Explanation: It enables items to wrap when there is insufficient space.

Question 12: Which value of the `display` property creates an element that behaves like a grid container but is inline?

A) inline-grid

B) inline-flex

C) inline-block

D) inline

Correct Answer: A

Explanation: `inline-grid` creates a grid container that behaves inline.

Question 13: In CSS Grid, what does the value `1fr` represent?

A) One fixed pixel

B) One fraction of the available space

C) One percentage of the container

D) One auto-sized column

Correct Answer: B

Explanation: The `fr` unit represents a fraction of the available space.

Question 14: How can you change the direction of flex items?

A) `flex-direction`

B) `direction`

C) `order`

D) `justify-content`

Correct Answer: A

Explanation: `flex-direction` determines the direction of the flex items.

Question 15: Which CSS property allows you to set gaps between grid items?

A) grid-gap

B) gap

C) grid-space

D) both A and B

Correct Answer: D

Explanation: Both `grid-gap` (legacy) and `gap` are used to set spacing in grids.

Question 16: What is the purpose of using media queries in responsive design?

    A) To apply conditional CSS rules based on device characteristics

    B) To add JavaScript functionality

    C) To reset default browser styles

    D) To create animations

    Correct Answer: A

Explanation: Media queries conditionally apply CSS rules based on the viewport and device features.

Question 17: Which display property is best for a navigation bar that needs to be responsive?

    A) inline

    B) block

    C) flex

    D) grid

    Correct Answer: C

Explanation: Flexbox is ideal for creating responsive navigation bars.

Question 18: In a grid layout, what does the function `repeat(auto-fit, minmax(200px, 1fr))` do?

    A) It creates a fixed number of columns

    B) It creates as many columns as will fit, each no smaller than 200px

    C) It repeats the grid rows

    D) It sets the grid gap to 200px

    Correct Answer: B

Explanation: It automatically fits as many columns as possible with a minimum width of 200px.

Question 19: Which property would you use to center flex items both horizontally and vertically?

    A) `justify-content: center;`

    B) `align-items: center;`

    C) Both A and B

D) `align-content: center;`

Correct Answer: C

Explanation: Use both properties to center items in a flex container.

Question 20: What is the key difference between Flexbox and Grid layout?

A) Flexbox is one-dimensional, while Grid is two-dimensional

B) Grid is only for text layouts

C) Flexbox cannot be used for responsive design

D) There is no difference

Correct Answer: A

Explanation: Flexbox handles one-dimensional layouts (row or column), whereas Grid manages two-dimensional layouts (rows and columns).

Question 21: Which of the following is a benefit of using CSS Grid over traditional layouts?

A) Easier complex, two-dimensional layouts

B) Automatically converts layouts to Flexbox

C) Reduces the need for media queries

D) Forces fixed widths on elements

Correct Answer: A

Explanation: CSS Grid excels at handling complex two-dimensional layouts.

Question 22: What does `align-self` do in a flex container?

A) Overrides the container's `align-items` for a specific item

B) Aligns the container itself

C) Sets the order of items

D) Applies only to grid layouts

Correct Answer: A

Explanation: `align-self` allows individual flex items to override the container's alignment settings.

Question 23: Which of the following best describes a "responsive layout"?

A) A layout that remains fixed in size

B) A layout that adapts to different screen sizes and orientations

C) A layout that uses only inline styles

D) A layout that requires JavaScript for adjustments

Correct Answer: B

Explanation: Responsive layouts adjust based on the device and viewport size.

Question 24: When would you use inline-flex over flex?

A) When you want the container to behave like an inline element

B) When you want a fixed layout

C) When you need grid functionality

D) Inline-flex is never used

Correct Answer: A

Explanation: Inline-flex creates a flex container that behaves like an inline element.

Question 25: Which layout technique is ideal for creating a complex webpage structure with headers, sidebars, and footers?

A) Only Flexbox

B) Only CSS Grid

C) A combination of Flexbox and CSS Grid

D) Inline styling

Correct Answer: C

Explanation: Combining Flexbox and CSS Grid leverages the strengths of both techniques to create robust, responsive layouts.

This comprehensive package for **Chapter 4: CSS Layout Techniques for Responsive Design** offers a detailed outline, in-depth content, 25 illustrative code snippets, 25 hands-on coding exercises with full code and explanations, and 25 multiple choice questions with detailed explanations. Use these resources to master display properties, Flexbox, and CSS Grid so you can build responsive designs that work beautifully on any device

Chapter 5: Media Queries and Breakpoints

Detailed Outline

1. **Introduction to Media Queries and Breakpoints**
   - **Purpose:**
     - Understand why responsive design is essential.
     - Learn how media queries enable styles to adapt to various devices.
   - **Key Concepts:**
     - What are media queries?
     - What are breakpoints?
2. **Syntax of Media Queries**
   - **Basic Structure:**
     - The `@media` rule.
     - Conditions enclosed in parentheses.
   - **Examples of Simple Media Queries.**
3. **Common Screen Size Breakpoints**
   - **Standard Breakpoints:**
     - Mobile (320px – 480px)
     - Tablet (481px – 768px)
     - Desktop (769px and above)
   - **Content-Driven Breakpoints:**
     - Choosing breakpoints based on content rather than device sizes.
4. **Using min-width and max-width**
   - **min-width:**
     - Building a mobile-first approach.
     - Example: Styles applied when the viewport is at least a certain width.
   - **max-width:**
     - Creating styles that apply up to a certain width.
     - Example: Adjusting layout for smaller screens.

Chapter Content

1. Introduction to Media Queries and Breakpoints

Responsive design is all about ensuring that your website looks and works well on any device — from mobile phones to large desktop monitors. **Media queries** are the cornerstone of this adaptability, allowing you to apply different CSS rules based on the characteristics of the device or viewport (such as width, height, resolution, or orientation). **Breakpoints** are the specific values (usually widths) at which your design changes to provide the best user experience.

2. Syntax of Media Queries

A media query starts with the `@media` rule followed by a condition in parentheses, then a block of CSS that applies if the condition is met. For example:

```
@media (max-width: 600px) {
    /* CSS rules for screens up to 600px wide */
}
```

This snippet applies styles only when the viewport width is 600px or less.

3. Common Screen Size Breakpoints

While breakpoints can be tailored to your content, common ranges are:

- **Mobile:** 320px to 480px
- **Tablet:** 481px to 768px
- **Desktop:** 769px and above

By using these ranges, you can design a layout that scales gracefully across devices.

4. Using min-width and max-width

min-width:

This condition applies styles when the viewport is *at least* a certain width. It is central to a **mobile-first** approach:

```
@media (min-width: 768px) {
    /* Styles for tablets and larger devices */
}
```

max-width:

This condition applies styles when the viewport is *no more than* a specified width. It's common in **desktop-first** designs:

```
@media (max-width: 480px) {
    /* Styles for mobile devices */
}
```

You can also combine them to target a specific range:

```
@media (min-width: 481px) and (max-width: 768px) {
    /* Styles for tablets only */
}
```

5. Applying Responsive Styles with Media Queries

Media queries allow you to override or adjust your base CSS rules. For example, you might increase font size on larger screens or adjust margins and padding for small devices. This flexible approach ensures your website remains usable and visually appealing across all platforms.

6. Mobile-First vs. Desktop-First Approach

- **Mobile-First:**
  Write base CSS for small screens, then use min-width queries to enhance the design for larger screens.
- **Desktop-First:**
  Start with styles for large screens and use max-width queries to tailor the design for smaller devices.

Mobile-first is generally recommended as it prioritizes performance and usability on the most constrained devices.

7. Conclusion and Next Steps

In this chapter, you learned:

- The syntax and purpose of media queries.
- How to use common breakpoints and the importance of content-driven breakpoints.
- The differences between min-width and max-width approaches.
- How to apply responsive styles using media queries.
- The benefits and tradeoffs of mobile-first versus desktop-first design strategies.

Practice these concepts with the examples and exercises below. As you progress, you'll be able to craft highly adaptable websites that provide a seamless experience for users on any device.

25 Code Snippets and Examples

Basic Media Query Syntax

```
@media (max-width: 600px) {
  body {
```

```
  background-color: #f0f0f0;
  }
}
```

1. *Explanation:* Changes the background color for viewports 600px wide or less.

Mobile-First Media Query

```
/* Base styles for mobile */
body { font-size: 14px; }
@media (min-width: 768px) {
  body { font-size: 16px; }
}
```

2. *Explanation:* Uses a mobile-first approach by increasing the font size on larger screens.

Desktop-First Media Query

```
/* Base styles for desktop */
body { font-size: 16px; }
@media (max-width: 480px) {
  body { font-size: 14px; }
}
```

3. *Explanation:* Reduces font size for smaller screens when starting with desktop styles.

Targeting Tablet Devices Only

```
@media (min-width: 481px) and (max-width:
768px) {
  .container { padding: 20px; }
}
```

4. *Explanation:* Applies styles exclusively to tablet-sized devices.

Using min-width for Responsive Images

```
img {
  width: 100%;
  height: auto;
}
@media (min-width: 768px) {
  img {
    width: 80%;
```

```
    }
}
```

5. *Explanation:* Adjusts image width based on the viewport, ensuring images scale appropriately.

Changing Layout at a Breakpoint

```
.sidebar {
  display: none;
}
@media (min-width: 768px) {
  .sidebar {
    display: block;
    width: 25%;
  }
}
```

6. *Explanation:* Hides the sidebar on small screens and shows it on larger ones.

Responsive Navigation Font Size

```
nav a {
  font-size: 14px;
}
@media (min-width: 768px) {
  nav a {
    font-size: 18px;
  }
}
```

7. *Explanation:* Increases navigation link size on larger screens.

Using max-width for Responsive Container

```
.container {
  width: 100%;
  max-width: 1200px;
  margin: 0 auto;
}
@media (max-width: 480px) {
  .container {
    padding: 10px;
```

```
  }
}
```

8. *Explanation:* Applies extra padding for smaller screens.

Multiple Conditions in a Media Query

```
@media (min-width: 600px) and (max-width:
900px) {
  .box {
    background-color: #ddd;
  }
}
```

9. *Explanation:* Styles .box only when the viewport is between 600px and 900px wide.

Responsive Typography Example

```
h1 {
  font-size: 2em;
}
@media (min-width: 768px) {
  h1 {
    font-size: 2.5em;
  }
}
```

10. *Explanation:* Adjusts heading size based on viewport width.

Adjusting Padding with max-width

```
.content {
  padding: 20px;
}
@media (max-width: 480px) {
  .content {
    padding: 10px;
  }
}
```

11. *Explanation:* Reduces padding for smaller screens.

Responsive Button Size

```
button {
```

```css
  padding: 10px 20px;
}
@media (min-width: 768px) {
  button {
    padding: 15px 30px;
  }
}
```

12. *Explanation:* Increases button padding on larger screens.

Changing Flex Direction with a Breakpoint

```css
.flex-container {
  display: flex;
  flex-direction: column;
}
@media (min-width: 768px) {
  .flex-container {
    flex-direction: row;
  }
}
```

13. *Explanation:* Stacks items in a column on mobile and rows on larger devices.

Using min-width in a Mobile-First Approach

```css
.menu {
  font-size: 14px;
}
@media (min-width: 768px) {
  .menu {
    font-size: 18px;
  }
}
```

14. *Explanation:* Increases menu font size when the viewport is at least 768px wide.

Responsive Layout for a Grid Container

```css
.grid {
  display: grid;
  grid-template-columns: 1fr;
```

```css
}
@media (min-width: 768px) {
  .grid {
    grid-template-columns: repeat(3, 1fr);
  }
}
```

15. *Explanation:* Uses a single column on small screens and a three-column layout on larger screens.

Applying a Border Only on Large Screens

```css
.card {
  padding: 20px;
}
@media (min-width: 1024px) {
  .card {
    border: 1px solid #ccc;
  }
}
```

16. *Explanation:* Adds a border to cards only when the screen is wide enough.

Responsive Footer Text Alignment

```css
footer {
  text-align: center;
}
@media (max-width: 600px) {
  footer {
    font-size: 14px;
  }
}
```

17. *Explanation:* Adjusts footer text size for small screens.

Using Both min-width and max-width

```css
@media (min-width: 500px) and (max-width:
800px) {
  .responsive-box {
    background-color: #f0f0f0;
  }
```

```
}
```

18. *Explanation:* Targets devices with widths between 500px and 800px.

Mobile-First Image Styling

```
img {
  width: 100%;
  height: auto;
}
@media (min-width: 768px) {
  img {
    width: 80%;
  }
}
```

19. *Explanation:* Uses a mobile-first approach to adjust image size.

Responsive Sidebar Width

```
.sidebar {
  width: 100%;
}
@media (min-width: 768px) {
  .sidebar {
    width: 25%;
  }
}
```

20. *Explanation:* The sidebar spans the full width on mobile and becomes narrower on larger screens.

Desktop-First Approach with max-width

```
.header {
  font-size: 24px;
}
@media (max-width: 600px) {
  .header {
    font-size: 18px;
  }
}
```

21. *Explanation:* Reduces header font size for small devices in a desktop-first design.

Responsive Margin Adjustment

```
.box {
  margin: 20px;
}
@media (max-width: 480px) {
  .box {
    margin: 10px;
  }
}
```

22. *Explanation:* Decreases margins on smaller screens to optimize space.

Using Media Queries for Device Orientation

```
@media (orientation: landscape) {
  .landscape-only {
    display: block;
  }
}
@media (orientation: portrait) {
  .landscape-only {
    display: none;
  }
}
```

23. *Explanation:* Shows or hides elements based on the device's orientation.

Applying Different Font Families with Breakpoints

```
body { font-family: Arial, sans-serif; }
@media (min-width: 1024px) {
  body { font-family: 'Georgia', serif; }
}
```

24. *Explanation:* Changes the base font family for larger screens.

Combining Multiple Breakpoints for a Responsive Layout

```
.layout {
  padding: 10px;
```

```css
}
@media (min-width: 480px) {
  .layout { padding: 20px; }
}
@media (min-width: 768px) {
  .layout { padding: 30px; }
}
@media (min-width: 1024px) {
  .layout { padding: 40px; }
}
```

25. *Explanation:* Gradually increases padding as the viewport widens.

25 Coding Exercises with Full Code and Explanations

Exercise 1: Basic Media Query Application

Task: Create a page that changes the background color on screens 600px wide or less.

HTML:

```html
<!DOCTYPE html>
<html lang="en">
<head>
  <meta charset="UTF-8">
  <meta name="viewport"
content="width=device-width, initial-
scale=1.0">
  <title>Media Query Background</title>
  <style>
    body { background-color: white; }
    @media (max-width: 600px) {
      body { background-color: #f0f0f0; }
    }
  </style>
</head>
<body>
  <h1>Resize the window</h1>
```

190

```html
<p>The background color changes when the
viewport is 600px or less.</p>
</body>
</html>
```

1. *Explanation:* The media query applies a new background color for small screens.

Exercise 2: Mobile-First Typography

Task: Set a base font size for mobile and increase it on larger screens using min-width.

HTML:

```html
<!DOCTYPE html>
<html lang="en">
<head>
  <meta charset="UTF-8">
  <meta name="viewport"
content="width=device-width, initial-
scale=1.0">
  <title>Responsive Typography</title>
  <style>
    body { font-size: 14px; }
    @media (min-width: 768px) {
      body { font-size: 16px; }
    }
  </style>
</head>
<body>
  <h1>Responsive Typography</h1>
  <p>This text size increases on screens
768px wide and above.</p>
</body>
</html>
```

2. *Explanation:* Uses a mobile-first approach to scale typography.

Exercise 3: Tablet-Specific Styles

Task: Apply a unique background color for tablets (481px to 768px).

HTML:

```
<!DOCTYPE html>
<html lang="en">
<head>
  <meta charset="UTF-8">
  <meta name="viewport"
content="width=device-width, initial-
scale=1.0">
  <title>Tablet Styles</title>
  <style>
    body { background-color: white; }
    @media (min-width: 481px) and (max-
width: 768px) {
      body { background-color: #e0ffe0; }
    }
  </style>
</head>
<body>
  <h1>Tablet Background</h1>
  <p>This background color appears on
tablets.</p>
</body>
</html>
```

3. *Explanation:* Targets tablet devices with specific min-width and max-width.

Exercise 4: Responsive Navigation Font Size

Task: Change the font size of navigation links for devices 600px or narrower.

HTML:

```
<!DOCTYPE html>
<html lang="en">
<head>
  <meta charset="UTF-8">
```

```html
    <meta name="viewport"
content="width=device-width, initial-
scale=1.0">
    <title>Responsive Nav</title>
    <style>
      nav a {
        font-size: 18px;
        color: #333;
        text-decoration: none;
        margin: 0 10px;
      }
      @media (max-width: 600px) {
        nav a {
          font-size: 14px;
        }
      }
    </style>
</head>
<body>
  <nav>
    <a href="#">Home</a>
    <a href="#">About</a>
    <a href="#">Contact</a>
  </nav>
</body>
</html>
```

4. *Explanation:* Adjusts the navigation links' font size on small screens.

Exercise 5: Sidebar Visibility

Task: Hide a sidebar on screens smaller than 768px.

HTML:

```html
<!DOCTYPE html>
<html lang="en">
<head>
  <meta charset="UTF-8">
```

```html
  <meta name="viewport"
content="width=device-width, initial-
scale=1.0">
  <title>Responsive Sidebar</title>
  <style>
    .sidebar { background: #ccc; padding:
20px; }
    @media (max-width: 768px) {
      .sidebar { display: none; }
    }
  </style>
</head>
<body>
  <div class="sidebar">This sidebar is
hidden on screens smaller than 768px.</div>
</body>
</html>
```

5. *Explanation:* Uses max-width to hide the sidebar on small devices.

Exercise 6: Responsive Image Scaling

Task: Ensure images scale down on small screens while retaining quality on larger ones.

HTML:

```html
<!DOCTYPE html>
<html lang="en">
<head>
  <meta charset="UTF-8">
  <meta name="viewport"
content="width=device-width, initial-
scale=1.0">
  <title>Responsive Image</title>
  <style>
    img { max-width: 100%; height: auto; }
  </style>
</head>
<body>
```

```html
<img src="example.jpg" alt="Responsive
Image">
</body>
</html>
```

6. *Explanation:* The image scales responsively with its container.

Exercise 7: Mobile-First Container Padding

Task: Define container padding for mobile and increase it on larger screens.

HTML:

```html
<!DOCTYPE html>
<html lang="en">
<head>
  <meta charset="UTF-8">
  <meta name="viewport"
content="width=device-width, initial-
scale=1.0">
  <title>Container Padding</title>
  <style>
    .container { padding: 10px; background:
#f9f9f9; }
    @media (min-width: 768px) {
      .container { padding: 30px; }
    }
  </style>
</head>
<body>
  <div class="container">Responsive
container with changing padding.</div>
</body>
</html>
```

7. *Explanation:* Adjusts padding using a mobile-first strategy.

Exercise 8: Desktop-First Font Adjustment

Task: Write a desktop-first media query that reduces font size on screens under 600px.

HTML:

```html
<!DOCTYPE html>
<html lang="en">
<head>
  <meta charset="UTF-8">
  <meta name="viewport"
content="width=device-width, initial-
scale=1.0">
  <title>Desktop-First Font Size</title>
  <style>
    body { font-size: 18px; }
    @media (max-width: 600px) {
      body { font-size: 16px; }
    }
  </style>
</head>
<body>
  <h1>Desktop-First Font Example</h1>
  <p>Font size reduces on smaller
screens.</p>
</body>
</html>
```

8. *Explanation:* Implements a desktop-first approach using max-width.

Exercise 9: Multiple Breakpoints for a Responsive Layout

Task: Use several media queries to adjust layout padding at different breakpoints.

HTML:

```html
<!DOCTYPE html>
<html lang="en">
<head>
  <meta charset="UTF-8">
```

```
  <meta name="viewport"
content="width=device-width, initial-
scale=1.0">
  <title>Multiple Breakpoints</title>
  <style>
    .layout { padding: 10px; background:
#eee; }
    @media (min-width: 480px) { .layout {
padding: 20px; } }
    @media (min-width: 768px) { .layout {
padding: 30px; } }
    @media (min-width: 1024px) { .layout {
padding: 40px; } }
  </style>
</head>
<body>
  <div class="layout">This layout's padding
changes with screen width.</div>
</body>
</html>
```

9. *Explanation:* Gradually increases padding as the viewport widens.

Exercise 10: Responsive Table Font Size

Task: Adjust table font size on smaller screens.

HTML:

```
<!DOCTYPE html>
<html lang="en">
<head>
  <meta charset="UTF-8">
  <meta name="viewport"
content="width=device-width, initial-
scale=1.0">
  <title>Responsive Table</title>
  <style>
    table { width: 100%; border-collapse:
collapse; }
```

```
    th, td { border: 1px solid #ccc;
padding: 8px; }
    @media (max-width: 600px) {
      table, th, td { font-size: 12px; }
    }
  </style>
</head>
<body>
  <table>
    <tr><th>Name</th><th>Age</th></tr>
    <tr><td>Alice</td><td>30</td></tr>
    <tr><td>Bob</td><td>25</td></tr>
  </table>
</body>
</html>
```

10. *Explanation:* Uses a media query to reduce font size for table elements on small screens.

Exercise 11: Responsive Call-to-Action Button

Task: Change the padding and font size of a button using media queries.

HTML:

```
<!DOCTYPE html>
<html lang="en">
<head>
  <meta charset="UTF-8">
  <meta name="viewport"
content="width=device-width, initial-
scale=1.0">
  <title>Responsive Button</title>
  <style>
    button {
      padding: 10px 20px;
      font-size: 16px;
    }
    @media (max-width: 600px) {
      button {
```

```
      padding: 8px 16px;
      font-size: 14px;
    }
  }
  </style>
</head>
<body>
  <button>Call to Action</button>
</body>
</html>
```

11. *Explanation:* Adjusts button styling on smaller devices.

Exercise 12: Mobile-First Layout for a Header

Task: Design a header with a mobile-first approach that increases in padding on larger screens.

HTML:

```
<!DOCTYPE html>
<html lang="en">
<head>
  <meta charset="UTF-8">
  <meta name="viewport"
content="width=device-width, initial-
scale=1.0">
  <title>Mobile-First Header</title>
  <style>
    header { background: #333; color: #fff;
padding: 10px; text-align: center; }
    @media (min-width: 768px) {
      header { padding: 20px; }
    }
  </style>
</head>
<body>
  <header>Responsive Header</header>
</body>
</html>
```

12. *Explanation:* Uses min-width to enhance header
    styling on larger screens.

Exercise 13: Desktop-First Navigation Menu

Task: Create a navigation menu designed for desktops and adjust for mobile using max-width.

HTML:

```html
<!DOCTYPE html>
<html lang="en">
<head>
  <meta charset="UTF-8">
  <meta name="viewport"
content="width=device-width, initial-
scale=1.0">
  <title>Desktop-First Nav</title>
  <style>
    nav a {
      font-size: 20px;
      margin: 0 15px;
      text-decoration: none;
      color: #333;
    }
    @media (max-width: 600px) {
      nav a {
        font-size: 16px;
        margin: 0 10px;
      }
    }
  </style>
</head>
<body>
  <nav>
    <a href="#">Home</a>
    <a href="#">About</a>
    <a href="#">Services</a>
    <a href="#">Contact</a>
  </nav>
```

```
</body>
</html>
```

13. *Explanation:* Uses max-width to adjust navigation for small screens.

Exercise 14: Responsive Card with Media Queries

Task: Create a card element that adjusts its padding and font size based on screen width.

HTML:

```
<!DOCTYPE html>
<html lang="en">
<head>
  <meta charset="UTF-8">
  <meta name="viewport"
content="width=device-width, initial-
scale=1.0">
  <title>Responsive Card</title>
  <style>
    .card { background: #fff; padding:
20px; border: 1px solid #ccc; }
    @media (max-width: 600px) {
      .card { padding: 10px; font-size:
14px; }
    }
    @media (min-width: 768px) {
      .card { padding: 30px; font-size:
16px; }
    }
  </style>
</head>
<body>
  <div class="card">
    <h2>Card Title</h2>
    <p>This card adjusts padding and font
size based on the screen width.</p>
  </div>
</body>
```

```
</html>
```

14. *Explanation:* Demonstrates responsive styling for a
    card component.

**Exercise 15: Using Both min-width and max-width in a
Query**

Task: Write a media query that applies styles only when the
viewport is between 500px and 800px.

HTML:

```
<!DOCTYPE html>
<html lang="en">
<head>
  <meta charset="UTF-8">
  <meta name="viewport"
content="width=device-width, initial-
scale=1.0">
  <title>Range Query</title>
  <style>
    .range-box { background: #ddd; padding:
20px; }
    @media (min-width: 500px) and (max-
width: 800px) {
        .range-box { background: #bada55; }
    }
  </style>
</head>
<body>
  <div class="range-box">This box changes
color between 500px and 800px.</div>
</body>
</html>
```

15. *Explanation:* Combines min-width and max-width to
    target a specific range.

Exercise 16: Responsive Form Layout

Task: Create a simple form whose layout adapts to mobile
and desktop using media queries.

HTML:

```
<!DOCTYPE html>
```

```
<html lang="en">
<head>
  <meta charset="UTF-8">
  <meta name="viewport"
content="width=device-width, initial-
scale=1.0">
  <title>Responsive Form</title>
  <style>
    form { width: 90%; max-width: 500px;
margin: 20px auto; padding: 20px; border:
1px solid #ccc; }
    input, textarea { width: 100%; padding:
10px; margin-bottom: 10px; }
    @media (max-width: 600px) {
      form { padding: 10px; }
    }
  </style>
</head>
<body>
  <form>
    <label for="email">Email:</label>
    <input type="email" id="email"
name="email">
    <label for="message">Message:</label>
    <textarea id="message"
name="message"></textarea>
    <input type="submit" value="Send">
  </form>
</body>
</html>
```

16. *Explanation:* The form layout adapts using media
    queries.

Exercise 17: Mobile-First Image Gallery

Task: Create an image gallery that displays one image per row on mobile and multiple images on larger screens.

HTML:

```
<!DOCTYPE html>
<html lang="en">
<head>
  <meta charset="UTF-8">
  <meta name="viewport"
content="width=device-width, initial-
scale=1.0">
  <title>Responsive Gallery</title>
  <style>
    .gallery { display: grid; grid-
template-columns: 1fr; gap: 10px; }
    @media (min-width: 768px) {
      .gallery { grid-template-columns:
repeat(3, 1fr); }
    }
  </style>
</head>
<body>
  <div class="gallery">
    <img src="img1.jpg" alt="Image 1">
    <img src="img2.jpg" alt="Image 2">
    <img src="img3.jpg" alt="Image 3">
  </div>
</body>
</html>
```

17. *Explanation:* Uses grid and media queries for a responsive gallery.

Exercise 18: Changing Layout Based on Orientation

Task: Write media queries that change styles based on device orientation.

HTML:

```
<!DOCTYPE html>
```

```html
<html lang="en">
<head>
  <meta charset="UTF-8">
  <meta name="viewport"
content="width=device-width, initial-
scale=1.0">
  <title>Orientation Query</title>
  <style>
    .orientation-box { padding: 20px;
background: #ccc; }
    @media (orientation: landscape) {
      .orientation-box { background: #aaf;
}
    }
    @media (orientation: portrait) {
      .orientation-box { background: #faa;
}
    }
  </style>
</head>
<body>
  <div class="orientation-box">Background
color changes based on orientation.</div>
</body>
</html>
```

18. *Explanation:* Alters styles when the device is in landscape versus portrait mode.

Exercise 19: Mobile-First vs. Desktop-First Comparison
Task: Create two sets of CSS rules — one using a mobile-first approach and one using a desktop-first approach — for the same element.

HTML (Mobile-First):

```html
<style>
  .box { background: #ddd; font-size: 14px;
}
  @media (min-width: 768px) {
```

```
  .box { font-size: 18px; }
  }
</style>
<div class="box">Mobile-first
approach</div>
```

HTML (Desktop-First):
```
<style>
  .box { background: #ddd; font-size: 18px;
}
  @media (max-width: 767px) {
    .box { font-size: 14px; }
  }
</style>
<div class="box">Desktop-first
approach</div>
```

19. *Explanation:* Compares two strategies for responsive
    font sizing.

Exercise 20: Adjusting Navigation Layout

Task: Create a navigation bar that changes layout direction
(row to column) based on screen width.

HTML:
```
<!DOCTYPE html>
<html lang="en">
<head>
  <meta charset="UTF-8">
  <meta name="viewport"
content="width=device-width, initial-
scale=1.0">
  <title>Responsive Navigation</title>
  <style>
    nav { display: flex; flex-direction:
row; background: #333; padding: 10px; }
    nav a { color: #fff; text-decoration:
none; margin: 5px; }
    @media (max-width: 600px) {
```

```
    nav { flex-direction: column; align-
items: center; }
    }
  </style>
</head>
<body>
  <nav>
    <a href="#">Home</a>
    <a href="#">About</a>
    <a href="#">Services</a>
    <a href="#">Contact</a>
  </nav>
</body>
</html>
```
20. *Explanation:* Changes the navigation bar layout on small screens.

Exercise 21: Responsive Pricing Section

Task: Build a pricing section that adjusts its layout at a breakpoint.

HTML:

```
<!DOCTYPE html>
<html lang="en">
<head>
  <meta charset="UTF-8">
  <meta name="viewport"
content="width=device-width, initial-
scale=1.0">
  <title>Responsive Pricing</title>
  <style>
    .pricing { display: flex; gap: 20px; }
    .plan { flex: 1; padding: 20px; border:
1px solid #ccc; }
    @media (max-width: 600px) {
      .pricing { flex-direction: column; }
    }
  </style>
```

```
</head>
<body>
  <div class="pricing">
    <div class="plan">Basic Plan</div>
    <div class="plan">Pro Plan</div>
    <div class="plan">Enterprise Plan</div>
  </div>
</body>
</html>
```

21. *Explanation:* Uses flex-direction change for pricing cards on small screens.

Exercise 22: Responsive Footer with Media Query

Task: Create a footer whose text size adjusts on devices with a width less than 600px.

HTML:

```
<!DOCTYPE html>
<html lang="en">
<head>
  <meta charset="UTF-8">
  <meta name="viewport"
content="width=device-width, initial-
scale=1.0">
  <title>Responsive Footer</title>
  <style>
    footer { text-align: center; padding:
20px; background: #222; color: #fff; }
    @media (max-width: 600px) {
      footer { font-size: 14px; }
    }
  </style>
</head>
<body>
  <footer>&copy; 2025 Responsive
Design</footer>
</body>
</html>
```

22. *Explanation:* Adjusts footer text size on smaller
    screens.

Exercise 23: Changing Layout Based on Resolution

Task: Use a media query targeting high-resolution devices
to load a different background image.

HTML:

```
<!DOCTYPE html>
<html lang="en">
<head>
  <meta charset="UTF-8">
  <meta name="viewport"
content="width=device-width, initial-
scale=1.0">
  <title>High-Resolution Background</title>
  <style>
    .hero { height: 300px; background:
url('hero.jpg') center/cover; }
    @media only screen and (min-resolution:
2dppx) {
      .hero { background:
url('hero@2x.jpg') center/cover; }
    }
  </style>
</head>
<body>
  <div class="hero"></div>
</body>
</html>
```

23. *Explanation:* Uses resolution-based media queries for
    high-DPI devices.

Exercise 24: Responsive Layout Debugging with Outlines

Task: Add CSS outlines to visualize element boundaries
during responsive design testing.

HTML:

```
<!DOCTYPE html>
<html lang="en">
```

```html
<head>
  <meta charset="UTF-8">
  <meta name="viewport"
content="width=device-width, initial-
scale=1.0">
  <title>Debug Outlines</title>
  <style>
    * { outline: 1px dashed red; }
  </style>
</head>
<body>
  <div>Use outlines to see layout
boundaries.</div>
</body>
</html>
```

24. *Explanation:* Outlines help debug spacing and element boundaries.

Exercise 25: Implement a Complete Mobile-First Responsive Page

Task: Build a complete HTML page using mobile-first CSS and media queries to adjust layout for tablets and desktops.

HTML:

```html
<!DOCTYPE html>
<html lang="en">
<head>
  <meta charset="UTF-8">
  <meta name="viewport"
content="width=device-width, initial-
scale=1.0">
  <title>Complete Mobile-First Page</title>
  <style>
    /* Base styles for mobile */
    body { font-family: sans-serif;
padding: 10px; }
```

```
    header, footer { background: #333;
color: #fff; text-align: center; padding:
10px; }
    nav { margin: 10px 0; }
    nav a { color: #fff; margin: 0 5px;
text-decoration: none; }
    .content { background: #f4f4f4;
padding: 10px; }
    /* Tablet and above */
    @media (min-width: 768px) {
      body { padding: 20px; }
      header, footer { padding: 20px; }
      .content { padding: 20px; }
    }
    /* Desktop */
    @media (min-width: 1024px) {
      .content { display: flex; }
      .content > div { flex: 1; margin:
10px; }
    }
  </style>
</head>
<body>
  <header><h1>My Responsive
Site</h1></header>
  <nav>
    <a href="#">Home</a>
    <a href="#">About</a>
    <a href="#">Services</a>
    <a href="#">Contact</a>
  </nav>
  <div class="content">
    <div>Main Content</div>
    <div>Sidebar</div>
  </div>
```

```
<footer>&copy; 2025 My Responsive
Site</footer>
</body>
</html>
```

25. *Explanation:* Combines mobile-first base styles with media queries for tablet and desktop enhancements.

25 Multiple Choice Questions with Full Explanations

Question 1: What is the primary purpose of a media query?

A) To import external fonts

B) To apply CSS rules based on device characteristics

C) To reset browser styles

D) To execute JavaScript

Correct Answer: B

Explanation: Media queries conditionally apply CSS based on factors like viewport size, orientation, or resolution.

Question 2: Which of the following is the correct syntax for a media query?

A) `@media screen and (max-width: 600px) { ... }`

B) `@media (max-width: 600px) screen { ... }`

C) `@media (max-width:600px): { ... }`

D) `media @ (max-width: 600px) { ... }`

Correct Answer: A

Explanation: The correct syntax places the media type first and the condition in parentheses.

Question 3: What does `min-width` indicate in a media query?

A) Styles apply when the viewport is no larger than the specified width

B) Styles apply when the viewport is at least the specified width

C) The minimum font size

D) The minimum height of an element

Correct Answer: B

Explanation: `min-width` applies styles when the viewport is at least the given width.

Question 4: Which property would you use to target devices with a viewport width up to 480px?

A) `@media (min-width: 480px)`

B) `@media (max-width: 480px)`

C) `@media (width: 480px)`

D) `@media (min-height: 480px)`

Correct Answer: B

Explanation: `max-width: 480px` applies styles to viewports of 480px or less.

Question 5: What is a breakpoint in responsive design?

A) The moment when JavaScript stops execution

B) A specific viewport width where the layout changes

C) A type of CSS selector

D) An error in the CSS code

Correct Answer: B

Explanation: Breakpoints are the viewport widths at which the design adjusts to improve usability.

Question 6: In a mobile-first approach, which media query is typically used?

A) `@media (max-width: ...)`

B) `@media (min-width: ...)`

C) `@media screen and (orientation: portrait)`

D) `@media (max-height: ...)`

Correct Answer: B

Explanation: Mobile-first starts with base styles for small screens and adds enhancements using `min-width`.

Question 7: What is the benefit of a mobile-first approach?

A) It loads fewer images

B) It prioritizes performance on devices with limited resources

C) It uses only fixed layouts

D) It ignores desktop styling

Correct Answer: B

Explanation: Mobile-first ensures that performance and usability are optimized for smaller, less powerful devices.

Question 8: Which of the following is a common mobile breakpoint?

A) 320px

B) 1024px

C) 1440px

D) 1920px

Correct Answer: A

Explanation: Mobile devices often have viewports as small as 320px.

Question 9: How can you combine conditions in a media query?

A) Using `or`

B) Using `and`

C) Using `,` (comma)

D) Using `+`

Correct Answer: B

Explanation: The `and` keyword is used to combine multiple conditions in a media query.

Question 10: Which of these is an example of a mobile-first media query?

A) `@media (max-width: 600px) { ... }`

B) `@media (min-width: 600px) { ... }`

C) `@media (min-width: 320px) { ... }`

D) `@media (max-height: 600px) { ... }`

Correct Answer: B

Explanation: Mobile-first base styles are defined first, and then `min-width` media queries enhance the layout for larger devices.

Question 11: What does the viewport meta tag do?

A) It defines the screen resolution

B) It instructs the browser on how to control the page's dimensions and scaling

C) It sets the font size

D) It adds media queries automatically

Correct Answer: B

Explanation: The viewport meta tag ensures the browser scales the page correctly on mobile devices.

Question 12: Which media query would apply styles for tablets?

```
A) @media (max-width: 480px)
B) @media (min-width: 481px) and (max-
width: 768px)
C) @media (min-width: 769px)
D) @media (max-width: 1024px)
```

Correct Answer: B

Explanation: This query targets devices between 481px and 768px, a common tablet range.

Question 13: In a desktop-first approach, which media query is commonly used?

```
A) @media (min-width: 768px)
B) @media (max-width: 768px)
C) @media (min-width: 480px)
D) @media (max-height: 768px)
```

Correct Answer: B

Explanation: Desktop-first starts with styles for large screens and uses max-width queries to adjust for smaller screens.

Question 14: Which CSS rule correctly changes the font size for devices wider than 1024px?

```
A) @media (min-width: 1024px) { body {
font-size: 20px; } }
B) @media (max-width: 1024px) { body {
font-size: 20px; } }
C) @media (min-width: 1024px) { body {
font-size: 14px; } }
```

D) `@media screen and (max-width: 1024px) { body { font-size: 20px; } }`

Correct Answer: A

Explanation: `min-width: 1024px` ensures the rule applies to devices 1024px wide or more.

Question 15: What does the following media query do?

`@media (min-width: 480px) and (max-width: 800px) { ... }`

A) Applies styles to devices smaller than 480px

B) Applies styles to devices between 480px and 800px wide

C) Applies styles to devices wider than 800px

D) Applies styles to all devices

Correct Answer: B

Explanation: The query targets devices with viewport widths between 480px and 800px.

Question 16: Which of the following is a best practice when writing media queries?

A) Define breakpoints based solely on popular device sizes

B) Base breakpoints on your content and design needs

C) Use as many media queries as possible

D) Avoid using media queries

Correct Answer: B

Explanation: It's best to define breakpoints based on when your design needs adjustment, not just device sizes.

Question 17: Which approach is generally recommended for responsive design?

A) Desktop-first

B) Mobile-first

C) Tablet-first

D) Fixed layout

Correct Answer: B

Explanation: Mobile-first is often recommended because it ensures a good baseline on the smallest devices.

Question 18: What is the effect of using `max-width: 100%;` on an image?

    A) The image will always be 100% of its intrinsic size

    B) The image will scale down to fit its container

    C) The image will scale up beyond its original size

    D) The image will be fixed at 100 pixels

    Correct Answer: B

    Explanation: It ensures that the image never exceeds the width of its container, making it responsive.

Question 19: In media queries, what unit is most commonly used to set breakpoints?

    A) em

    B) rem

    C) px

    D) %

    Correct Answer: C

    Explanation: Pixels (px) are the most common unit for defining breakpoints.

Question 20: Which statement best describes a mobile-first approach?

    A) Base styles are written for mobile devices, with enhancements added for larger screens

    B) Base styles are written for desktops, with modifications for smaller devices

    C) Media queries are not needed

    D) The layout is fixed for mobile devices

    Correct Answer: A

    Explanation: Mobile-first involves creating base styles for mobile and enhancing for larger viewports with min-width queries.

Question 21: What is the role of the viewport meta tag in responsive design?

    A) It sets the screen resolution

    B) It controls the layout scaling on mobile devices

    C) It imports media queries

D) It disables responsive design

Correct Answer: B

Explanation: The viewport meta tag is essential for ensuring the browser renders the page at the correct scale on mobile devices.

Question 22: How can you target high-resolution devices using media queries?

A) `@media (min-resolution: 2dppx)`
B) `@media (max-resolution: 2dppx)`
C) `@media (min-width: 2dppx)`
D) `@media (max-width: 2dppx)`

Correct Answer: A

Explanation: This query targets devices with a resolution of at least 2 device pixels per CSS pixel.

Question 23: What does the following media query achieve?

```
@media (max-width: 480px) {
  .menu { display: none; }
}
```

A) Hides the menu on devices wider than 480px
B) Hides the menu on devices 480px wide or less
C) Shows the menu only on mobile devices
D) Does nothing

Correct Answer: B

Explanation: It hides the menu on small screens (480px wide or less).

Question 24: When using a mobile-first approach, which media query condition is typically added?

A) `@media (max-width: ... )`
B) `@media (min-width: ... )`
C) `@media (orientation: landscape)`
D) `@media (max-height: ... )`

Correct Answer: B

Explanation: Enhancements are added for larger screens using `min-width`.

Question 25: Why are content-driven breakpoints important in responsive design?

A) They are based on the design's needs rather than arbitrary device sizes

B) They ensure all devices display the same layout

C) They eliminate the need for media queries

D) They are not important

Correct Answer: A

Explanation: Content-driven breakpoints adapt the design based on where the layout needs to change for optimal readability and usability.

This comprehensive package for **Chapter 5: Media Queries and Breakpoints** provides a detailed outline, in-depth chapter content, 25 illustrative code snippets, 25 practical coding exercises with full code and explanations, and 25 multiple choice questions with detailed explanations. Use these resources to master the art of writing responsive CSS that adapts seamlessly across devices.

Chapter 6: Responsive Typography and Images

Detailed Outline

1. **Introduction**
   - Overview of responsive design for text and images.
   - Why scalable typography and adaptable images are essential for modern websites.
   - Learning objectives for the chapter.

2. **Scalable Font Sizes with Relative Units**
   - Understanding absolute vs. relative units (px vs. em, rem, %).
   - Benefits of using relative units for accessibility and responsiveness.
   - Examples of setting font sizes using em and rem.

3. **The vw, vh, and clamp() Functions**
   - Explanation of viewport units: vw (viewport width) and vh (viewport height).
   - How the clamp() function can create dynamic font sizing.
   - Examples demonstrating how to use these functions for fluid typography.

4. **Using @media for Typography**
   - How media queries can adjust font sizes and styles at different breakpoints.
   - Examples showing typography changes for mobile, tablet, and desktop.
   - Best practices for typography in responsive design.

5. **Responsive Images with max-width: 100%**
   - Techniques to ensure images scale down with their containers.
   - The importance of setting max-width: 100% and height: auto.

Chapter Content

1. Introduction

Responsive typography and images are critical for ensuring your content looks great on every device. As screen sizes and resolutions vary dramatically, setting fixed sizes (like pixels) can lead to text that's too small on mobile devices or images that overflow their containers. This chapter explores methods to create fluid, scalable typography and images that adapt to the user's viewport.

2. Scalable Font Sizes with Relative Units

Relative units such as **em, rem,** and percentages allow your fonts to scale in relation to the parent or root element. This improves readability and accessibility.

Example:

```
body {
  font-size: 16px; /* Base size */
}
h1 {
```

```
    font-size: 2rem; /* 2 times the root font
size */
}
p {
    font-size: 1em; /* Same as its parent */
}
```

3. The vw, vh, and clamp() Functions

Viewport units — **vw** (viewport width) and **vh** (viewport height) — let you size fonts relative to the viewport dimensions. The **clamp()** function is especially useful for setting fluid font sizes that have a minimum, preferred, and maximum value.

Example using clamp():

```
h1 {
    font-size: clamp(1.5rem, 5vw, 3rem);
}
```

This means the font will never be smaller than 1.5rem or larger than 3rem, but will ideally be 5vw.

4. Using @media for Typography

Media queries let you adjust typography for different devices. For example, you might increase the font size on larger screens to improve readability.

Example:

```
body {
    font-size: 16px;
}
@media (min-width: 768px) {
    body {
        font-size: 18px;
    }
}
@media (min-width: 1024px) {
    body {
        font-size: 20px;
    }
}
```

5. Responsive Images with max-width: 100%

Setting an image's **max-width** to 100% ensures that it scales down as its container shrinks, while **height: auto** maintains its aspect ratio.

Example:

```
img {
  max-width: 100%;
  height: auto;
}
```

6. The Picture Element and srcset for Different Resolutions

The `<picture>` element, along with the **srcset** and **sizes** attributes, gives you control over which image is served based on device resolution and layout. This technique improves performance by delivering appropriately sized images.

Example:

```
<picture>
  <source media="(min-width: 1024px)"
srcset="large.jpg">
  <source media="(min-width: 768px)"
srcset="medium.jpg">
  <img src="small.jpg" alt="Responsive
Image">
</picture>
```

7. Conclusion and Next Steps

In this chapter, you learned how to:

- Use relative units for scalable typography.
- Employ viewport units and clamp() for fluid text sizing.
- Apply media queries to adjust typography across devices.
- Ensure images remain responsive with max-width: 100%.
- Utilize the picture element and srcset to deliver optimized images.

Practice these techniques to build web pages that provide an optimal reading experience and display images beautifully on any device.

25 Code Snippets and Examples

Relative Font Size Using rem

```
html { font-size: 16px; }
h1 { font-size: 2rem; }
p { font-size: 1rem; }
```

1. *Explanation:* Sets scalable font sizes relative to the root element.

Font Size Using em

```
.container { font-size: 16px; }
.container h2 { font-size: 1.5em; }
```

2. *Explanation:* Font size for h2 is 1.5 times the container's font size.

Percentage-Based Font Size

```
p { font-size: 100%; }
```

3. *Explanation:* Sets font size relative to the parent's computed value.

Using vw for Typography

```
h1 { font-size: 5vw; }
```

4. *Explanation:* The h1 font size scales with the viewport width.

Using vh for Typography

```
h2 { font-size: 5vh; }
```

5. *Explanation:* The h2 font size scales with the viewport height.

Clamp() for Fluid Font Sizing

```
h1 { font-size: clamp(1.5rem, 5vw, 3rem); }
```

6. *Explanation:* Ensures h1 font size remains between 1.5rem and 3rem while scaling with 5vw.

Media Query for Typography (Mobile-First)

```
body { font-size: 16px; }
@media (min-width: 768px) {
  body { font-size: 18px; }
}
```

7. *Explanation:* Increases base font size on larger screens.

Media Query for Headings

```
h1 { font-size: 2rem; }
@media (min-width: 1024px) {
  h1 { font-size: 2.5rem; }
}
```

8. *Explanation:* Adjusts heading size on desktops.

Responsive Image with max-width

```
img { max-width: 100%; height: auto; }
```

9. *Explanation:* Ensures images scale with their container.

Simple HTML for a Responsive Image

```
<img src="example.jpg" alt="Example Image">
```

10. *Explanation:* Use with the CSS snippet above for responsive images.

Picture Element for Multiple Resolutions

```
<picture>
  <source media="(min-width: 1024px)"
srcset="large.jpg">
  <source media="(min-width: 768px)"
srcset="medium.jpg">
  <img src="small.jpg" alt="Responsive
Image">
</picture>
```

11. *Explanation:* Serves different images based on viewport width.

Using srcset with img Tag

```
<img src="small.jpg"
     srcset="small.jpg 480w, medium.jpg
768w, large.jpg 1024w"
     sizes="(max-width: 480px) 100vw, (max-
width: 768px) 50vw, 33vw"
     alt="Responsive Image">
```

12. *Explanation:* The browser selects the best image based on viewport width.

Combining Relative Units with vw

```
h2 { font-size: calc(1rem + 1vw); }
```

13. *Explanation:* Combines fixed and viewport-based sizing for fluid typography.

Using clamp() in a Paragraph

```
p { font-size: clamp(1rem, 2vw, 1.5rem); }
```

14. *Explanation:* Ensures paragraph text scales between 1rem and 1.5rem.

Responsive Typography with Multiple Media Queries

```
body { font-size: 14px; }
@media (min-width: 480px) { body { font-size: 15px; } }
@media (min-width: 768px) { body { font-size: 16px; } }
@media (min-width: 1024px) { body { font-size: 18px; } }
```

15. *Explanation:* Adjusts body font size at several breakpoints.

Setting a Base Font Size Using Percentages

```
body { font-size: 100%; }
```

16. *Explanation:* Inherits font size from the browser's default (often 16px).

Responsive Heading with rem and clamp()

```
h1 { font-size: clamp(2rem, 4vw, 3rem); }
```

17. *Explanation:* Fluid heading size with minimum and maximum limits.

Using @media to Change Line-Height

```
p { line-height: 1.4; }
@media (min-width: 768px) {
  p { line-height: 1.6; }
}
```

18. *Explanation:* Adjusts line spacing on larger screens.

Responsive Font Weight Change with Media Query

```
h2 { font-weight: 600; }
@media (max-width: 600px) {
  h2 { font-weight: 400; }
}
```

19. *Explanation:* Changes font weight for smaller devices.

Combining max-width and clamp() for Typography

```
h3 {
   font-size: clamp(1.2rem, 3vw, 2rem);
   max-width: 90%;
}
```

20. *Explanation:* Ensures h3 text scales fluidly while not exceeding container width.

Responsive Navigation Typography

```
nav a { font-size: 1rem; }
@media (min-width: 768px) {
   nav a { font-size: 1.2rem; }
}
```

21. *Explanation:* Increases navigation link size on larger screens.

Responsive Caption for Images

```
figcaption { font-size: 0.9rem; }
@media (min-width: 768px) {
   figcaption { font-size: 1rem; }
}
```

22. *Explanation:* Adjusts caption text size for responsiveness.

Fluid Layout with Scalable Typography

```
.content { font-size: calc(1rem + 0.5vw); }
```

23. *Explanation:* Dynamically scales content font size based on viewport width.

Using CSS Variables for Scalable Typography

```
:root { --base-font: 16px; }
body { font-size: var(--base-font); }
h1 { font-size: calc(var(--base-font) * 2);
}
```

24. *Explanation:* Uses custom properties to maintain consistent scaling.

Responsive Image Gallery with Typography Overlays

```
<style>
   .gallery { display: grid; gap: 10px; }
```

```css
@media (min-width: 768px) {
    .gallery { grid-template-columns:
repeat(3, 1fr); }
   }
   .gallery img { max-width: 100%; height:
auto; }
   .gallery figcaption { text-align: center;
font-size: clamp(0.8rem, 2vw, 1rem); }
</style>
<figure class="gallery">
   <img src="gallery1.jpg" alt="Gallery
Image">
   <figcaption>Image Caption</figcaption>
</figure>
```

    25. *Explanation:* Combines responsive images with overlaying scalable typography.

25 Coding Exercises with Full Code and Explanations

Exercise 1: Base Page with Scalable Typography

Task: Create a simple HTML page that sets the base font size using rem units.

Code:

```html
<!DOCTYPE html>
<html lang="en">
<head>
   <meta charset="UTF-8">
   <meta name="viewport"
content="width=device-width, initial-
scale=1.0">
   <title>Scalable Typography</title>
   <style>
     html { font-size: 16px; }
     body { font-family: Arial, sans-serif;
}
     h1 { font-size: 2rem; }
```

```
    p { font-size: 1rem; }
  </style>
</head>
<body>
  <h1>Responsive Typography</h1>
  <p>This text scales with the root font
size.</p>
</body>
</html>
```

1. *Explanation:* Demonstrates setting up a base font size using rem.

Exercise 2: Using em for Nested Elements

Task: Create a container where nested headings use em units for scalable sizing.

Code:

```
<!DOCTYPE html>
<html lang="en">
<head>
  <meta charset="UTF-8">
  <meta name="viewport"
content="width=device-width, initial-
scale=1.0">
  <title>em Units Example</title>
  <style>
    .container { font-size: 16px; }
    .container h2 { font-size: 1.5em; }
  </style>
</head>
<body>
  <div class="container">
    <h2>Heading using em</h2>
    <p>Text size relative to container font
size.</p>
  </div>
</body>
</html>
```

2. *Explanation:* The heading scales based on the container's font size.

Exercise 3: Fluid Font Size with vw

Task: Create a heading that scales its size using the vw unit.

Code:

```
<!DOCTYPE html>
<html lang="en">
<head>
  <meta charset="UTF-8">
  <meta name="viewport"
content="width=device-width, initial-
scale=1.0">
  <title>Viewport Width Typography</title>
  <style>
    h1 { font-size: 5vw; }
  </style>
</head>
<body>
  <h1>Fluid Heading</h1>
</body>
</html>
```

3. *Explanation:* The heading's size adjusts relative to the viewport width.

Exercise 4: Using clamp() for Responsive Headings

Task: Implement a heading that uses clamp() to set a fluid font size with min and max limits.

Code:

```
<!DOCTYPE html>
<html lang="en">
<head>
  <meta charset="UTF-8">
  <meta name="viewport"
content="width=device-width, initial-
scale=1.0">
  <title>Clamp Function Example</title>
  <style>
```

```
      h1 { font-size: clamp(1.5rem, 5vw,
3rem); }
    </style>
</head>
<body>
    <h1>Clamped Heading</h1>
</body>
</html>
```
   4. *Explanation:* The heading's font size will not drop
      below 1.5rem or exceed 3rem.

Exercise 5: Media Query for Typography

Task: Adjust the body font size for devices with a viewport
width of 768px or more.

Code:

```
<!DOCTYPE html>
<html lang="en">
<head>
    <meta charset="UTF-8">
    <meta name="viewport"
content="width=device-width, initial-
scale=1.0">
    <title>Media Query Typography</title>
    <style>
      body { font-size: 16px; }
      @media (min-width: 768px) {
        body { font-size: 18px; }
      }
    </style>
</head>
<body>
    <p>This text grows larger on wider
screens.</p>
</body>
</html>
```
   5. *Explanation:* Uses min-width media query to
      enhance typography on larger screens.

Exercise 6: Responsive Image Scaling

Task: Create an HTML page with an image that scales responsively.

Code:

```
<!DOCTYPE html>
<html lang="en">
<head>
  <meta charset="UTF-8">
  <meta name="viewport"
content="width=device-width, initial-
scale=1.0">
  <title>Responsive Image</title>
  <style>
    img { max-width: 100%; height: auto; }
  </style>
</head>
<body>
  <img src="example.jpg" alt="Example
Image">
</body>
</html>
```

6. *Explanation:* Ensures the image adapts to the container's width.

Exercise 7: Picture Element for Multiple Resolutions

Task: Use the `<picture>` element to serve different images based on viewport width.

Code:

```
<!DOCTYPE html>
<html lang="en">
<head>
  <meta charset="UTF-8">
  <meta name="viewport"
content="width=device-width, initial-
scale=1.0">
  <title>Picture Element Example</title>
</head>
```

```
<body>
  <picture>
    <source media="(min-width: 1024px)"
srcset="large.jpg">
    <source media="(min-width: 768px)"
srcset="medium.jpg">
    <img src="small.jpg" alt="Responsive
Picture">
  </picture>
</body>
</html>
```

7. *Explanation:* Serves different image files based on device width.

Exercise 8: Using srcset with img

Task: Create an image tag that uses srcset for responsive images.

Code:

```
<!DOCTYPE html>
<html lang="en">
<head>
  <meta charset="UTF-8">
  <meta name="viewport"
content="width=device-width, initial-
scale=1.0">
  <title>srcset Example</title>
</head>
<body>
  <img src="small.jpg"
        srcset="small.jpg 480w, medium.jpg
768w, large.jpg 1024w"
        sizes="(max-width: 480px) 100vw,
(max-width: 768px) 50vw, 33vw"
        alt="Responsive Image with srcset">
</body>
</html>
```

8. *Explanation:* The browser selects the most appropriate image based on screen size.

Exercise 9: Responsive Figure with Caption

Task: Create a figure with an image and a responsive figcaption.

Code:

```html
<!DOCTYPE html>
<html lang="en">
<head>
  <meta charset="UTF-8">
  <meta name="viewport"
content="width=device-width, initial-
scale=1.0">
  <title>Figure and Figcaption</title>
  <style>
    img { max-width: 100%; height: auto; }
    figcaption { font-size: clamp(0.8rem,
2vw, 1rem); text-align: center; }
  </style>
</head>
<body>
  <figure>
    <img src="example.jpg" alt="Example">
    <figcaption>Responsive Image
Caption</figcaption>
  </figure>
</body>
</html>
```

9. *Explanation:* The figcaption adjusts its size fluidly with clamp().

Exercise 10: Adjusting Line-Height with Media Queries

Task: Change the line-height of paragraphs for larger screens.

Code:

```html
<!DOCTYPE html>
<html lang="en">
```

```
<head>
  <meta charset="UTF-8">
  <meta name="viewport"
content="width=device-width, initial-
scale=1.0">
  <title>Responsive Line-Height</title>
  <style>
    p { line-height: 1.4; }
    @media (min-width: 768px) {
      p { line-height: 1.6; }
    }
  </style>
</head>
<body>
  <p>This paragraph has increased line-
height on wider screens.</p>
</body>
</html>
```

   10. *Explanation:* Improves readability on larger
      viewports.

Exercise 11: Responsive Navigation Typography

Task: Create a navigation bar with font sizes that adjust
based on viewport width.

Code:

```
<!DOCTYPE html>
<html lang="en">
<head>
  <meta charset="UTF-8">
  <meta name="viewport"
content="width=device-width, initial-
scale=1.0">
  <title>Responsive Nav Typography</title>
  <style>
    nav a { font-size: 1rem; color: #333;
text-decoration: none; margin: 0 10px; }
    @media (min-width: 768px) {
```

```
      nav a { font-size: 1.2rem; }
    }
  </style>
</head>
<body>
  <nav>
    <a href="#">Home</a>
    <a href="#">Services</a>
    <a href="#">Contact</a>
  </nav>
</body>
</html>
```

11. *Explanation:* Uses media queries to adjust navigation
    link sizes.

Exercise 12: Responsive Blog Post Typography

Task: Adjust the typography of a blog post for different
screen sizes.

Code:

```
<!DOCTYPE html>
<html lang="en">
<head>
  <meta charset="UTF-8">
  <meta name="viewport"
content="width=device-width, initial-
scale=1.0">
  <title>Blog Post Typography</title>
  <style>
    body { font-size: 16px; line-height:
1.5; }
    @media (min-width: 768px) {
      body { font-size: 18px; }
    }
  </style>
</head>
<body>
  <h1>Blog Post Title</h1>
```

```
<p>This blog post adjusts its typography
based on the device.</p>
</body>
</html>
```
    12. *Explanation:* Uses a mobile-first approach with
        media queries.

Exercise 13: Using vw and clamp() Together

Task: Create a heading that uses both viewport units and
clamp() for fluid sizing.

Code:
```
<!DOCTYPE html>
<html lang="en">
<head>
  <meta charset="UTF-8">
  <meta name="viewport"
content="width=device-width, initial-
scale=1.0">
  <title>vw and clamp Combination</title>
  <style>
    h1 { font-size: clamp(2rem, 4vw, 3rem);
}
  </style>
</head>
<body>
  <h1>Fluid Heading</h1>
</body>
</html>
```
    13. *Explanation:* Combines both techniques for optimal
        fluid typography.

Exercise 14: Responsive Footer with Scalable Text

Task: Create a footer where the text scales using relative
units and media queries.

Code:
```
<!DOCTYPE html>
<html lang="en">
<head>
```

```html
  <meta charset="UTF-8">
  <meta name="viewport"
content="width=device-width, initial-
scale=1.0">
  <title>Responsive Footer</title>
  <style>
    footer { font-size: 0.9rem; text-align:
center; background: #333; color: #fff;
padding: 20px; }
    @media (min-width: 768px) {
      footer { font-size: 1rem; }
    }
  </style>
</head>
<body>
  <footer>&copy; 2025 Responsive
Site</footer>
</body>
</html>
```

14. *Explanation:* Adjusts footer text size based on
viewport width.

Exercise 15: Responsive Card with Scalable Caption
Task: Build a card component with an image and caption
that scales responsively.
Code:

```html
<!DOCTYPE html>
<html lang="en">
<head>
  <meta charset="UTF-8">
  <meta name="viewport"
content="width=device-width, initial-
scale=1.0">
  <title>Responsive Card</title>
  <style>
    .card { border: 1px solid #ccc;
padding: 15px; }
```

```css
    .card img { max-width: 100%; height:
auto; }
    .card figcaption { font-size:
clamp(0.8rem, 2vw, 1rem); text-align:
center; }
  </style>
</head>
<body>
  <figure class="card">
    <img src="card.jpg" alt="Card Image">
    <figcaption>Card Caption</figcaption>
  </figure>
</body>
</html>
```

15. *Explanation:* Uses clamp() for a responsive caption.

Exercise 16: Implement a Responsive Hero Section with Scalable Text

Task: Create a hero section that uses relative and viewport units for text and a responsive background image.

Code:

```html
<!DOCTYPE html>
<html lang="en">
<head>
  <meta charset="UTF-8">
  <meta name="viewport"
content="width=device-width, initial-
scale=1.0">
  <title>Responsive Hero</title>
  <style>
    .hero {
      position: relative;
      background: url('hero.jpg') no-repeat
center/cover;
      height: 60vh;
      display: flex;
      justify-content: center;
```

```
      align-items: center;
      color: #fff;
    }
    .hero h1 {
      font-size: clamp(2rem, 5vw, 4rem);
    }
  </style>
</head>
<body>
  <div class="hero">
    <h1>Welcome to Our Site</h1>
  </div>
</body>
</html>
```

16. *Explanation:* The hero section text scales fluidly while the background image covers the viewport.

Exercise 17: Using @media to Adjust Image Margin

Task: Change the margin around an image based on screen size.

Code:

```
<!DOCTYPE html>
<html lang="en">
<head>
  <meta charset="UTF-8">
  <meta name="viewport"
content="width=device-width, initial-
scale=1.0">
  <title>Responsive Image Margin</title>
  <style>
    img { max-width: 100%; height: auto;
margin: 10px; }
    @media (min-width: 768px) {
      img { margin: 20px; }
    }
  </style>
</head>
```

```
<body>
  <img src="margin.jpg" alt="Margin
Example">
</body>
</html>
```

17. *Explanation:* Adjusts image margin with a media query.

Exercise 18: Responsive Block Quote with Scalable Font

Task: Create a block quote that adjusts font size using relative units and media queries.

Code:

```
<!DOCTYPE html>
<html lang="en">
<head>
  <meta charset="UTF-8">
  <meta name="viewport"
content="width=device-width, initial-
scale=1.0">
  <title>Responsive Block Quote</title>
  <style>
    blockquote { font-size: 1rem; border-
left: 4px solid #ccc; padding-left: 10px; }
    @media (min-width: 768px) {
      blockquote { font-size: 1.2rem; }
    }
  </style>
</head>
<body>
  <blockquote>
    "Responsive design is not a trend; it's
a necessity."
  </blockquote>
</body>
</html>
```

18. *Explanation:* Enhances readability of block quotes on larger devices.

Exercise 19: Responsive Headings with Media Queries

Task: Adjust multiple heading levels for different devices using media queries.

Code:

```html
<!DOCTYPE html>
<html lang="en">
<head>
  <meta charset="UTF-8">
  <meta name="viewport"
content="width=device-width, initial-
scale=1.0">
  <title>Responsive Headings</title>
  <style>
    h1 { font-size: 2rem; }
    h2 { font-size: 1.5rem; }
    @media (min-width: 768px) {
      h1 { font-size: 2.5rem; }
      h2 { font-size: 2rem; }
    }
  </style>
</head>
<body>
  <h1>Main Heading</h1>
  <h2>Subheading</h2>
</body>
</html>
```

19. *Explanation:* Adjusts heading sizes based on screen width.

Exercise 20: Using CSS Variables for Consistent Responsive Typography

Task: Create a stylesheet that uses CSS custom properties to control typography across breakpoints.

Code:

```html
<!DOCTYPE html>
<html lang="en">
<head>
```

```html
  <meta charset="UTF-8">
  <meta name="viewport"
content="width=device-width, initial-
scale=1.0">
  <title>CSS Variables Typography</title>
  <style>
    :root { --base-font: 16px; }
    body { font-size: var(--base-font); }
    h1 { font-size: calc(var(--base-font) *
2); }
    @media (min-width: 768px) {
      :root { --base-font: 18px; }
    }
  </style>
</head>
<body>
  <h1>Variable-Based Heading</h1>
  <p>Text scales with the base font defined
in CSS variables.</p>
</body>
</html>
```

20. *Explanation:* CSS variables ensure consistent scaling across the document.

Exercise 21: Responsive Figure with Both Picture Element and CSS

Task: Create a figure that uses the picture element for image selection and CSS for responsive typography on the caption.

Code:

```html
<!DOCTYPE html>
<html lang="en">
<head>
  <meta charset="UTF-8">
  <meta name="viewport"
content="width=device-width, initial-
scale=1.0">
```

```html
    <title>Responsive Figure</title>
    <style>
      figcaption { font-size: clamp(0.8rem,
2vw, 1rem); text-align: center; }
    </style>
</head>
<body>
  <figure>
    <picture>
      <source media="(min-width: 1024px)"
srcset="large.jpg">
      <source media="(min-width: 768px)"
srcset="medium.jpg">
      <img src="small.jpg" alt="Figure
Image">
    </picture>
    <figcaption>Adaptive Image
Caption</figcaption>
  </figure>
</body>
</html>
```

21. *Explanation:* Combines responsive image selection
    with scalable caption text.

**Exercise 22: Responsive Call-to-Action with Scalable
Typography**

Task: Create a call-to-action section where the button text
and padding adjust based on the viewport.

Code:

```html
<!DOCTYPE html>
<html lang="en">
<head>
  <meta charset="UTF-8">
  <meta name="viewport"
content="width=device-width, initial-
scale=1.0">
  <title>Responsive CTA</title>
```

```html
<style>
    .cta { text-align: center; padding:
20px; }
    .cta button { font-size: clamp(1rem,
2vw, 1.5rem); padding: 10px 20px; }
  </style>
</head>
<body>
  <div class="cta">
    <button>Click Here</button>
  </div>
</body>
</html>
```
22. *Explanation:* Uses clamp() for button text and
ensures padding adjusts responsively.

Exercise 23: Responsive Article with Adaptive Typography and Images

Task: Create a simple article layout where both the text and images scale responsively.

Code:
```html
<!DOCTYPE html>
<html lang="en">
<head>
  <meta charset="UTF-8">
  <meta name="viewport"
content="width=device-width, initial-
scale=1.0">
  <title>Responsive Article</title>
  <style>
    article { padding: 15px; }
    article h1 { font-size: clamp(1.8rem,
4vw, 2.5rem); }
    article p { font-size: 1rem; }
    article img { max-width: 100%; height:
auto; margin: 10px 0; }
  </style>
```

245

```
</head>
<body>
  <article>
    <h1>Article Title</h1>
    <img src="article.jpg" alt="Article
Image">
    <p>This article adjusts its layout for
responsive reading.</p>
  </article>
</body>
</html>
```

23. *Explanation:* Integrates scalable typography and responsive images in an article.

Exercise 24: Debugging Responsive Typography with Outlines

Task: Add CSS outlines to all typography elements to check their boundaries during development.

Code:

```
<!DOCTYPE html>
<html lang="en">
<head>
  <meta charset="UTF-8">
  <meta name="viewport"
content="width=device-width, initial-
scale=1.0">
  <title>Debug Typography</title>
  <style>
    * { outline: 1px dashed red; }
  </style>
</head>
<body>
  <h1>Debug Heading</h1>
  <p>Use outlines to see the boundaries of
typography elements.</p>
</body>
</html>
```

24. *Explanation:* Outlines help visualize spacing and
    element boundaries.

Exercise 25: Build a Complete Responsive Page Focusing on Typography and Images

Task: Create a full HTML page that uses mobile-first CSS for scalable typography and responsive images.

Code:

```
<!DOCTYPE html>
<html lang="en">
<head>
  <meta charset="UTF-8">
  <meta name="viewport"
content="width=device-width, initial-
scale=1.0">
  <title>Complete Responsive Page</title>
  <style>
    :root { font-size: 16px; }
    body { font-family: Arial, sans-serif;
margin: 0; padding: 10px; }
    header, footer { background: #333;
color: #fff; text-align: center; padding:
15px; }
    h1 { font-size: clamp(2rem, 4vw, 3rem);
}
    p { font-size: 1rem; line-height: 1.5;
}
    img { max-width: 100%; height: auto; }
    @media (min-width: 768px) {
      body { padding: 20px; }
      header, footer { padding: 20px; }
    }
  </style>
</head>
<body>
  <header><h1>My Responsive
Site</h1></header>
```

```
<main>
  <article>
    <h1>Article Title</h1>
    <img src="article.jpg" alt="Article
Image">
      <p>This article demonstrates
responsive typography and images using
mobile-first design principles.</p>
  </article>
</main>
<footer>&copy; 2025 My Responsive
Site</footer>
</body>
</html>
```

25. *Explanation:* Combines all the learned techniques to build a complete, responsive page.

25 Multiple Choice Questions with Full Explanations

Question 1: What is the primary benefit of using relative units (em, rem) for font sizes?

    A) They set a fixed size

    B) They scale based on parent or root font size

    C) They are easier to write

    D) They do not change with screen size

    Correct Answer: B

    Explanation: Relative units scale according to their parent (em) or root (rem) font size, enhancing responsiveness.

Question 2: What does the vw unit represent?

    A) Viewport width

    B) Virtual width

    C) Variable width

    D) Visible width

    Correct Answer: A

    Explanation: 1vw equals 1% of the viewport's width.

Question 3: Which CSS function allows you to set a value with a minimum, preferred, and maximum?

A) calc()

B) min()

C) clamp()

D) var()

Correct Answer: C

Explanation: The clamp() function constrains a value between a defined minimum and maximum.

Question 4: How does setting `max-width: 100%` on an image help responsiveness?

A) It makes the image fixed

B) It ensures the image does not exceed its container's width

C) It sets the image width to 100 pixels

D) It removes the image

Correct Answer: B

Explanation: It ensures the image scales down with its container while retaining its aspect ratio.

Question 5: What is the purpose of the `<picture>` element?

A) To add captions to images

B) To serve different images based on media conditions

C) To style images with CSS

D) To link to external images

Correct Answer: B

Explanation: The `<picture>` element lets you specify multiple sources for an image based on media queries.

Question 6: Which attribute is used in the `<img>` tag to define multiple image resolutions?

A) alt

B) srcset

C) sizes

D) href
Correct Answer: B
Explanation: The srcset attribute provides the browser with a list of image sources and their corresponding widths.
Question 7: What does the clamp() function do in CSS?
A) It calculates a sum
B) It sets a value within a defined range
C) It sets a fixed value
D) It converts units
Correct Answer: B
Explanation: clamp() ensures that a CSS property's value stays between a minimum and maximum.
Question 8: Which is a mobile-first strategy for typography?
A) Using max-width queries to adjust text for mobile
B) Writing base styles for mobile and enhancing them with min-width queries
C) Designing for desktop and scaling down
D) Using fixed pixel sizes
Correct Answer: B
Explanation: Mobile-first involves designing for small screens first, then using min-width media queries to enhance for larger screens.
Question 9: How does using the srcset attribute improve performance?
A) It compresses images
B) It allows the browser to choose the most appropriate image size
C) It caches images
D) It converts images to text
Correct Answer: B
Explanation: srcset helps deliver an image that is the right size for the device, reducing unnecessary bandwidth.
Question 10: What is the effect of setting an image's height to auto when using max-width: 100%?

A) It stretches the image vertically
B) It maintains the image's aspect ratio
C) It fixes the height
D) It hides the image

Correct Answer: B

Explanation: height: auto ensures that the image scales proportionally.

Question 11: Which unit is most appropriate for fluid typography?

A) px
B) em or rem
C) cm
D) pt

Correct Answer: B

Explanation: em and rem are relative units that adjust based on context and help create fluid typography.

Question 12: What does the sizes attribute in an img tag do?

A) It defines the display size of the image
B) It tells the browser how much space the image will take up
C) It sets the font size for captions
D) It changes the image resolution

Correct Answer: B

Explanation: The sizes attribute helps the browser determine which image from srcset to load.

Question 13: Why is it important to use responsive typography?

A) To ensure text is legible on all devices
B) To increase website load times
C) To use more pixels
D) To avoid media queries

Correct Answer: A

Explanation: Responsive typography improves readability and user experience across devices.

Question 14: What is the default behavior of an image without max-width: 100% in responsive design?

A) It scales to its container
B) It may overflow its container
C) It disappears
D) It automatically centers

Correct Answer: B

Explanation: Without max-width: 100%, images might exceed the container width and break the layout.

Question 15: Which of the following is a benefit of a mobile-first approach?

A) It creates larger images by default
B) It optimizes performance on smaller devices
C) It requires more media queries
D) It ignores desktop layouts

Correct Answer: B

Explanation: Mobile-first design ensures that performance is optimized for devices with limited resources.

Question 16: What does the viewport unit "vh" represent?

A) 1% of the viewport's width
B) 1% of the viewport's height
C) A fixed value
D) The device's pixel density

Correct Answer: B

Explanation: 1vh equals 1% of the viewport's height.

Question 17: In the following code, what is the minimum font size for h1?

```
h1 { font-size: clamp(1.5rem, 5vw, 3rem); }
```

A) 1.5rem
B) 5vw
C) 3rem
D) Depends on the viewport

Correct Answer: A

Explanation: The clamp() function ensures the font size does not go below 1.5rem.

Question 18: Which media query technique is used to adjust typography?

A) Using max-width queries

B) Using min-width queries
C) Both A and B
D) Neither
Correct Answer: C
Explanation: Both max-width and min-width media queries can be used to fine-tune typography for various screen sizes.

Question 19: How does the picture element enhance responsive images?
A) It compresses images automatically
B) It allows for conditional loading of different images based on media conditions
C) It increases image quality
D) It is used only for decorative images
Correct Answer: B
Explanation: The picture element gives control over which image file to load based on conditions like screen width.

Question 20: Which attribute would you use with the picture element to specify a source for large screens?
A) media
B) srcset
C) alt
D) sizes
Correct Answer: A
Explanation: The media attribute in a source element specifies the media condition.

Question 21: What is the primary purpose of using relative units for font sizes in responsive design?
A) To ensure text remains fixed
B) To allow text to scale proportionally with the viewport or parent element
C) To use fewer pixels
D) To create more media queries
Correct Answer: B
Explanation: Relative units ensure text scales in harmony with its container and viewport.

Question 22: What is the effect of setting an image's width to 100%?

    A) The image fills its container's width
    B) The image becomes 100 pixels wide
    C) The image is cropped
    D) The image loses quality

    Correct Answer: A

    Explanation: It makes the image responsive by filling the container.

Question 23: Which of the following best describes the srcset attribute?

    A) It specifies multiple image sources for different display densities and sizes
    B) It defines a single image source
    C) It sets the alt text for an image
    D) It links to an external stylesheet

    Correct Answer: A

    Explanation: srcset enables the browser to choose from multiple image sources based on device needs.

Question 24: Why is it important to test responsive typography on different devices?

    A) To ensure consistent readability and usability
    B) To increase page load time
    C) To eliminate the need for images
    D) To use fixed layouts

    Correct Answer: A

    Explanation: Testing ensures that text remains legible and well-formatted on all devices.

Question 25: Which approach helps ensure that images look sharp on high-resolution devices?

    A) Using a single image for all devices
    B) Using the picture element with srcset and sizes
    C) Avoiding media queries
    D) Setting image dimensions in pixels

    Correct Answer: B

    Explanation: The picture element with srcset allows serving higher-resolution images to high-DPI devices.

This comprehensive package for **Chapter 6: Responsive Typography and Images** includes a detailed outline, in-depth chapter content, 25 code snippets and examples, 25 hands-on coding exercises with full code and explanations, and 25 multiple choice questions with detailed explanations. Use these resources to master the art of creating fluid, adaptable typography and images that ensure an optimal user experience on every device

Chapter 7: Responsive Navigation Menus

Detailed Outline

1. **Introduction to Navigation Menus**
   - Overview of different types of navigation menus:
     - Horizontal navigation bars
     - Vertical side menus
     - Hamburger (mobile) menus
   - Importance of navigation in user experience and site structure

2. **Building a Basic Responsive Menu**
   - Setting up HTML for a simple navigation menu
   - Using semantic elements like `<nav>`, `<ul>`, and `<li>`
   - Basic CSS styling for desktop menus

3. **Using CSS Flexbox for Navigation**
   - Creating a flex container for navigation items
   - Horizontal alignment and spacing with Flexbox
   - Adjusting navigation layout for responsiveness

4. **Creating a Mobile-Friendly Hamburger Menu**
   - Designing a hamburger icon using HTML and CSS
   - Hiding/showing the full menu on mobile screens
   - Using media queries to control the menu display

5. **Enhancing Navigation with JavaScript**
   - Adding interactivity to the hamburger menu (toggle open/close)
   - Basic JavaScript for menu button functionality
   - Improving accessibility with ARIA attributes

6. **Conclusion and Best Practices**
    - ○ Recap of key techniques: basic menu, Flexbox layout, hamburger menus, and JavaScript enhancements
    - ○ Tips for testing and refining navigation menus
    - ○ Preview of next topics (e.g., advanced navigation interactions)

Chapter Content

1. Introduction to Navigation Menus

Navigation is one of the most critical parts of a website, guiding users through content and features. In this chapter, we will explore several types of navigation menus, from traditional horizontal menus to mobile-friendly hamburger menus. A well-designed responsive navigation menu adapts to different devices, ensuring that users can easily access your site's content regardless of screen size.

2. Building a Basic Responsive Menu

We start with the fundamentals by creating a simple HTML structure using semantic elements such as `<nav>`, `<ul>`, and `<li>`. Basic CSS will style the menu, providing a solid foundation for more advanced responsive techniques.

3. Using CSS Flexbox for Navigation

Flexbox is a powerful tool for aligning and distributing space among navigation items. By setting a navigation container to `display: flex;`, you can easily center items, space them evenly, and allow the menu to adapt to various screen sizes without much extra effort.

4. Creating a Mobile-Friendly Hamburger Menu

On mobile devices, screen space is limited. A hamburger menu is a compact solution that hides the navigation links behind an icon until the user is ready to access them. We'll build a hamburger menu using HTML and CSS, then use media queries to show or hide elements based on screen width.

5. Enhancing Navigation with JavaScript

To add interactivity to your hamburger menu, you can use JavaScript to toggle the menu's visibility. We'll demonstrate a simple script that listens for a click event on the hamburger icon, expanding or collapsing the navigation links. We'll also discuss how to include ARIA attributes to improve accessibility.

6. Conclusion and Best Practices

We've covered the basics of building responsive navigation menus using HTML, CSS Flexbox, media queries, and JavaScript enhancements. As you develop your navigation, remember to test across devices and use best practices to ensure both usability and accessibility.

25 Code Snippets and Examples

Basic HTML Navigation Structure

```
<nav>
  <ul>
    <li><a href="#">Home</a></li>
    <li><a href="#">About</a></li>
    <li><a href="#">Services</a></li>
    <li><a href="#">Contact</a></li>
  </ul>
</nav>
```

1. *Explanation:* A simple semantic navigation using <nav>, <ul>, and <li>.

Basic CSS Styling for Navigation

```
nav ul {
  list-style: none;
  margin: 0;
  padding: 0;
  display: flex;
}
nav li {
  margin: 0 15px;
}
nav a {
  text-decoration: none;
```

```css
  color: #333;
}
```

2. *Explanation:* Styles the navigation for a horizontal desktop layout.

Responsive Navigation Container with Flexbox

```css
.nav-container {
  display: flex;
  justify-content: space-around;
  background: #f8f8f8;
  padding: 10px;
}
```

3. *Explanation:* Creates a flex container for evenly spaced navigation items.

Centering Navigation Items with Flexbox

```css
.nav-container {
  display: flex;
  justify-content: center;
  gap: 20px;
}
```

4. *Explanation:* Centers items horizontally and uses gap for spacing.

Vertical Navigation Menu

```css
.vertical-nav ul {
  list-style: none;
  padding: 0;
}
.vertical-nav li {
  margin-bottom: 10px;
}
```

5. *Explanation:* Styles for a vertical (sidebar) navigation menu.

Media Query for Hiding Navigation on Mobile

```css
@media (max-width: 600px) {
  .nav-container { display: none; }
}
```

6. *Explanation:* Hides the standard navigation on screens 600px wide or less.

Hamburger Icon with CSS

```html
<div class="hamburger">
  <span></span>
  <span></span>
  <span></span>
</div>
```

```css
.hamburger span {
  display: block;
  width: 25px;
  height: 3px;
  background: #333;
  margin: 5px 0;
}
```

7. *Explanation:* Creates a hamburger icon using three stacked spans.

Media Query to Display Hamburger Menu

```css
@media (max-width: 600px) {
  .hamburger { display: block; }
  .nav-container { display: none; }
}
```

8. *Explanation:* Shows the hamburger icon on small screens while hiding the full menu.

Toggle Navigation Menu (CSS Only)

```css
.nav-menu { display: none; }
.nav-menu.active { display: block; }
```

9. *Explanation:* CSS class to toggle menu visibility.

Basic JavaScript Toggle for Hamburger Menu

```html
<script>

document.querySelector('.hamburger').addEve
ntListener('click', function() {
    document.querySelector('.nav-
menu').classList.toggle('active');
  });
</script>
```

10. *Explanation:* Simple script to toggle the navigation menu on click.

Flexbox Navigation with Space-Between

```css
.nav-container {
  display: flex;
  justify-content: space-between;
  align-items: center;
  padding: 10px 20px;
  background: #eee;
}
```

11. *Explanation:* Distributes navigation items evenly with space between.

Fixed Navigation Bar at the Top

```css
nav {
  position: fixed;
  top: 0;
  width: 100%;
  background: #fff;
  box-shadow: 0 2px 4px rgba(0,0,0,0.1);
}
```

12. *Explanation:* Keeps the navigation fixed at the top of the page.

Responsive Navigation with Dropdown (Basic)

```html
<nav>
  <ul>
    <li><a href="#">Home</a></li>
    <li>
      <a href="#">Services</a>
      <ul class="dropdown">
        <li><a href="#">Design</a></li>
        <li><a
href="#">Development</a></li>
      </ul>
    </li>
    <li><a href="#">Contact</a></li>
  </ul>
```

```
</nav>
```

13. *Explanation:* A nested list for a dropdown menu.

CSS for Dropdown Menu

```css
nav ul li { position: relative; }
nav ul li ul.dropdown {
  display: none;
  position: absolute;
  top: 100%;
  left: 0;
  list-style: none;
  background: #fff;
  box-shadow: 0 2px 4px rgba(0,0,0,0.1);
}
nav ul li:hover ul.dropdown { display:
block; }
```

14. *Explanation:* Displays the dropdown on hover.

Responsive Hamburger Menu with Transition

```css
.hamburger {
  cursor: pointer;
  transition: all 0.3s ease;
}
.hamburger.active span:nth-child(1) {
transform: rotate(45deg) translate(5px,
5px); }
.hamburger.active span:nth-child(2) {
opacity: 0; }
.hamburger.active span:nth-child(3) {
transform: rotate(-45deg) translate(5px, -
5px); }
```

15. *Explanation:* Adds a transition to animate the hamburger icon into a cross.

Basic HTML for a Responsive Navigation Menu

```html
<header>
  <div
class="hamburger"><span></span><span></span
><span></span></div>
```

```
<nav class="nav-menu">
  <ul>
    <li><a href="#">Home</a></li>
    <li><a href="#">About</a></li>
    <li><a href="#">Services</a></li>
    <li><a href="#">Contact</a></li>
  </ul>
</nav>
</header>
```

16. *Explanation:* Complete structure for a responsive navigation header.

CSS Media Query to Switch from Full Menu to Hamburger

```
@media (max-width: 600px) {
  .nav-menu { display: none; }
  .hamburger { display: block; }
}
@media (min-width: 601px) {
  .nav-menu { display: block; }
  .hamburger { display: none; }
}
```

17. *Explanation:* Shows full menu on larger screens and hamburger on small screens.

CSS Styling for Mobile Navigation Menu

```
@media (max-width: 600px) {
  .nav-menu ul {
    flex-direction: column;
    align-items: center;
  }
  .nav-menu li { margin: 10px 0; }
}
```

18. *Explanation:* Stacks navigation items vertically on mobile.

Accessible Hamburger Menu with ARIA

```
<div class="hamburger" aria-label="Menu"
aria-expanded="false" role="button">
```

```
<span></span><span></span><span></span>
</div>
```

19. *Explanation:* Adds ARIA attributes to improve accessibility.

JavaScript to Toggle ARIA Attribute

```
<script>
  const hamburger =
document.querySelector('.hamburger');
  hamburger.addEventListener('click',
function() {
    const expanded =
this.getAttribute('aria-expanded') ===
'true' || false;
    this.setAttribute('aria-expanded',
!expanded);
    document.querySelector('.nav-
menu').classList.toggle('active');
  });
</script>
```

20. *Explanation:* Toggles the ARIA attribute along with menu visibility.

CSS for Smooth Transition in Navigation

```
.nav-menu {
  transition: all 0.3s ease;
}
```

21. *Explanation:* Adds smooth animation when toggling the menu.

Responsive Navigation with Border and Shadow

```
nav {
  border-bottom: 1px solid #ddd;
  box-shadow: 0 2px 4px rgba(0,0,0,0.05);
}
```

22. *Explanation:* Enhances the visual separation of the navigation bar.

CSS to Change Link Color on Hover

```
nav a:hover {
```

```css
  color: #007bff;
}
```

23. *Explanation:* Provides visual feedback when hovering over links.

CSS for Fixed Navigation on Scroll
```css
header {
  position: fixed;
  top: 0;
  width: 100%;
  z-index: 1000;
}
```

24. *Explanation:* Keeps the navigation visible at the top while scrolling.

Combining Flexbox and Media Queries for Navigation Layout
```css
.nav-container {
  display: flex;
  justify-content: space-between;
  align-items: center;
  padding: 10px;
  background: #fff;
}
@media (max-width: 600px) {
  .nav-container { flex-direction: column;
}
}
```

25. *Explanation:* Adjusts navigation container layout based on screen size.

25 Coding Exercises with Full Code and Explanations

Exercise 1: Create a Basic Navigation Bar
Task: Build a simple horizontal navigation bar using semantic HTML and basic CSS.
Code:
```html
<!DOCTYPE html>
<html lang="en">
```

```html
<head>
  <meta charset="UTF-8">
  <meta name="viewport"
content="width=device-width, initial-
scale=1.0">
  <title>Basic Navigation</title>
  <style>
    nav ul { list-style: none; padding: 0;
display: flex; }
    nav li { margin: 0 15px; }
    nav a { text-decoration: none; color:
#333; }
  </style>
</head>
<body>
  <nav>
    <ul>
      <li><a href="#">Home</a></li>
      <li><a href="#">About</a></li>
      <li><a href="#">Services</a></li>
      <li><a href="#">Contact</a></li>
    </ul>
  </nav>
</body>
</html>
```

1. *Explanation:* This exercise introduces the basic structure and styling of a navigation bar.

Exercise 2: Style Navigation with Flexbox

Task: Use Flexbox to center and space navigation items evenly.

Code:

```html
<!DOCTYPE html>
<html lang="en">
<head>
  <meta charset="UTF-8">
```

```html
    <meta name="viewport"
content="width=device-width, initial-
scale=1.0">
    <title>Flex Navigation</title>
    <style>
      nav { display: flex; justify-content:
center; gap: 20px; background: #f0f0f0;
padding: 10px; }
      nav a { text-decoration: none; color:
#333; }
    </style>
</head>
<body>
    <nav>
      <a href="#">Home</a>
      <a href="#">About</a>
      <a href="#">Services</a>
      <a href="#">Contact</a>
    </nav>
</body>
</html>
```

2. *Explanation:* Demonstrates using Flexbox to create a centered navigation layout.

Exercise 3: Build a Vertical Sidebar Navigation

Task: Create a vertical navigation menu suitable for a sidebar.

Code:

```html
<!DOCTYPE html>
<html lang="en">
<head>
    <meta charset="UTF-8">
    <meta name="viewport"
content="width=device-width, initial-
scale=1.0">
    <title>Vertical Sidebar</title>
    <style>
```

```
    .vertical-nav ul { list-style: none;
padding: 0; }
    .vertical-nav li { margin: 10px 0; }
    .vertical-nav a { text-decoration:
none; color: #333; }
  </style>
</head>
<body>
  <div class="vertical-nav">
    <ul>
      <li><a href="#">Dashboard</a></li>
      <li><a href="#">Profile</a></li>
      <li><a href="#">Settings</a></li>
      <li><a href="#">Logout</a></li>
    </ul>
  </div>
</body>
</html>
```

3. *Explanation:* Provides a vertical navigation layout using a simple list.

Exercise 4: Create a Responsive Navigation with Media Queries

Task: Build a navigation menu that displays as a full menu on desktops and hides on screens 600px or less.

Code:

```
<!DOCTYPE html>
<html lang="en">
<head>
  <meta charset="UTF-8">
  <meta name="viewport"
content="width=device-width, initial-
scale=1.0">
  <title>Responsive Navigation</title>
  <style>
    .nav-menu { display: block; }
    @media (max-width: 600px) {
```

```
      .nav-menu { display: none; }
    }
  </style>
</head>
<body>
  <nav class="nav-menu">
    <ul>
      <li><a href="#">Home</a></li>
      <li><a href="#">About</a></li>
      <li><a href="#">Services</a></li>
      <li><a href="#">Contact</a></li>
    </ul>
  </nav>
</body>
</html>
```

4. *Explanation:* Uses a media query to hide the full menu on mobile devices.

Exercise 5: Design a Hamburger Icon

Task: Create a hamburger icon using HTML and CSS.

Code:

```
<!DOCTYPE html>
<html lang="en">
<head>
  <meta charset="UTF-8">
  <meta name="viewport"
content="width=device-width, initial-
scale=1.0">
  <title>Hamburger Icon</title>
  <style>
    .hamburger span {
      display: block;
      width: 25px;
      height: 3px;
      background: #333;
      margin: 5px 0;
    }
```

```
    </style>
  </head>
  <body>
    <div class="hamburger">
      <span></span>
      <span></span>
      <span></span>
    </div>
  </body>
</html>
```

5. *Explanation:* Builds a simple hamburger icon with three bars.

Exercise 6: Toggle Navigation with JavaScript

Task: Implement a script to toggle the visibility of the navigation menu when the hamburger icon is clicked.

Code:

```
<!DOCTYPE html>
<html lang="en">
<head>
  <meta charset="UTF-8">
  <meta name="viewport"
content="width=device-width, initial-
scale=1.0">
  <title>Toggle Navigation</title>
  <style>
    .nav-menu { display: none; }
    .nav-menu.active { display: block; }
    .hamburger { cursor: pointer; }
    .hamburger span { display: block;
width: 25px; height: 3px; background: #333;
margin: 5px 0; }
  </style>
</head>
<body>
  <div class="hamburger">
    <span></span>
```

```
    <span></span>
    <span></span>
  </div>
  <nav class="nav-menu">
    <ul>
      <li><a href="#">Home</a></li>
      <li><a href="#">About</a></li>
      <li><a href="#">Services</a></li>
      <li><a href="#">Contact</a></li>
    </ul>
  </nav>
  <script>

document.querySelector('.hamburger').addEve
ntListener('click', function() {
    document.querySelector('.nav-
menu').classList.toggle('active');
    });
  </script>
</body>
</html>
```

6. *Explanation:* JavaScript toggles the "active" class on the navigation menu when the hamburger is clicked.

Exercise 7: Responsive Hamburger Menu with Media Queries

Task: Show the hamburger icon on screens 600px or less and hide the full navigation.

Code:

```
<!DOCTYPE html>
<html lang="en">
<head>
  <meta charset="UTF-8">
  <meta name="viewport"
content="width=device-width, initial-
scale=1.0">
```

```html
<title>Responsive Hamburger</title>
<style>
   .hamburger { display: none; cursor: pointer; }
   .hamburger span { display: block; width: 25px; height: 3px; background: #333; margin: 5px 0; }
   @media (max-width: 600px) {
      .hamburger { display: block; }
      .nav-menu { display: none; }
   }
</style>
</head>
<body>
  <div class="hamburger">
    <span></span>
    <span></span>
    <span></span>
  </div>
  <nav class="nav-menu">
    <ul>
      <li><a href="#">Home</a></li>
      <li><a href="#">About</a></li>
      <li><a href="#">Services</a></li>
      <li><a href="#">Contact</a></li>
    </ul>
  </nav>
</body>
</html>
```

7. *Explanation:* Uses media queries to display the hamburger and hide the full menu on mobile.

Exercise 8: Enhance Hamburger with Transition Effects

Task: Add CSS transitions to animate the hamburger icon when toggled.

Code:

```html
<!DOCTYPE html>
```

```html
<html lang="en">
<head>
  <meta charset="UTF-8">
  <meta name="viewport"
content="width=device-width, initial-
scale=1.0">
  <title>Hamburger Transition</title>
  <style>
    .hamburger { cursor: pointer;
transition: all 0.3s ease; }
    .hamburger span { display: block;
width: 25px; height: 3px; background: #333;
margin: 5px 0; transition: all 0.3s ease; }
    .hamburger.active span:nth-child(1) {
transform: rotate(45deg) translate(5px,
5px); }
    .hamburger.active span:nth-child(2) {
opacity: 0; }
    .hamburger.active span:nth-child(3) {
transform: rotate(-45deg) translate(5px, -
5px); }
  </style>
</head>
<body>
  <div class="hamburger" id="hamburger">
    <span></span>
    <span></span>
    <span></span>
  </div>
  <script>

document.getElementById('hamburger').addEve
ntListener('click', function() {
      this.classList.toggle('active');
    });
  </script>
```

```
</body>
</html>
```

8. *Explanation:* Animates the hamburger icon into a cross when clicked.

Exercise 9: Navigation with Dropdown Submenu

Task: Create a navigation menu with a dropdown submenu that appears on hover.

Code:

```
<!DOCTYPE html>
<html lang="en">
<head>
  <meta charset="UTF-8">
  <meta name="viewport"
content="width=device-width, initial-
scale=1.0">
  <title>Dropdown Navigation</title>
  <style>
    nav ul { list-style: none; padding: 0;
margin: 0; display: flex; }
    nav li { position: relative; margin: 0
15px; }
    nav li ul.dropdown { display: none;
position: absolute; top: 100%; left: 0;
background: #fff; box-shadow: 0 2px 4px
rgba(0,0,0,0.1); }
    nav li:hover ul.dropdown { display:
block; }
    nav a { text-decoration: none; color:
#333; padding: 5px 0; }
  </style>
</head>
<body>
  <nav>
    <ul>
      <li><a href="#">Home</a></li>
      <li>
```

```
          <a href="#">Services</a>
          <ul class="dropdown">
            <li><a href="#">Design</a></li>
            <li><a
href="#">Development</a></li>
          </ul>
        </li>
        <li><a href="#">Contact</a></li>
      </ul>
    </nav>
</body>
</html>
```

9. *Explanation:* Demonstrates a dropdown submenu that appears on hover.

Exercise 10: Fixed Navigation on Scroll

Task: Create a navigation bar that stays fixed at the top of the viewport.

Code:

```
<!DOCTYPE html>
<html lang="en">
<head>
  <meta charset="UTF-8">
  <meta name="viewport"
content="width=device-width, initial-
scale=1.0">
  <title>Fixed Navigation</title>
  <style>
    nav { position: fixed; top: 0; width:
100%; background: #fff; box-shadow: 0 2px
4px rgba(0,0,0,0.1); padding: 10px; }
    body { padding-top: 60px; }
  </style>
</head>
<body>
  <nav>
```

```html
    <ul style="display: flex; list-style:
none; justify-content: space-around;">
      <li><a href="#">Home</a></li>
      <li><a href="#">About</a></li>
      <li><a href="#">Services</a></li>
      <li><a href="#">Contact</a></li>
    </ul>
  </nav>
  <p>Scroll down to see the fixed
navigation bar.</p>
</body>
</html>
```

10. *Explanation:* Fixes the navigation bar at the top while allowing content to scroll beneath it.

Exercise 11: Accessible Hamburger with ARIA

Task: Enhance the hamburger menu for accessibility using ARIA attributes.

Code:

```html
<!DOCTYPE html>
<html lang="en">
<head>
  <meta charset="UTF-8">
  <meta name="viewport"
content="width=device-width, initial-
scale=1.0">
  <title>Accessible Hamburger</title>
  <style>
    .hamburger { cursor: pointer; }
    .hamburger span { display: block;
width: 25px; height: 3px; background: #333;
margin: 5px 0; }
  </style>
</head>
<body>
```

```html
<div class="hamburger" aria-label="Menu"
aria-expanded="false" role="button"
id="hamburger">
    <span></span>
    <span></span>
    <span></span>
  </div>
  <script>

document.getElementById('hamburger').addEve
ntListener('click', function() {
      let expanded =
this.getAttribute('aria-expanded') ===
'true';
      this.setAttribute('aria-expanded',
!expanded);
    });
  </script>
</body>
</html>
```

11. *Explanation:* Adds ARIA attributes for improved accessibility.

Exercise 12: Responsive Navigation with Combined Flexbox and Media Queries

Task: Build a navigation container that changes its layout based on screen width.

Code:

```html
<!DOCTYPE html>
<html lang="en">
<head>
  <meta charset="UTF-8">
  <meta name="viewport"
content="width=device-width, initial-
scale=1.0">
  <title>Responsive Flex Navigation</title>
  <style>
```

```css
    .nav-container {
      display: flex;
      justify-content: space-between;
      align-items: center;
      padding: 10px;
      background: #fff;
    }
    @media (max-width: 600px) {
      .nav-container { flex-direction:
column; }
    }
  </style>
</head>
```
```html
<body>
  <header class="nav-container">
    <div class="logo">Logo</div>
    <nav>
      <a href="#">Home</a>
      <a href="#">About</a>
      <a href="#">Services</a>
      <a href="#">Contact</a>
    </nav>
  </header>
</body>
</html>
```
12. *Explanation:* Adjusts the layout direction based on screen size.

Exercise 13: Build a Hamburger Menu with Dropdown Animation

Task: Create a hamburger menu that expands with a smooth animation.

Code:
```html
<!DOCTYPE html>
<html lang="en">
<head>
  <meta charset="UTF-8">
```

```html
  <meta name="viewport"
content="width=device-width, initial-
scale=1.0">
  <title>Animated Hamburger Menu</title>
  <style>
    .nav-menu { display: none; transition:
max-height 0.3s ease; overflow: hidden; }
    .nav-menu.active { display: block; }
    .hamburger { cursor: pointer; }
    .hamburger span { display: block;
width: 25px; height: 3px; background: #333;
margin: 5px 0; }
  </style>
</head>
<body>
  <div class="hamburger" id="hamburger">
    <span></span>
    <span></span>
    <span></span>
  </div>
  <nav class="nav-menu" id="navMenu">
    <ul>
      <li><a href="#">Home</a></li>
      <li><a href="#">Portfolio</a></li>
      <li><a href="#">Blog</a></li>
      <li><a href="#">Contact</a></li>
    </ul>
  </nav>
  <script>

document.getElementById('hamburger').addEve
ntListener('click', function() {

document.getElementById('navMenu').classLis
t.toggle('active');
    });
```

```
    </script>
  </body>
</html>
```

13. *Explanation:* Adds a smooth transition when toggling the dropdown navigation.

Exercise 14: Create a Sticky Navigation Bar

Task: Implement a navigation bar that remains at the top during scrolling.

Code:

```
<!DOCTYPE html>
<html lang="en">
<head>
  <meta charset="UTF-8">
  <meta name="viewport"
content="width=device-width, initial-
scale=1.0">
  <title>Sticky Navigation</title>
  <style>
    nav {
      position: sticky;
      top: 0;
      background: #fff;
      padding: 10px;
      box-shadow: 0 2px 4px
rgba(0,0,0,0.1);
    }
  </style>
</head>
<body>
  <nav>
    <ul style="display: flex; list-style:
none; justify-content: space-around;">
      <li><a href="#">Home</a></li>
      <li><a href="#">About</a></li>
      <li><a href="#">Services</a></li>
      <li><a href="#">Contact</a></li>
```

```html
    </ul>
  </nav>
  <div style="height: 2000px;">Scroll down
to see the sticky nav in action.</div>
</body>
</html>
```
14. *Explanation:* Uses CSS sticky positioning for a
    navigation bar that stays in view.

Exercise 15: Responsive Hamburger with JavaScript and ARIA

Task: Combine JavaScript toggle with ARIA attributes for an accessible hamburger menu.

Code:
```html
<!DOCTYPE html>
<html lang="en">
<head>
  <meta charset="UTF-8">
  <meta name="viewport"
content="width=device-width, initial-
scale=1.0">
  <title>Accessible Hamburger Menu</title>
  <style>
    .hamburger { cursor: pointer; }
    .hamburger span { display: block;
width: 25px; height: 3px; background: #333;
margin: 5px 0; }
    .nav-menu { display: none; }
    .nav-menu.active { display: block; }
  </style>
</head>
<body>
  <div class="hamburger" id="hamburger"
aria-label="Menu" aria-expanded="false"
role="button">
    <span></span>
    <span></span>
```

```html
      <span></span>
    </div>
    <nav class="nav-menu" id="navMenu">
      <ul>
        <li><a href="#">Home</a></li>
        <li><a href="#">Services</a></li>
        <li><a href="#">Contact</a></li>
      </ul>
    </nav>
    <script>
      const hamburger =
document.getElementById('hamburger');
      const navMenu =
document.getElementById('navMenu');
      hamburger.addEventListener('click',
function() {
        let expanded =
this.getAttribute('aria-expanded') ===
'true';
        this.setAttribute('aria-expanded',
!expanded);
        navMenu.classList.toggle('active');
      });
    </script>
</body>
</html>
```

15. *Explanation:* Enhances the hamburger menu with accessibility features and interactivity.

Exercise 16: Creating a Horizontal Dropdown in a Responsive Menu

Task: Build a horizontal navigation bar with a dropdown submenu that works on desktop.

Code:

```html
<!DOCTYPE html>
<html lang="en">
<head>
```

```html
    <meta charset="UTF-8">
    <meta name="viewport"
content="width=device-width, initial-
scale=1.0">
    <title>Horizontal Dropdown</title>
    <style>
      nav ul { list-style: none; padding: 0;
display: flex; }
      nav li { position: relative; margin: 0
15px; }
      nav li ul.dropdown {
        display: none;
        position: absolute;
        top: 100%;
        left: 0;
        background: #fff;
        box-shadow: 0 2px 4px
rgba(0,0,0,0.1);
        padding: 10px;
        list-style: none;
      }
      nav li:hover ul.dropdown { display:
block; }
      nav a { text-decoration: none; color:
#333; }
    </style>
</head>
<body>
  <nav>
    <ul>
      <li><a href="#">Home</a></li>
      <li>
        <a href="#">Products</a>
        <ul class="dropdown">
          <li><a href="#">Product
1</a></li>
```

```html
          <li><a href="#">Product
2</a></li>
        </ul>
      </li>
      <li><a href="#">Contact</a></li>
    </ul>
  </nav>
</body>
</html>
```

16. *Explanation:* Shows a desktop dropdown submenu in a horizontal navigation bar.

Exercise 17: Responsive Navigation with Social Media Icons

Task: Add social media icons to a navigation bar that adapt responsively.

Code:

```html
<!DOCTYPE html>
<html lang="en">
<head>
  <meta charset="UTF-8">
  <meta name="viewport"
content="width=device-width, initial-
scale=1.0">
  <title>Navigation with Icons</title>
  <style>
    nav { display: flex; justify-content:
space-between; align-items: center;
padding: 10px; background: #fff; }
    nav ul { list-style: none; display:
flex; margin: 0; padding: 0; }
    nav li { margin: 0 10px; }
    nav a { text-decoration: none; color:
#333; }
    .social { display: flex; }
    .social a { margin-left: 10px; }
  </style>
```

```html
  </head>
<body>
  <nav>
    <ul>
      <li><a href="#">Home</a></li>
      <li><a href="#">About</a></li>
    </ul>
    <div class="social">
      <a href="#"><img src="facebook.png"
alt="Facebook" width="20"></a>
      <a href="#"><img src="twitter.png"
alt="Twitter" width="20"></a>
    </div>
  </nav>
</body>
</html>
```

17. *Explanation:* Integrates social media icons into the navigation.

Exercise 18: Navigation with Submenu for Mobile

Task: Create a mobile-friendly navigation where clicking a menu item reveals a submenu.

Code:

```html
<!DOCTYPE html>
<html lang="en">
<head>
  <meta charset="UTF-8">
  <meta name="viewport"
content="width=device-width, initial-
scale=1.0">
  <title>Mobile Submenu</title>
  <style>
    .nav-menu ul { list-style: none;
padding: 0; }
    .nav-menu li { position: relative; }
    .submenu { display: none; }
```

```
    .nav-menu li.active .submenu { display:
block; }
    @media (max-width: 600px) {
      .nav-menu ul { display: block; }
      .nav-menu li { margin: 10px 0; }
    }
  </style>
</head>
<body>
  <nav class="nav-menu">
    <ul>
      <li><a href="#">Home</a></li>
      <li id="mobileSubmenu">
        <a href="#">Services</a>
        <ul class="submenu">
          <li><a href="#">Design</a></li>
          <li><a
href="#">Development</a></li>
        </ul>
      </li>
    </ul>
  </nav>
  <script>

document.getElementById('mobileSubmenu').ad
dEventListener('click', function(e) {
      e.preventDefault();
      this.classList.toggle('active');
    });
  </script>
</body>
</html>
```

18. *Explanation:* Uses JavaScript to toggle a submenu in a mobile navigation.

Exercise 19: Animated Navigation Link Hover Effect

Task: Add a hover effect to navigation links that underlines them smoothly.

Code:

```
<!DOCTYPE html>
<html lang="en">
<head>
  <meta charset="UTF-8">
  <meta name="viewport"
content="width=device-width, initial-
scale=1.0">
  <title>Link Hover Effect</title>
  <style>
    nav a {
      position: relative;
      color: #333;
      text-decoration: none;
      padding-bottom: 5px;
    }
    nav a::after {
      content: '';
      position: absolute;
      left: 0;
      bottom: 0;
      width: 0;
      height: 2px;
      background: #007bff;
      transition: width 0.3s;
    }
    nav a:hover::after { width: 100%; }
  </style>
</head>
<body>
  <nav>
    <a href="#">Home</a>
    <a href="#">About</a>
```

```
    </nav>
</body>
</html>
```

19. *Explanation:* Creates a smooth underline effect on hover.

Exercise 20: Fixed Header with Responsive Navigation

Task: Create a fixed header that contains a responsive navigation menu.

Code:

```
<!DOCTYPE html>
<html lang="en">
<head>
  <meta charset="UTF-8">
  <meta name="viewport"
content="width=device-width, initial-
scale=1.0">
  <title>Fixed Responsive Header</title>
  <style>
    header {
      position: fixed;
      top: 0;
      width: 100%;
      background: #fff;
      box-shadow: 0 2px 4px
rgba(0,0,0,0.1);
      z-index: 1000;
      padding: 10px;
    }
    body { padding-top: 60px; }
    nav ul { list-style: none; display:
flex; justify-content: space-around; }
    nav a { text-decoration: none; color:
#333; }
    @media (max-width: 600px) {
      nav ul { flex-direction: column; }
    }
```

```html
    </style>
</head>
<body>
  <header>
    <nav>
      <ul>
        <li><a href="#">Home</a></li>
        <li><a href="#">Services</a></li>
        <li><a href="#">Contact</a></li>
      </ul>
    </nav>
  </header>
  <div style="height: 2000px;">Scroll to
see the fixed header.</div>
</body>
</html>
```

20. *Explanation:* Implements a fixed header with a responsive navigation menu.

Exercise 21: Toggle Navigation with Fade Effect

Task: Create a navigation menu that fades in/out when toggled.

Code:

```html
<!DOCTYPE html>
<html lang="en">
<head>
  <meta charset="UTF-8">
  <meta name="viewport"
content="width=device-width, initial-
scale=1.0">
  <title>Fade Toggle Menu</title>
  <style>
    .nav-menu {
      display: none;
      opacity: 0;
      transition: opacity 0.5s;
    }
```

```
    .nav-menu.active {
      display: block;
      opacity: 1;
    }
  </style>
</head>
<body>
  <div class="hamburger"
id="hamburger">Menu</div>
  <nav class="nav-menu" id="navMenu">
    <ul>
      <li><a href="#">Home</a></li>
      <li><a href="#">Blog</a></li>
      <li><a href="#">Contact</a></li>
    </ul>
  </nav>
  <script>

document.getElementById('hamburger').addEve
ntListener('click', function() {

document.getElementById('navMenu').classLis
t.toggle('active');
    });
  </script>
</body>
</html>
```
21. *Explanation:* Adds a fade-in/out effect when toggling the menu.

Exercise 22: Navigation with Logo and Search Bar
Task: Create a navigation header that includes a logo, navigation links, and a search bar.
Code:
```
<!DOCTYPE html>
<html lang="en">
<head>
```

```
  <meta charset="UTF-8">
  <meta name="viewport"
content="width=device-width, initial-
scale=1.0">
  <title>Logo and Search Navigation</title>
  <style>
    header {
      display: flex;
      justify-content: space-between;
      align-items: center;
      padding: 10px;
      background: #fff;
      box-shadow: 0 2px 4px
rgba(0,0,0,0.1);
    }
    .logo { font-size: 1.5rem; font-weight:
bold; }
    nav ul { list-style: none; display:
flex; gap: 15px; }
    .search input { padding: 5px; }
  </style>
</head>
<body>
  <header>
    <div class="logo">MySite</div>
    <nav>
      <ul>
        <li><a href="#">Home</a></li>
        <li><a href="#">About</a></li>
        <li><a href="#">Services</a></li>
      </ul>
    </nav>
    <div class="search">
      <input type="text"
placeholder="Search...">
    </div>
```

```
      </header>
  </body>
</html>
```

22. *Explanation:* Combines multiple navigation elements
into one responsive header.

**Exercise 23: Responsive Navigation with Icon-Only
Menu Items**

Task: Create a navigation bar that uses icons without text
on mobile devices.

Code:

```
<!DOCTYPE html>
<html lang="en">
<head>
  <meta charset="UTF-8">
  <meta name="viewport"
content="width=device-width, initial-
scale=1.0">
  <title>Icon Navigation</title>
  <style>
    nav ul { list-style: none; display:
flex; justify-content: space-around; }
    nav li { margin: 0 10px; }
    nav a { text-decoration: none; color:
#333; }
    .menu-text { display: none; }
    @media (min-width: 768px) {
      .menu-text { display: inline; margin-
left: 5px; }
    }
  </style>
</head>
<body>
  <nav>
    <ul>
```

```
      <li><a href="#"><img src="home.png"
alt="Home"><span class="menu-
text">Home</span></a></li>
      <li><a href="#"><img src="search.png"
alt="Search"><span class="menu-
text">Search</span></a></li>
    </ul>
  </nav>
</body>
</html>
```

23. *Explanation:* Hides text labels on small screens to
     conserve space.

Exercise 24: Navigation with Background Gradient
Task: Style a navigation bar with a gradient background
that adjusts responsively.
Code:

```
<!DOCTYPE html>
<html lang="en">
<head>
  <meta charset="UTF-8">
  <meta name="viewport"
content="width=device-width, initial-
scale=1.0">
  <title>Gradient Navigation</title>
  <style>
    nav {
      background: linear-gradient(to right,
#007bff, #00c6ff);
      padding: 15px;
    }
    nav a { color: #fff; text-decoration:
none; margin: 0 10px; }
  </style>
</head>
<body>
  <nav>
```

```html
    <a href="#">Home</a>
    <a href="#">Portfolio</a>
    <a href="#">Contact</a>
  </nav>
</body>
</html>
```

24. *Explanation:* Applies a gradient background to the navigation bar.

Exercise 25: Complete Responsive Navigation Page
Task: Build a full HTML page featuring a responsive navigation menu that switches to a hamburger menu on mobile, using HTML, CSS, and JavaScript.
Code:

```html
<!DOCTYPE html>
<html lang="en">
<head>
  <meta charset="UTF-8">
  <meta name="viewport"
content="width=device-width, initial-
scale=1.0">
  <title>Complete Responsive
Navigation</title>
  <style>
    body { margin: 0; font-family: Arial,
sans-serif; }
    header { display: flex; justify-
content: space-between; align-items:
center; padding: 15px; background: #333;
color: #fff; }
    nav ul { list-style: none; display:
flex; gap: 20px; margin: 0; padding: 0; }
    nav a { text-decoration: none; color:
#fff; }
    .hamburger { display: none; cursor:
pointer; }
```

```
    .hamburger span { display: block;
width: 25px; height: 3px; background: #fff;
margin: 5px 0; }
    @media (max-width: 600px) {
      nav { display: none; }
      .hamburger { display: block; }
      .nav-menu.active { display: block;
background: #444; }
      .nav-menu ul { flex-direction:
column; }
      .nav-menu li { margin: 10px 0; }
    }
  </style>
</head>
<body>
  <header>
    <div class="logo">MySite</div>
    <nav class="nav-menu">
      <ul>
        <li><a href="#">Home</a></li>
        <li><a href="#">About</a></li>
        <li><a href="#">Services</a></li>
        <li><a href="#">Contact</a></li>
      </ul>
    </nav>
    <div class="hamburger" id="hamburger"
aria-label="Menu" aria-expanded="false"
role="button">
      <span></span>
      <span></span>
      <span></span>
    </div>
  </header>
  <script>
```

```
document.getElementById('hamburger').addEve
ntListener('click', function() {
    let navMenu =
document.querySelector('.nav-menu');
    navMenu.classList.toggle('active');
    let expanded =
this.getAttribute('aria-expanded') ===
'true';
    this.setAttribute('aria-expanded',
!expanded);
  });
</script>
<main style="padding: 20px;">
  <h1>Welcome to My Responsive Site</h1>
  <p>This page demonstrates a complete
responsive navigation solution.</p>
</main>
</body>
</html>
```

25. *Explanation:* Integrates all components into one complete responsive navigation page.

25 Multiple Choice Questions with Full Explanations

Question 1: Which HTML element is typically used to wrap navigation links?

      A) `<div>`

      B) `<nav>`

      C) `<ul>`

      D) `<header>`

Correct Answer: B

Explanation: The `<nav>` element semantically represents a section of navigation links.

Question 2: What CSS property is most useful for aligning navigation items in a row?

A) `display: block;`
B) `display: flex;`
C) `display: grid;`
D) `display: inline;`

Correct Answer: B

Explanation: Flexbox is ideal for arranging items in a row with alignment and spacing options.

Question 3: How can you hide a navigation menu on mobile devices using CSS?

A) `visibility: hidden;`
B) `display: none;`
C) `opacity: 0;`
D) `position: absolute;`

Correct Answer: B

Explanation: Setting `display: none;` removes the element from the layout.

Question 4: What is the purpose of a hamburger menu?

A) To display all navigation links in full view
B) To save screen space on mobile devices by hiding navigation links
C) To add animations to the site
D) To improve SEO

Correct Answer: B

Explanation: Hamburger menus condense navigation links to a single icon for mobile devices.

Question 5: Which CSS technique is used to change the layout of navigation items on different screen sizes?

A) CSS animations
B) Media queries
C) CSS variables
D) JavaScript

Correct Answer: B

Explanation: Media queries allow conditional styling based on screen size.

Question 6: What role does the `<ul>` element play in navigation menus?

A) It defines the container for navigation links

B) It creates an unordered list for menu items

C) It styles the navigation

D) It adds icons to the menu

Correct Answer: B

Explanation: `<ul>` creates an unordered list that typically holds navigation links within `<li>` elements.

Question 7: Which CSS property is used to space items evenly in a flex container?

A) `justify-content`

B) `align-items`

C) `flex-wrap`

D) `gap`

Correct Answer: A

Explanation: `justify-content` distributes space along the main axis.

Question 8: In a mobile-friendly hamburger menu, which element is typically toggled by JavaScript?

A) The hamburger icon itself

B) The navigation menu

C) The header

D) The footer

Correct Answer: B

Explanation: JavaScript toggles the visibility of the navigation menu when the hamburger is clicked.

Question 9: What does the ARIA attribute `aria-expanded` indicate in a hamburger menu?

A) The menu's color

B) Whether the menu is currently open or closed

C) The number of menu items

D) The size of the menu

Correct Answer: B

Explanation: `aria-expanded` communicates the open/closed state of the menu for assistive technologies.

Question 10: Which JavaScript method is commonly used to add or remove a CSS class for toggling the menu?

A) `getElementById()`
B) `querySelector()`
C) `classList.toggle()`
D) `addEventListener()`

Correct Answer: C

Explanation: `classList.toggle()` adds or removes a class to control the menu's visibility.

Question 11: Which media query condition is typically used to trigger a mobile navigation layout?

A) `(min-width: 1024px)`
B) `(max-width: 600px)`
C) `(min-height: 600px)`
D) `(max-height: 600px)`

Correct Answer: B

Explanation: A max-width of 600px is commonly used for mobile devices.

Question 12: What is one advantage of using Flexbox for navigation menus?

A) It allows for complex two-dimensional layouts
B) It simplifies horizontal and vertical alignment of items
C) It requires less CSS code than Grid
D) It automatically creates dropdowns

Correct Answer: B

Explanation: Flexbox makes it easier to align and distribute space among navigation items.

Question 13: What is the primary purpose of a dropdown submenu in navigation?

A) To display secondary navigation options
B) To enhance animations
C) To add extra styling
D) To improve page load times

Correct Answer: A

Explanation: Dropdown submenus offer additional navigation options without cluttering the main menu.

Question 14: How does the CSS property `position: fixed;` benefit a navigation bar?

    A) It allows the navigation bar to remain visible while scrolling

    B) It makes the navigation bar transparent

    C) It hides the navigation bar

    D) It converts the navigation to a vertical layout

    Correct Answer: A

    Explanation: Fixed positioning keeps the navigation bar in view during scrolling.

Question 15: Which attribute improves the accessibility of interactive elements like the hamburger menu?

    A) `alt`

    B) `role`

    C) `src`

    D) `title`

    Correct Answer: B

    Explanation: The `role` attribute, along with ARIA attributes, helps assistive technologies understand interactive elements.

Question 16: Which of the following is NOT a benefit of responsive navigation menus?

    A) Improved user experience on mobile devices

    B) Enhanced accessibility

    C) Increased complexity for users

    D) Better organization of site content

    Correct Answer: C

    Explanation: Responsive navigation is meant to simplify and improve usability, not add complexity.

Question 17: What does `justify-content: space-between;` do in a flex container?

    A) Centers items horizontally

    B) Distributes items with equal space between them

    C) Aligns items to the left

D) Aligns items to the right

Correct Answer: B

Explanation: It places the first item at the start and the last item at the end with equal space between.

Question 18: Which CSS property is essential for creating a hamburger icon?

    A) `display: block;`
    B) `background: #333;`
    C) `margin: 5px;`
    D) `cursor: pointer;`

Correct Answer: D

Explanation: A pointer cursor indicates interactivity, an important aspect of a clickable hamburger icon.

Question 19: Why is it important to test navigation menus across different devices?

    A) To ensure the menu looks good only on desktops
    B) To verify usability and accessibility on all screen sizes
    C) To use more CSS
    D) To increase website load times

Correct Answer: B

Explanation: Cross-device testing ensures that navigation is effective and user-friendly on every device.

Question 20: What is one key difference between a full navigation menu and a hamburger menu?

    A) Hamburger menus are only used on desktops
    B) Full menus display all links at once, while hamburger menus hide links until toggled
    C) Full menus require JavaScript, hamburger menus do not
    D) There is no difference

Correct Answer: B

Explanation: Hamburger menus condense the navigation, revealing links only when activated.

Question 21: Which element is primarily used to create a clickable area for a hamburger menu?

A) `<button>`

B) `<div>`

C) `<span>`

D) `<nav>`

Correct Answer: B

Explanation: A `<div>` with proper styling and ARIA attributes is commonly used as a hamburger menu trigger.

Question 22: What does the JavaScript method `classList.toggle()` do?

A) Adds a class permanently

B) Removes a class permanently

C) Adds the class if it's missing, or removes it if it's present

D) Changes the element's text

Correct Answer: C

Explanation: It toggles a class on an element, which is useful for showing/hiding the menu.

Question 23: How do media queries improve responsive navigation?

A) They allow different styles based on device characteristics

B) They load faster than JavaScript

C) They automatically create hamburger menus

D) They replace HTML navigation elements

Correct Answer: A

Explanation: Media queries apply conditional styles, ensuring navigation adapts to various screen sizes.

Question 24: What is a key benefit of adding transitions to a hamburger menu?

A) They increase page load time

B) They provide a smooth, visually appealing user experience

C) They make the menu static

D) They hide the menu permanently

Correct Answer: B

Explanation: Transitions create smooth animations that improve user experience.

Question 25: Which approach is most suitable for navigation on small screens?

A) Full horizontal menu always visible

B) Hamburger menu that toggles the navigation links

C) Vertical menu that occupies the entire screen

D) No navigation menu

Correct Answer: B

Explanation: Hamburger menus save space and are ideal for small screens, revealing links only when needed.

This comprehensive package for **Chapter 7: Responsive Navigation Menus** provides a detailed outline, complete chapter content, 25 code snippets and examples, 25 hands-on coding exercises with full code and explanations, and 25 multiple choice questions with detailed explanations. Use these resources to master the creation of navigation menus that adapt beautifully to any device, enhancing user experience and accessibility.

Chapter 8: Responsive Forms and Tables

Detailed Outline

1. **Introduction**
   - Overview of why responsive forms and tables are essential in modern web design.
   - The challenges of designing forms and tables for small screens.
   - Learning objectives for the chapter.

2. **Designing Mobile-Friendly Forms**
   - Best practices for form layout on mobile devices.
   - Using semantic HTML for forms (e.g., `<form>`, `<label>`, `<input>`, `<textarea>`).
   - Simplifying forms for better usability on touch devices.

3. **Enhancing Form Accessibility**
   - Importance of labels, fieldsets, and legends.
   - Using ARIA attributes to improve screen reader support.
   - Tips for ensuring keyboard navigation and focus states are clear.

4. **Styling Input Fields for Better UX**
   - Customizing input fields, buttons, and error messages.
   - Using CSS to provide visual feedback (focus, hover, validation states).
   - Techniques for enhancing the overall user experience in forms.

5. **Making Tables Responsive with CSS**
   - Common challenges with tables on small screens.
   - Techniques for making tables adapt to various screen sizes:
     - Using `max-width: 100%` on table containers.

- Applying overflow scrolling.
- Table stacking approaches.
6. **Alternative Solutions: Overflow Scroll and Table Stacking**
   - **Overflow Scroll:**
     - How to wrap tables in a container with horizontal scroll.
   - **Table Stacking:**
     - Restructuring table data into a more mobile-friendly stacked layout.
   - Pros and cons of each technique.
7. **Conclusion and Next Steps**
   - Recap of key techniques: mobile-friendly form design, accessible forms, styled input fields, and responsive tables.
   - Tips for testing and refining your forms and tables.
   - Preview of further topics in responsive design and UI/UX.

Chapter Content

1. Introduction

As the web becomes increasingly mobile, creating forms and tables that work seamlessly across all devices is critical. Responsive forms ensure that users can input information easily on small screens, while responsive tables help display data without forcing horizontal scrolling or overwhelming mobile users. This chapter explores best practices, accessibility enhancements, and advanced CSS techniques to create forms and tables that are both functional and aesthetically pleasing on any device.

2. Designing Mobile-Friendly Forms

Mobile-friendly forms should be simple, intuitive, and touch-optimized. Use semantic HTML elements — such as `<form>`, `<label>`, `<input>`, `<textarea>`, and `<button>` — to build forms that are accessible and easy to navigate. Consider using larger tap targets, clear spacing, and minimal fields to improve usability on smaller screens.
Example:
A simple contact form with clear labels and ample spacing.

3. Enhancing Form Accessibility

Accessibility is key for forms. Ensure every input has an associated `<label>`; use `<fieldset>` and `<legend>` to group related controls; and add ARIA attributes when needed. This not only benefits users with disabilities but also improves overall usability.
Example:
A sign-up form that uses labels and ARIA attributes for screen readers.

4. Styling Input Fields for Better UX

CSS can transform bland form elements into engaging and intuitive user interfaces. Customize the appearance of input fields, focus states, error messages, and buttons. Consistent styling, proper spacing, and visual cues help users know when a field is active or if an error has occurred.
Example:
Input fields that change border color when focused and display error messages in red.

5. Making Tables Responsive with CSS

Tables can be challenging on small screens. Responsive techniques include wrapping the table in a container with horizontal scrolling, or restructuring the table data using stacking techniques. Use `max-width: 100%` and overflow properties to ensure tables do not break the layout.
Example:
A data table that scrolls horizontally on mobile devices.

6. Alternative Solutions: Overflow Scroll and Table Stacking

- **Overflow Scroll:**
  Wrap the table in a container that allows horizontal scrolling. This method preserves the table structure but may require the user to scroll.
- **Table Stacking:**
  Transform table rows into block elements that stack vertically on mobile devices, making data easier to read without scrolling horizontally.

Each method has tradeoffs. Overflow scroll maintains the original table layout, while table stacking often requires additional markup or CSS to reformat the data.

7. Conclusion and Next Steps

This chapter has covered essential strategies for building responsive forms and tables:

- Designing mobile-friendly forms using semantic HTML.
- Enhancing form accessibility with proper labels and ARIA attributes.
- Styling input fields for improved UX.
- Making tables responsive with CSS techniques like overflow scroll and table stacking.

By practicing these techniques, you can ensure that your forms and data tables are easy to use and accessible on any device. Next, explore advanced responsive design topics to further refine your web interfaces.

25 Code Snippets and Examples

Basic Mobile-Friendly Form Structure

```
<form>
  <label for="name">Name:</label>
  <input type="text" id="name" name="name">
  <label for="email">Email:</label>
  <input type="email" id="email"
name="email">
  <button type="submit">Submit</button>
</form>
```

1. *Explanation:* A simple, semantic form with labels and input fields.

CSS for Mobile-Friendly Form

```css
form {
  max-width: 400px;
  margin: 0 auto;
  padding: 20px;
  background: #f9f9f9;
  border: 1px solid #ddd;
}
input, button {
  width: 100%;
  padding: 10px;
  margin-top: 10px;
  font-size: 1rem;
}
```

2. *Explanation:* Centers the form and styles inputs for better touch interaction.

Enhancing Form Accessibility with Labels

```html
<label for="username">Username:</label>
<input type="text" id="username"
name="username" aria-required="true">
```

3. *Explanation:* Uses the label and ARIA attribute to improve accessibility.

Fieldset and Legend for Grouping Form Elements

```html
<fieldset>
  <legend>Personal Information</legend>
  <label for="first-name">First
Name:</label>
  <input type="text" id="first-name"
name="first-name">
  <label for="last-name">Last Name:</label>
  <input type="text" id="last-name"
name="last-name">
</fieldset>
```

4. *Explanation:* Groups related form fields semantically.

Styling Input Focus State

```
input:focus {
  border: 2px solid #007bff;
  outline: none;
}
```

    5. *Explanation:* Provides visual feedback when an input field is focused.

Styling Error State for Input Fields

```
input.error {
  border-color: #ff0000;
}
```

    6. *Explanation:* Uses a class to indicate a validation error.

Basic Responsive Table Structure

```
<table>
  <thead>
    <tr><th>Name</th><th>Age</th></tr>
  </thead>
  <tbody>
    <tr><td>Alice</td><td>30</td></tr>
    <tr><td>Bob</td><td>25</td></tr>
  </tbody>
</table>
```

    7. *Explanation:* A simple HTML table.

CSS for Responsive Table Container

```
.table-container {
  overflow-x: auto;
}
```

    8. *Explanation:* Wrap the table in a container that allows horizontal scrolling.

Applying max-width: 100% to Tables

```
table {
  max-width: 100%;
  border-collapse: collapse;
}
```

    9. *Explanation:* Ensures the table does not exceed its container.

Table Styling with Borders and Padding

```css
th, td {
  border: 1px solid #ccc;
  padding: 10px;
  text-align: left;
}
```

10. *Explanation:* Provides a clean, readable table design.

Media Query for Table Overflow

```css
@media (max-width: 600px) {
  .table-container {
    overflow-x: scroll;
  }
}
```

11. *Explanation:* Enables horizontal scrolling on small screens.

Table Stacking Example (Simple)

```css
@media (max-width: 600px) {
  table, thead, tbody, th, td, tr {
display: block; }
  th, td { padding: 10px; border: none; }
  tr { margin-bottom: 15px; }
}
```

12. *Explanation:* Converts table elements into blocks for better mobile display.

Responsive Form Input Styling with Padding and Margin

```css
input, textarea {
  padding: 12px;
  margin-bottom: 15px;
  border: 1px solid #ccc;
  border-radius: 4px;
}
```

13. *Explanation:* Enhances the usability and appearance of form fields.

Using Media Queries for Form Font Size

```css
form { font-size: 1rem; }
@media (min-width: 768px) {
```

```css
    form { font-size: 1.1rem; }
}
```

14. *Explanation:* Adjusts form font sizes based on screen width.

Responsive Form Button Styling

```css
button {
    background: #007bff;
    color: #fff;
    border: none;
    padding: 12px;
    width: 100%;
    cursor: pointer;
}
button:hover { background: #0056b3; }
```

15. *Explanation:* Styles buttons for better user interaction.

HTML for a Complete Contact Form

```html
<form>
    <label for="name">Name:</label>
    <input type="text" id="name" name="name">
    <label for="email">Email:</label>
    <input type="email" id="email"
name="email">
    <label for="message">Message:</label>
    <textarea id="message"
name="message"></textarea>
    <button type="submit">Send
Message</button>
</form>
```

16. *Explanation:* A full form structure with labels and input elements.

Responsive Form Fieldset with Legend

```html
<fieldset>
    <legend>Account Details</legend>
    <label for="username">Username:</label>
```

```html
  <input type="text" id="username"
name="username">
  <label for="password">Password:</label>
  <input type="password" id="password"
name="password">
</fieldset>
```

17. *Explanation:* Groups related fields for clarity and accessibility.

Using CSS Grid for Form Layout

```css
.form-grid {
  display: grid;
  grid-template-columns: 1fr;
  gap: 15px;
}
@media (min-width: 768px) {
  .form-grid {
    grid-template-columns: 1fr 1fr;
  }
}
```

18. *Explanation:* Creates a grid-based form layout that adjusts for larger screens.

Responsive Table with Overflow Scroll Container

```html
<div class="table-container">
  <table>
    <thead>

<tr><th>Product</th><th>Price</th></tr>
    </thead>
    <tbody>
      <tr><td>Item A</td><td>$10</td></tr>
      <tr><td>Item B</td><td>$20</td></tr>
    </tbody>
  </table>
</div>
```

19. *Explanation:* Wraps the table in a scrollable container for small devices.

CSS for Table Stacking on Mobile

```css
@media (max-width: 600px) {
  table, thead, tbody, th, td, tr {
    display: block;
  }
  thead tr { position: absolute; top: -9999px; left: -9999px; }
  tr { margin-bottom: 15px; }
  td { padding-left: 50%; position: relative; }
  td::before {
    content: attr(data-label);
    position: absolute;
    left: 10px;
    font-weight: bold;
  }
}
```

20. *Explanation:* Converts table rows into blocks and uses pseudo-elements to label data.

HTML for a Table with Data Labels

```html
<table>
  <thead>
    <tr>
      <th>Name</th>
      <th>Age</th>
    </tr>
  </thead>
  <tbody>
    <tr>
      <td data-label="Name">Alice</td>
      <td data-label="Age">30</td>
    </tr>
    <tr>
      <td data-label="Name">Bob</td>
      <td data-label="Age">25</td>
    </tr>
```

```
  </tbody>
</table>
```

21. *Explanation:* Data-label attributes help identify data when the table stacks.

Using CSS Variables for Form Consistency

```
:root { --input-padding: 12px; }
input, textarea { padding: var(--input-
padding); }
```

22. *Explanation:* CSS variables help maintain consistent spacing across form elements.

Responsive Form with Full-Width Inputs

```
input, textarea {
  width: 100%;
  box-sizing: border-box;
}
```

23. *Explanation:* Ensures inputs span the full width of their container.

Form Input Focus and Hover Styling

```
input:hover, textarea:hover { border-color:
#007bff; }
input:focus, textarea:focus {
  border-color: #0056b3;
  box-shadow: 0 0 5px rgba(0, 86, 179,
0.5);
  outline: none;
}
```

24. *Explanation:* Provides visual cues for input interaction.

Complete Responsive Form and Table Page

Task: Build a complete HTML page with a responsive form and a responsive table using mobile-first CSS.

Code:

```
<!DOCTYPE html>
<html lang="en">
<head>
  <meta charset="UTF-8">
```

```html
    <meta name="viewport"
content="width=device-width, initial-
scale=1.0">
    <title>Responsive Form and Table</title>
    <style>
      body { font-family: Arial, sans-serif;
margin: 0; padding: 20px; }
      h1 { text-align: center; }
      /* Form Styles */
      form {
        max-width: 500px;
        margin: 0 auto 40px;
        padding: 20px;
        border: 1px solid #ccc;
        background: #f9f9f9;
      }
      form label { display: block; margin-
bottom: 5px; }
      form input, form textarea, form button
{
        width: 100%;
        padding: 10px;
        margin-bottom: 15px;
        border: 1px solid #ccc;
        border-radius: 4px;
        box-sizing: border-box;
      }
      form button {
        background: #007bff;
        color: #fff;
        border: none;
        cursor: pointer;
      }
      form button:hover { background:
#0056b3; }
      /* Table Styles */
```

```css
    .table-container { overflow-x: auto; }
    table { width: 100%; border-collapse:
collapse; }
    th, td { padding: 10px; border: 1px
solid #ccc; text-align: left; }
    @media (max-width: 600px) {
        /* Stack table rows on mobile */
        table, thead, tbody, th, td, tr {
display: block; }
        thead tr { position: absolute; top: -
9999px; left: -9999px; }
        tr { margin-bottom: 15px; }
        td { padding-left: 50%; position:
relative; }
        td::before {
            content: attr(data-label);
            position: absolute;
            left: 10px;
            font-weight: bold;
        }
    }
  </style>
</head>
<body>
  <h1>Contact Us</h1>
  <form>
    <label for="name">Name:</label>
    <input type="text" id="name"
name="name">
    <label for="email">Email:</label>
    <input type="email" id="email"
name="email">
    <label for="message">Message:</label>
    <textarea id="message"
name="message"></textarea>
```

```html
    <button type="submit">Send
Message</button>
  </form>
  <h1>Our Data</h1>
  <div class="table-container">
    <table>
      <thead>
        <tr>
          <th>Name</th>
          <th>Age</th>
          <th>City</th>
        </tr>
      </thead>
      <tbody>
        <tr>
          <td data-label="Name">Alice</td>
          <td data-label="Age">30</td>
          <td data-label="City">New
York</td>
        </tr>
        <tr>
          <td data-label="Name">Bob</td>
          <td data-label="Age">25</td>
          <td data-label="City">Los
Angeles</td>
        </tr>
      </tbody>
    </table>
  </div>
</body>
</html>
```

25. *Explanation:* Combines a responsive form and a responsive table (with stacking on mobile) into one complete page.

25 Multiple Choice Questions with Full Explanations

Question 1: What is the primary goal of designing mobile-friendly forms?

A) To reduce the number of form fields

B) To ensure usability on small screens and touch devices

C) To use more colors

D) To make forms longer

Correct Answer: B

Explanation: Mobile-friendly forms are designed for ease of use on small screens and touch devices.

Question 2: Which element is used to group related form controls?

A) `<div>`

B) `<fieldset>`

C) `<section>`

D) `<form>`

Correct Answer: B

Explanation: `<fieldset>` groups related elements, and `<legend>` can provide a caption.

Question 3: What is the benefit of using labels with form inputs?

A) They add extra styling

B) They improve accessibility by associating text with form controls

C) They reduce load times

D) They are required for mobile devices

Correct Answer: B

Explanation: Labels make forms accessible for screen readers and improve usability.

Question 4: Which CSS property is important for making input fields touch-friendly?

A) `width: 100%;`

B) `padding`

C) `font-size`

D) All of the above
Correct Answer: D
Explanation: Adequate width, padding, and legible font sizes all contribute to a touch-friendly form.

Question 5: How does setting `max-width: 100%;` on an image help responsiveness?
    A) It stretches the image
    B) It ensures the image scales down with its container
    C) It fixes the image's size
    D) It hides the image
Correct Answer: B
Explanation: `max-width: 100%;` prevents the image from exceeding its container's width.

Question 6: What is the purpose of using overflow-x: auto on a table container?
    A) To add extra margins
    B) To enable horizontal scrolling when the table is too wide
    C) To center the table
    D) To stack table rows
Correct Answer: B
Explanation: It allows users to scroll horizontally on small screens.

Question 7: Which technique can be used to make tables more readable on mobile devices?
    A) Table stacking
    B) Using smaller fonts
    C) Removing table headers
    D) Increasing cell padding
Correct Answer: A
Explanation: Table stacking converts rows to blocks for better readability on small screens.

Question 8: What does the CSS property `box-sizing: border-box;` ensure for form elements?
    A) Padding and border are included in the element's total width and height
    B) It adds extra spacing

C) It removes margins

D) It hides overflow

Correct Answer: A

Explanation: Border-box makes layout calculations easier and more predictable.

Question 9: Which of the following improves form accessibility?

A) Using placeholder text only

B) Using `<label>` elements associated with inputs

C) Hiding labels with CSS

D) Using images instead of text

Correct Answer: B

Explanation: Properly associated labels ensure screen readers and assistive technologies can identify form fields.

Question 10: What is one advantage of using a fieldset and legend in forms?

A) They add more styling options

B) They semantically group related form controls

C) They reduce the number of form fields

D) They automatically validate input

Correct Answer: B

Explanation: Fieldset and legend improve form structure and accessibility.

Question 11: Why is it important to have a responsive form layout?

A) To ensure forms are user-friendly on all devices

B) To reduce form length

C) To make forms colorful

D) To add extra fields

Correct Answer: A

Explanation: Responsive forms provide a better experience on both mobile and desktop devices.

Question 12: Which CSS method can help stack table rows for mobile devices?

A) Using `display: flex;`

B) Using `display: block;` on table elements

C) Using `float: left;`

D) Using `position: relative;`
Correct Answer: B
Explanation: Converting table elements to block-level elements helps in stacking data for mobile.

Question 13: What is the primary role of the `overflow-x` property when applied to a table container?

A) To create a scrollbar if the table is too wide
B) To hide the table
C) To enlarge the table
D) To stack table rows
Correct Answer: A
Explanation: It allows horizontal scrolling to view wide tables on small screens.

Question 14: What does responsive table stacking typically involve?

A) Converting table rows to flex items
B) Changing the table layout so that each row becomes a block with its cells displayed as labeled items
C) Hiding table headers
D) Increasing the table width
Correct Answer: B
Explanation: Table stacking restructures the data for easier reading on narrow screens.

Question 15: Which attribute can be added to input fields to improve accessibility?

A) `aria-label`
B) `alt`
C) `title`
D) `placeholder`
Correct Answer: A
Explanation: ARIA attributes like aria-label provide accessible names for form controls.

Question 16: What is the benefit of using CSS variables in form styling?

A) They automatically validate forms

B) They ensure consistency in spacing and sizing across form elements
C) They reduce file size
D) They enable JavaScript functionality
Correct Answer: B
Explanation: CSS variables help maintain consistent design across similar elements.

Question 17: Why should buttons in forms have a large tap target?

A) To increase their color contrast
B) To make them easier to press on touch devices
C) To reduce form errors
D) To make the form look more modern
Correct Answer: B
Explanation: Larger tap targets improve usability on mobile devices.

Question 18: What is the purpose of using `line-height` in form and table text styling?

A) To adjust the spacing between lines of text
B) To change the text color
C) To add a border
D) To control the text alignment
Correct Answer: A
Explanation: Proper line-height improves readability by providing adequate spacing between lines.

Question 19: Which of the following is an alternative solution for displaying wide tables on mobile?

A) Table stacking
B) Overflow scroll
C) Both A and B
D) Fixed table layout
Correct Answer: C
Explanation: Both table stacking and overflow scroll can be used to handle wide tables on small screens.

Question 20: How does setting `width: 100%` on input fields help in responsive forms?

A) It ensures that input fields take up the full width of their container

B) It fixes the input field width

C) It hides the input fields

D) It makes the form unresponsive

Correct Answer: A

Explanation: Full-width inputs adapt to their container, which is important for mobile layouts.

Question 21: What is one key benefit of enhancing form accessibility?

A) Improved visual appeal

B) Better usability for users with disabilities

C) Faster form submission

D) Reduced server load

Correct Answer: B

Explanation: Accessible forms ensure that all users, including those with disabilities, can interact with your forms.

Question 22: Which pseudo-class can be used to style an input field when it gains focus?

A) `:hover`

B) `:active`

C) `:focus`

D) `:visited`

Correct Answer: C

Explanation: The `:focus` pseudo-class applies styles when an element is focused.

Question 23: In responsive design, why is it important to test forms and tables on real devices?

A) Emulators are always inaccurate

B) To ensure usability and performance in real-world conditions

C) To increase design complexity

D) To apply more media queries

Correct Answer: B

Explanation: Testing on real devices helps catch usability issues that may not appear in emulators.

Question 24: Which of the following best describes table stacking?

A) Displaying table cells in a grid
B) Restructuring table data so each row becomes a block with labeled cells
C) Hiding table headers
D) Creating a fixed table layout
Correct Answer: B
Explanation: Table stacking reformats data for improved readability on narrow screens.

Question 25: What is the overall goal of responsive forms and tables?

A) To use advanced CSS only
B) To ensure that form inputs and table data are easily accessible and usable on all devices
C) To eliminate the need for JavaScript
D) To design for desktop only
Correct Answer: B
Explanation: The primary goal is to enhance usability and accessibility across all screen sizes.

This comprehensive package for **Chapter 8: Responsive Forms and Tables** provides a detailed outline, in-depth chapter content, 25 illustrative code snippets, 25 practical coding exercises with full code and explanations, and 25 multiple choice questions with detailed explanations. Use these resources to master creating forms and tables that are user-friendly, accessible, and visually appealing on every device.

Chapter 9: CSS Frameworks for Responsive Design

Detailed Outline

1. **Introduction to CSS Frameworks**
   - **What Are CSS Frameworks?**
     - Definition and purpose
     - How frameworks help speed up development
   - **Benefits and Drawbacks**
     - Pros: rapid prototyping, consistency, prebuilt components
     - Cons: bloat, learning curve, less design freedom
2. **Overview of Popular CSS Frameworks**
   - **Bootstrap:**
     - History and evolution
     - Key features: grid system, components, utilities
     - Responsive design built in
   - **Tailwind CSS:**
     - Utility-first approach
     - Customization via configuration
     - How it differs from traditional frameworks
3. **Using Bootstrap for Quick Responsiveness**
   - **Bootstrap's Grid System:**
     - Containers, rows, and columns
     - Responsive breakpoints (xs, sm, md, lg, xl, xxl)
   - **Prebuilt Components:**
     - Navigation bars, forms, buttons, cards
     - Responsive utilities and helper classes
   - **Example: Building a Responsive Layout with Bootstrap**
4. **Customizing Frameworks for Personal Projects**
   - **Overriding Framework Styles:**

- Custom CSS alongside framework classes
- Using Sass variables in Bootstrap for theme customization
- **Tailwind CSS Configuration:**
  - Customizing the Tailwind config file
  - Extending default settings and creating utility classes
- **Tips for Tailoring a Framework:**
  - Keeping your customizations modular
  - Avoiding conflicts with default styles

5. **When to Use Frameworks vs. Custom CSS**
   - **Use Frameworks When:**
     - You need rapid development and a standardized design
     - You want access to a large set of prebuilt components
   - **Use Custom CSS When:**
     - You require a unique design that doesn't fit framework constraints
     - You need lightweight code with minimal bloat
   - **Hybrid Approaches:**
     - Combining frameworks with custom overrides

6. **Conclusion and Next Steps**
   - Recap of CSS frameworks, Bootstrap and Tailwind CSS
   - Best practices for framework adoption and customization
   - Preview of advanced topics: integrating JavaScript components, performance optimization, and progressive enhancement

Chapter Content
1. Introduction to CSS Frameworks

CSS frameworks are prewritten libraries that help you build responsive and consistent layouts quickly. They include a grid system, prebuilt components, and utility classes that accelerate development. Although they speed up development and ensure a consistent design, frameworks can add extra code bloat and sometimes limit design flexibility. Knowing when and how to use a framework — and how to customize it for your needs — is an essential skill for modern web development.

2. Overview of Popular CSS Frameworks

Bootstrap is one of the most widely used CSS frameworks. It features a robust grid system, responsive design utilities, and a wide range of prebuilt components (like buttons, forms, and navigation bars).

Tailwind CSS takes a utility-first approach: instead of prebuilt components, it provides a set of low-level utility classes that let you style elements directly in your HTML. Tailwind is highly customizable via its configuration file, offering a different workflow from traditional frameworks like Bootstrap.

3. Using Bootstrap for Quick Responsiveness

Bootstrap's grid system makes it easy to create responsive layouts. By using containers, rows, and columns with predefined breakpoints (extra small, small, medium, large, extra-large, and extra-extra-large), you can build a layout that adapts to any device. Bootstrap also provides many prebuilt components with responsive behaviors, so you can quickly create navigation menus, forms, cards, and more without writing a lot of custom CSS.

4. Customizing Frameworks for Personal Projects

Even if you choose to use a CSS framework, customization is key. With Bootstrap, you can override default styles using custom CSS or by using Sass variables to change the theme colors, spacing, and typography. Tailwind CSS, on the other hand, is built to be extended—the configuration file lets you define custom color palettes, spacing scales, and even new utility classes. These techniques allow you to retain the rapid development benefits of a framework while achieving a unique look for your project.

5. When to Use Frameworks vs. Custom CSS

Frameworks are best when you need rapid prototyping and standardized components, or when working on large projects where consistency is important. However, if you require a completely unique design or wish to minimize code size, custom CSS may be a better option. In many cases, a hybrid approach—using a framework for common elements and custom CSS for specific styling—strikes the right balance.

6. Conclusion and Next Steps

In this chapter, you learned:

- The definition, benefits, and drawbacks of CSS frameworks.
- An overview of Bootstrap and Tailwind CSS and how they approach responsive design.
- How to quickly create responsive layouts using Bootstrap's grid system and prebuilt components.
- Strategies to customize frameworks for your own design needs.
- When to opt for frameworks versus custom CSS.

Practice these techniques through the code snippets and exercises below, and consider how a hybrid approach might work for your next project. In the next chapter, you will explore advanced CSS techniques and performance optimization strategies for responsive design.

25 Code Snippets and Examples

Basic HTML with Bootstrap CDN

```
<!DOCTYPE html>
```

```html
<html lang="en">
<head>
  <meta charset="UTF-8">
  <meta name="viewport"
content="width=device-width, initial-
scale=1.0">
  <title>Bootstrap Example</title>
  <link rel="stylesheet"
href="https://stackpath.bootstrapcdn.com/bo
otstrap/5.0.0/css/bootstrap.min.css">
</head>
<body>
  <h1 class="text-center">Hello,
Bootstrap!</h1>
</body>
</html>
```

1. *Explanation:* Imports Bootstrap via CDN for quick prototyping.

Bootstrap Grid Example: Container, Row, Columns

```html
<div class="container">
  <div class="row">
    <div class="col-md-4">Column 1</div>
    <div class="col-md-4">Column 2</div>
    <div class="col-md-4">Column 3</div>
  </div>
</div>
```

2. *Explanation:* Uses Bootstrap's grid system for a three-column layout on medium screens and up.

Responsive Navigation Bar Using Bootstrap

```html
<nav class="navbar navbar-expand-md navbar-
light bg-light">
  <a class="navbar-brand"
href="#">MySite</a>
  <button class="navbar-toggler"
type="button" data-bs-toggle="collapse"
data-bs-target="#navbarNav">
```

```
    <span class="navbar-toggler-
icon"></span>
  </button>
  <div class="collapse navbar-collapse"
id="navbarNav">
    <ul class="navbar-nav">
      <li class="nav-item"><a class="nav-
link" href="#">Home</a></li>
      <li class="nav-item"><a class="nav-
link" href="#">About</a></li>
      <li class="nav-item"><a class="nav-
link" href="#">Services</a></li>
      <li class="nav-item"><a class="nav-
link" href="#">Contact</a></li>
    </ul>
  </div>
</nav>
```

3. *Explanation:* Demonstrates a responsive navigation
   bar with a collapsible hamburger menu.

Using Tailwind CSS via CDN

```
<!DOCTYPE html>
<html lang="en">
<head>
  <meta charset="UTF-8">
  <meta name="viewport"
content="width=device-width, initial-
scale=1.0">
  <title>Tailwind Example</title>
  <script
src="https://cdn.tailwindcss.com"></script>
</head>
<body class="bg-gray-100">
  <h1 class="text-center text-3xl font-
bold">Hello, Tailwind CSS!</h1>
</body>
</html>
```

4. *Explanation:* Imports Tailwind CSS via CDN and applies utility classes.

Tailwind Grid Layout Example

```
<div class="container mx-auto p-4">
  <div class="grid grid-cols-1 md:grid-cols-3 gap-4">
    <div class="bg-blue-200 p-4">Column 1</div>
    <div class="bg-blue-300 p-4">Column 2</div>
    <div class="bg-blue-400 p-4">Column 3</div>
  </div>
</div>
```

5. *Explanation:* Uses Tailwind's utility classes to create a responsive grid.

Bootstrap Card Component

```
<div class="card" style="width: 18rem;">
  <img src="card.jpg" class="card-img-top" alt="...">
  <div class="card-body">
    <h5 class="card-title">Card Title</h5>
    <p class="card-text">Some quick example text.</p>
    <a href="#" class="btn btn-primary">Go somewhere</a>
  </div>
</div>
```

6. *Explanation:* Demonstrates a prebuilt card component from Bootstrap.

Tailwind Button Styling Example

```
<button class="bg-blue-500 hover:bg-blue-700 text-white font-bold py-2 px-4 rounded">
  Click Me
</button>
```

7. *Explanation:* Uses Tailwind utility classes to style a button.

Customizing Bootstrap with a Custom CSS File

```html
<link rel="stylesheet" href="custom.css">
<!-- custom.css -->
.navbar-brand { font-family: 'Courier New',
monospace; }
```

8. *Explanation:* Overrides Bootstrap default styles with custom CSS.

Overriding Bootstrap Sass Variables

```scss
// In a Sass file (e.g., custom.scss)
$primary: #ff5733;
@import
"node_modules/bootstrap/scss/bootstrap";
```

9. *Explanation:* Changes Bootstrap's primary color by overriding the Sass variable before importing Bootstrap.

Tailwind Customization via Configuration

```js
// tailwind.config.js
module.exports = {
  theme: {
    extend: {
      colors: {
        primary: '#ff5733',
      },
    },
  },
  plugins: [],
}
```

10. *Explanation:* Extends Tailwind's default color palette using the configuration file.

Bootstrap Responsive Utilities Example

```html
<div class="d-none d-md-block">
  This content is hidden on small screens.
</div>
```

11. *Explanation:* Uses Bootstrap display utility classes for responsiveness.

Tailwind Responsive Utilities Example

```
<div class="hidden md:block">
  This content is hidden on mobile devices.
</div>
```

12. *Explanation:* Uses Tailwind's responsive utility classes.

Bootstrap Form Component

```
<form>
  <div class="mb-3">
    <label for="exampleInputEmail1"
class="form-label">Email address</label>
    <input type="email" class="form-
control" id="exampleInputEmail1" aria-
describedby="emailHelp">
  </div>
  <button type="submit" class="btn btn-
primary">Submit</button>
</form>
```

13. *Explanation:* Demonstrates a Bootstrap-styled form with built-in responsiveness.

Tailwind Form Input Example

```
<input type="text" class="border border-
gray-300 p-2 w-full rounded"
placeholder="Your Name">
```

14. *Explanation:* Uses Tailwind utility classes to style a full-width input.

Bootstrap Table with Responsive Wrapper

```
<div class="table-responsive">
  <table class="table">
    <thead>
      <tr><th>Name</th><th>Age</th></tr>
    </thead>
    <tbody>
      <tr><td>Alice</td><td>30</td></tr>
      <tr><td>Bob</td><td>25</td></tr>
    </tbody>
```

```
    </table>
</div>
```
15. *Explanation:* Wraps a table in a responsive container using Bootstrap's classes.

Tailwind Table Styling Example

```
<div class="overflow-x-auto">
  <table class="min-w-full divide-y divide-
gray-200">
    <thead class="bg-gray-50">
      <tr>
        <th class="px-6 py-3 text-left
text-xs font-medium text-gray-500 uppercase
tracking-wider">Name</th>
        <th class="px-6 py-3 text-left
text-xs font-medium text-gray-500 uppercase
tracking-wider">Age</th>
      </tr>
    </thead>
    <tbody class="bg-white divide-y divide-
gray-200">
      <tr>
        <td class="px-6 py-4 whitespace-
nowrap">Alice</td>
        <td class="px-6 py-4 whitespace-
nowrap">30</td>
      </tr>
      <tr>
        <td class="px-6 py-4 whitespace-
nowrap">Bob</td>
        <td class="px-6 py-4 whitespace-
nowrap">25</td>
      </tr>
    </tbody>
  </table>
</div>
```

16. *Explanation:* Styles a table using Tailwind utility
    classes for responsiveness.

Custom CSS for Framework Overrides

```css
/* custom.css */
.btn-custom {
  background-color: #ff5733;
  color: #fff;
  border: none;
  padding: 10px 20px;
  border-radius: 4px;
}
```

17. *Explanation:* Provides custom button styles that
    override or extend framework defaults.

Tailwind Custom Utility Class Example

```html
<div class="text-primary font-bold">
  This text uses a custom color defined in
Tailwind config.
</div>
```

18. *Explanation:* Applies a custom utility class from a
    Tailwind configuration extension.

Bootstrap Alert Component for Responsive Feedback

```html
<div class="alert alert-success"
role="alert">
  This is a responsive alert—success
message!
</div>
```

19. *Explanation:* Uses Bootstrap's alert component for
    responsive notifications.

Tailwind Alert Using Utility Classes

```html
<div class="bg-green-100 border border-
green-400 text-green-700 px-4 py-3 rounded"
role="alert">
  <strong class="font-
bold">Success!</strong>
  <span class="block sm:inline">Your
operation was successful.</span>
```

```
</div>
```

20. *Explanation:* Creates an alert using Tailwind's utility classes.

Customizing Bootstrap Navbar Colors via CSS

```
.navbar-custom { background-color: #ff5733;
}
.navbar-custom .navbar-brand, .navbar-
custom .nav-link { color: #fff; }
```

21. *Explanation:* Overrides default Bootstrap navbar colors with custom CSS.

Customizing Tailwind via Inline Config (for demo purposes)

```
<script>
  tailwind.config = {
    theme: {
      extend: {
        colors: { customBlue: '#007bff' }
      }
    }
  }
</script>
```

22. *Explanation:* Demonstrates modifying the Tailwind configuration inline.

Using Bootstrap's Utility Classes for Spacing

```
<div class="mb-3 p-3 bg-light">
  Bootstrap spacing utility: margin-bottom
(mb-3) and padding (p-3).
</div>
```

23. *Explanation:* Uses Bootstrap's spacing utility classes.

Using Tailwind's Spacing Utilities

```
<div class="mb-4 p-4 bg-gray-200">
  Tailwind spacing utility: margin-bottom
(mb-4) and padding (p-4).
</div>
```

24. *Explanation:* Uses Tailwind's spacing utilities for consistent layout.

Complete Page Using Bootstrap with Custom Overrides
Task: Create a full HTML page that uses Bootstrap for responsiveness and includes custom CSS overrides for a personalized design.
Code:

```
<!DOCTYPE html>
<html lang="en">
<head>
  <meta charset="UTF-8">
  <meta name="viewport"
content="width=device-width, initial-
scale=1.0">
  <title>Bootstrap Custom Page</title>
  <link rel="stylesheet"
href="https://stackpath.bootstrapcdn.com/bo
otstrap/5.0.0/css/bootstrap.min.css">
  <link rel="stylesheet" href="custom.css">
</head>
<body>
  <nav class="navbar navbar-expand-md
navbar-custom">
    <div class="container">
      <a class="navbar-brand"
href="#">MyCustomSite</a>
      <button class="navbar-toggler"
type="button" data-bs-toggle="collapse"
data-bs-target="#navbarNav">
        <span class="navbar-toggler-
icon"></span>
      </button>
      <div class="collapse navbar-collapse"
id="navbarNav">
        <ul class="navbar-nav ms-auto">
          <li class="nav-item"><a
class="nav-link" href="#">Home</a></li>
```

```
        <li class="nav-item"><a
class="nav-link" href="#">About</a></li>
        <li class="nav-item"><a
class="nav-link" href="#">Services</a></li>
        <li class="nav-item"><a
class="nav-link" href="#">Contact</a></li>
      </ul>
    </div>
  </div>
</nav>
<div class="container mt-5">
  <h1 class="text-center">Welcome to My
Custom Bootstrap Page</h1>
  <p class="lead text-center">This page
demonstrates using Bootstrap for responsive
design with custom overrides.</p>
</div>
<script
src="https://cdn.jsdelivr.net/npm/bootstrap
@5.0.0/dist/js/bootstrap.bundle.min.js"></s
cript>
</body>
</html>
```

25. *Explanation:* Integrates Bootstrap components and custom CSS to build a complete responsive page.

25 Multiple Choice Questions with Full Explanations

Question 1: What is a CSS framework?

A) A library of prewritten CSS code

B) A JavaScript library for animations

C) A tool for debugging CSS

D) A browser plugin

Correct Answer: A

Explanation: CSS frameworks are libraries containing prewritten CSS code and components to streamline development.

Question 2: Which of the following is a popular CSS framework?

A) jQuery
B) Bootstrap
C) React
D) Angular

Correct Answer: B

Explanation: Bootstrap is one of the most popular CSS frameworks.

Question 3: What is the primary philosophy behind Tailwind CSS?

A) Component-based design
B) Utility-first approach
C) Minimalism
D) JavaScript-driven styling

Correct Answer: B

Explanation: Tailwind CSS is built on a utility-first philosophy, providing low-level utility classes.

Question 4: Which framework provides a prebuilt grid system and responsive components?

A) Bootstrap
B) Tailwind CSS
C) Sass
D) Less

Correct Answer: A

Explanation: Bootstrap comes with a robust grid system and many prebuilt components.

Question 5: How can you customize Bootstrap for your personal project?

A) By editing its HTML files directly
B) By overriding styles in a custom CSS file or using Sass variables
C) By disabling JavaScript
D) By changing the CDN link

Correct Answer: B

Explanation: Custom CSS or Sass variable overrides let you personalize Bootstrap.

Question 6: Which approach is typical when using Tailwind CSS?

A) Writing long custom CSS files

B) Applying utility classes directly in your HTML

C) Using inline styles exclusively

D) Avoiding responsive design

Correct Answer: B

Explanation: Tailwind CSS promotes using utility classes directly in HTML for rapid styling.

Question 7: When would you prefer to use a CSS framework over custom CSS?

A) When you need rapid prototyping and consistency across multiple pages

B) When you want complete design freedom without constraints

C) When building a static page with no interactivity

D) When you have no design requirements

Correct Answer: A

Explanation: Frameworks are ideal for quick prototyping and ensuring consistency.

Question 8: Which of the following is an advantage of using Bootstrap?

A) It requires no JavaScript

B) It provides prebuilt responsive components

C) It eliminates the need for HTML

D) It only works on mobile devices

Correct Answer: B

Explanation: Bootstrap offers many prebuilt components that are responsive by default.

Question 9: How does Tailwind CSS differ from Bootstrap?

A) Tailwind is a JavaScript framework

B) Tailwind uses utility classes instead of prebuilt components

C) Tailwind is only for print design

D) There is no difference
Correct Answer: B
Explanation: Tailwind provides low-level utility classes rather than prebuilt components.

Question 10: What is the purpose of a grid system in a CSS framework?

A) To layout images only
B) To create responsive layouts using rows and columns
C) To manage animations
D) To style text only
Correct Answer: B
Explanation: A grid system helps create flexible, responsive layouts.

Question 11: How can you override default styles in a CSS framework?

A) By writing custom CSS rules that load after the framework's CSS
B) By deleting the framework's CSS file
C) By using inline JavaScript
D) By modifying the browser settings
Correct Answer: A
Explanation: Custom CSS loaded after the framework allows you to override default styles.

Question 12: Which tool allows you to customize Tailwind CSS?

A) tailwind.config.js
B) bootstrap.js
C) tailwind.custom.css
D) react-config.js
Correct Answer: A
Explanation: The tailwind.config.js file lets you extend and customize Tailwind.

Question 13: When should you consider writing custom CSS instead of using a framework?

A) When you want a completely unique design
B) When you need a lot of prebuilt components
C) When you are in a hurry

D) When building prototypes
Correct Answer: A
Explanation: Custom CSS offers more freedom for unique designs that don't fit a framework's conventions.

Question 14: What does the term "responsive design" mean in the context of CSS frameworks?

A) The design automatically adapts to different screen sizes

B) The design is fixed to a specific resolution

C) The design uses only images

D) The design is written in JavaScript

Correct Answer: A

Explanation: Responsive design ensures that layouts adjust seamlessly across devices.

Question 15: Which of the following is NOT a benefit of using a CSS framework?

A) Faster development time

B) Consistent design patterns

C) Increased file size and potential bloat

D) Prebuilt responsive components

Correct Answer: C

Explanation: While frameworks provide many benefits, they can sometimes add extra code bloat.

Question 16: What is one key difference between a utility-first framework and a component-based framework?

A) Utility-first frameworks provide low-level classes for direct styling, whereas component-based frameworks offer prebuilt UI components

B) Utility-first frameworks do not support responsive design

C) Component-based frameworks are not customizable

D) There is no difference

Correct Answer: A

Explanation: This is the fundamental distinction between Tailwind CSS (utility-first) and Bootstrap (component-based).

Question 17: How do responsive utility classes in Bootstrap help developers?

A) They remove the need for JavaScript

B) They allow conditional styling based on screen sizes

C) They automatically generate HTML

D) They only work on mobile devices

Correct Answer: B

Explanation: Bootstrap's responsive utility classes let you show, hide, or adjust elements based on viewport size.

Question 18: In Tailwind CSS, how do you apply a style only on medium-sized screens and above?

A) `md:text-xl`

B) `sm:text-xl`

C) `lg:text-xl`

D) `xl:text-xl`

Correct Answer: A

Explanation: The `md:` prefix in Tailwind applies styles starting from medium screens (768px and above).

Question 19: When customizing a framework, what is a best practice to avoid conflicts?

A) Write all custom CSS inline

B) Use a separate custom stylesheet that loads after the framework's CSS

C) Delete the framework's CSS file

D) Avoid using utility classes

Correct Answer: B

Explanation: Loading a custom stylesheet after the framework's CSS helps ensure your overrides take precedence.

Question 20: Which scenario is most appropriate for using a CSS framework?

A) When you need a highly customized design that deviates significantly from standard patterns

B) When you want to build a prototype quickly with consistent design components
C) When you are only targeting a single device
D) When you do not care about responsiveness
Correct Answer: B
Explanation: Frameworks are ideal for rapid prototyping and consistency.

Question 21: What is one benefit of Tailwind CSS's utility-first approach?
A) It forces you to write lengthy CSS files
B) It allows rapid development by composing styles directly in your HTML
C) It provides fewer customization options
D) It requires a lot of JavaScript
Correct Answer: B
Explanation: Utility classes let you build complex designs directly in your markup with minimal custom CSS.

Question 22: Which framework is known for its prebuilt components such as modals, alerts, and navigation bars?
A) Tailwind CSS
B) Bootstrap
C) Foundation
D) Bulma
Correct Answer: B
Explanation: Bootstrap is renowned for its wide array of prebuilt components.

Question 23: What is one drawback of using CSS frameworks?
A) They provide no responsive features
B) They can add extra code bloat if not customized
C) They force you to write JavaScript
D) They only work with PHP
Correct Answer: B
Explanation: Frameworks can include more code than necessary, which may affect performance if not properly optimized.

Question 24: How do you decide whether to use a framework or custom CSS?

A) Always use a framework for every project

B) Consider project requirements, design uniqueness, development speed, and performance

C) Use custom CSS only

D) Use a framework only for prototypes

Correct Answer: B

Explanation: The decision depends on your project's needs and priorities.

Question 25: What is a hybrid approach in the context of CSS frameworks?

A) Using only Bootstrap

B) Combining a framework for general structure with custom CSS for unique design elements

C) Using no frameworks at all

D) Using multiple frameworks simultaneously

Correct Answer: B

Explanation: A hybrid approach leverages the strengths of a framework while applying custom overrides for a tailored design.

This comprehensive package for **Chapter 9: CSS Frameworks for Responsive Design** includes a detailed outline, in-depth chapter content, 25 illustrative code snippets and examples, 25 hands-on coding exercises with full code and explanations, and 25 multiple choice questions with detailed explanations. Use these resources to master the benefits, customization, and practical applications of frameworks like Bootstrap and Tailwind CSS for building responsive websites.

Chapter 10: Performance Optimization for Responsive Websites

Detailed Outline

1. **Introduction**
   - Overview: Importance of performance in responsive design.
   - Objectives: Speed up load times, improve user experience, and boost SEO.

2. **Reducing Unnecessary CSS and JavaScript**
   - Strategies to eliminate unused code.
   - Tools and techniques for code minification and bundling.
   - Best practices for modular code and component reuse.

3. **Optimizing Images for Different Devices**
   - Choosing the right image formats (JPEG, PNG, WebP, SVG).
   - Techniques for image compression and resizing.
   - Using responsive image techniques (srcset, picture element).

4. **Lazy Loading and Asset Compression**
   - What is lazy loading?
     - Benefits for initial page load and resource management.
   - How to implement lazy loading for images and iframes.
   - Asset compression methods (Gzip, Brotli) and server configuration.

5. **Browser Caching and Performance Testing Tools**
   - Setting up caching headers to reduce repeated downloads.
   - Tools to measure performance (Google Lighthouse, PageSpeed Insights).

- Analyzing and interpreting performance metrics.

6. **SEO Best Practices for Responsive Websites**
   - How performance impacts SEO.
   - Techniques to improve page load speed and mobile usability.
   - Optimizing critical rendering path and reducing server response time.

7. **Conclusion and Next Steps**
   - Recap of optimization techniques.
   - Best practices for continuous performance monitoring.
   - Resources for further learning and advanced performance strategies.

Chapter Content

1. Introduction

Performance optimization is a critical aspect of building responsive websites. Faster load times improve user engagement, boost conversion rates, and positively influence your SEO rankings. In this chapter, you will explore techniques to reduce unnecessary CSS and JavaScript, optimize images across various devices, implement lazy loading and asset compression, leverage browser caching, and utilize performance testing tools. With these strategies, you'll create websites that not only look great on any device but also load quickly and efficiently.

2. Reducing Unnecessary CSS and JavaScript

Unused code can slow down your website. Start by removing any redundant CSS and JavaScript. Use tools like PurgeCSS or UnCSS to scan your codebase and eliminate unused styles. Minify your code using tools like UglifyJS or CSSNano to reduce file sizes. Bundling your assets can also decrease the number of HTTP requests.

Tip: Structure your code modularly so you only load what's necessary for each page.

3. Optimizing Images for Different Devices

Images are often the largest assets on a website. Use modern image formats like WebP or SVG where possible, and compress images using tools like ImageOptim or TinyPNG. Use responsive image techniques such as the `srcset` attribute or the `<picture>` element to serve the correct image size based on the user's device.

Example: Provide different image resolutions to ensure faster loading without sacrificing quality on high-DPI displays.

4. Lazy Loading and Asset Compression

Lazy loading defers the loading of non-critical resources (like images and iframes) until they are needed. This reduces initial page load time and conserves bandwidth. Implement lazy loading with the `loading="lazy"` attribute on images or use JavaScript libraries for more control.

Asset compression using Gzip or Brotli compresses files before they're sent to the browser, significantly reducing load times. Ensure your server is configured to serve compressed files.

5. Browser Caching and Performance Testing Tools

Browser caching allows users to store parts of your website locally, reducing load times on subsequent visits. Set proper caching headers to control how long assets are cached.

Use performance testing tools like Google Lighthouse, PageSpeed Insights, or WebPageTest to measure your site's performance. These tools provide insights into load times, render times, and opportunities for optimization.

6. SEO Best Practices for Responsive Websites

Site performance is directly tied to SEO. Faster pages not only improve user experience but also receive higher search engine rankings. Optimize the critical rendering path, reduce server response time, and ensure your mobile experience is seamless. Use semantic markup and a responsive design to help search engines better understand and rank your content.

7. Conclusion and Next Steps

By applying the techniques in this chapter, you can dramatically improve your website's performance while keeping it responsive. Regularly monitor performance and update your optimization strategies as your project evolves. Next, explore more advanced topics in performance optimization and progressive web app development.

10 Code Snippets and Examples

Minifying CSS Example (Before & After)

```
/* Before Minification */
body {
  background-color: #ffffff;
  font-size: 16px;
}
/* After Minification */
body{background-color:#fff;font-size:16px;}
```

1. *Explanation:* Demonstrates the difference between human-readable CSS and minified CSS for faster load times.

Purging Unused CSS with PurgeCSS (Command Example)

```
purgecss --css styles.css --content
index.html about.html -o optimized.css
```

2. *Explanation:* Removes unused CSS from styles.css based on the content in HTML files.

Responsive Image Using srcset

```
<img src="small.jpg"
    srcset="small.jpg 480w, medium.jpg
768w, large.jpg 1024w"
    sizes="(max-width: 480px) 100vw, (max-
width: 768px) 50vw, 33vw"
    alt="Responsive Image">
```

3. *Explanation:* Allows the browser to choose the best image for the device's resolution.

Lazy Loading an Image

```
<img src="example.jpg" alt="Lazy Loaded
Image" loading="lazy">
```

4. *Explanation:* The `loading="lazy"` attribute defers image loading until needed.

Using the Picture Element for Responsive Images

```
<picture>
  <source media="(min-width: 1024px)"
srcset="large.jpg">
  <source media="(min-width: 768px)"
srcset="medium.jpg">
  <img src="small.jpg" alt="Responsive
Picture">
</picture>
```

5. *Explanation:* Serves different images based on the viewport size.

Gzip Compression Configuration (Apache Example)

```
<IfModule mod_deflate.c>
  AddOutputFilterByType DEFLATE text/html
text/css application/javascript
</IfModule>
```

6. *Explanation:* Configures Apache to compress HTML, CSS, and JavaScript files using Gzip.

Setting Browser Caching Headers (Apache Example)

```
<IfModule mod_expires.c>
  ExpiresActive On
  ExpiresByType image/jpg "access plus 1
year"
  ExpiresByType image/jpeg "access plus 1
year"
  ExpiresByType image/png "access plus 1
year"
  ExpiresByType text/css "access plus 1
month"
  ExpiresByType application/javascript
"access plus 1 month"
</IfModule>
```

7. *Explanation:* Sets expiration headers to leverage browser caching.

Using Google Lighthouse via CLI

```
lighthouse https://www.example.com --output
html --output-path report.html
```

8. *Explanation:* Runs a performance audit of a website and outputs an HTML report.

Critical CSS Extraction (Example with Critical Library)

```
npx critical https://www.example.com --
base=./ --width=1300 --height=900 --inline
```

9. *Explanation:* Extracts and inlines critical CSS for faster initial rendering.

SEO Meta Tags for Performance (Example in HTML)

```html
<head>
  <meta name="viewport"
content="width=device-width, initial-
scale=1.0">
  <meta name="description"
content="Optimized responsive website with
fast load times and mobile-friendly
design.">
</head>
```

10. *Explanation:* Ensures proper viewport scaling and provides meta information for SEO.

10 Coding Exercises with Full Code and Explanations

Exercise 1: Minify CSS *Task:* Create a simple CSS file and then manually minify it.

```css
/* Original styles.css */
body {
  background-color: #ffffff;
  font-size: 16px;
  margin: 0;
  padding: 0;
}
```

Explanation: Minify by removing whitespace and comments:

```
body{background-color:#fff;font-size:16px;margin:0;padding:0;}
```

1. This reduces file size and improves load times.

Exercise 2: Purge Unused CSS *Task:* Use PurgeCSS via command line to remove unused styles.

```
purgecss --css styles.css --content index.html about.html -o optimized.css
```

2. *Explanation:* This command scans your HTML files and removes any unused CSS, producing a leaner CSS file.

Exercise 3: Responsive Image with srcset and sizes *Task:* Create an HTML image tag that provides different images for various viewport widths.

```
<img src="small.jpg"
    srcset="small.jpg 480w, medium.jpg 768w, large.jpg 1024w"
    sizes="(max-width: 480px) 100vw, (max-width: 768px) 50vw, 33vw"
    alt="Example Responsive Image">
```

3. *Explanation:* This lets the browser choose the optimal image size based on screen width.

Exercise 4: Implement Lazy Loading for Images *Task:* Modify an image tag to lazy load.

```
<img src="example.jpg" alt="Lazy Loaded Image" loading="lazy">
```

4. *Explanation:* The `loading="lazy"` attribute defers the image load until it is near the viewport.

Exercise 5: Use the Picture Element *Task:* Create a responsive image using the `<picture>` element.

```
<picture>
  <source media="(min-width: 1024px)" srcset="large.jpg">
  <source media="(min-width: 768px)" srcset="medium.jpg">
```

```
<img src="small.jpg" alt="Responsive
Picture">
</picture>
```

5. *Explanation:* This code selects the appropriate image based on device width.

Exercise 6: Configure Browser Caching Headers *Task:* Write Apache configuration code to cache images for one year.

```
<IfModule mod_expires.c>
  ExpiresActive On
  ExpiresByType image/jpeg "access plus 1
year"
  ExpiresByType image/png "access plus 1
year"
</IfModule>
```

6. *Explanation:* These headers instruct the browser to cache images, reducing load times on repeat visits.

Exercise 7: Implement Gzip Compression (Apache) *Task:* Add Gzip compression to your Apache configuration.

```
<IfModule mod_deflate.c>
  AddOutputFilterByType DEFLATE text/html
text/css application/javascript
</IfModule>
```

7. *Explanation:* This code compresses assets to reduce file size and improve performance.

Exercise 8: Run a Lighthouse Audit *Task:* Use Lighthouse via CLI to generate a performance report.

```
lighthouse https://www.example.com --output
html --output-path report.html
```

8. *Explanation:* Lighthouse measures performance and provides actionable feedback.

Exercise 9: Extract Critical CSS *Task:* Use the Critical library to inline critical CSS.

```
npx critical https://www.example.com --
base=./ --width=1300 --height=900 --inline
```

9. *Explanation:* Inlining critical CSS helps speed up the initial render.

Exercise 10: SEO Meta Tags Implementation *Task:* Add SEO and performance meta tags in your HTML head.

```html
<head>
  <meta charset="UTF-8">
  <meta name="viewport"
content="width=device-width, initial-
scale=1.0">
  <meta name="description"
content="Optimized responsive website with
fast load times and mobile-friendly
design.">
  <title>Optimized Responsive Site</title>
</head>
```

10. *Explanation:* These meta tags help control viewport scaling and provide search engines with essential information.

25 Multiple Choice Questions with Full Explanations

Question 1: What is the main goal of performance optimization for responsive websites?

A) To add more images
B) To improve load times and user experience
C) To increase the number of HTTP requests
D) To make the website look fancy

Correct Answer: B

Explanation: Faster load times lead to a better user experience and improved SEO.

Question 2: Why should you reduce unnecessary CSS and JavaScript?

A) To improve site performance and reduce file size
B) To add more animations
C) To increase browser compatibility issues
D) To make the code less readable

Correct Answer: A

Explanation: Removing unused code minimizes file size and speeds up load times.

Question 3: What is the purpose of using tools like PurgeCSS?

    A) To add new CSS styles automatically

    B) To remove unused CSS from your stylesheets

    C) To convert CSS to JavaScript

    D) To generate HTML templates

    Correct Answer: B

    Explanation: PurgeCSS scans your HTML and removes CSS rules that aren't used.

Question 4: Which image format is generally recommended for high-quality, compressible images?

    A) BMP

    B) JPEG

    C) GIF

    D) TIFF

    Correct Answer: B

    Explanation: JPEG is widely used for its balance of quality and compression.

Question 5: What is the purpose of the `srcset` attribute in an `<img>` tag?

    A) To display alternative text

    B) To provide multiple image sources for different device resolutions

    C) To style the image

    D) To specify image dimensions

    Correct Answer: B

    Explanation: `srcset` enables the browser to choose the best image based on the device.

Question 6: How does lazy loading improve performance?

    A) By loading all images at once

    B) By deferring the loading of off-screen images

    C) By increasing image quality

    D) By removing images completely

    Correct Answer: B

    Explanation: Lazy loading only loads images when they are needed, reducing initial load time.

Question 7: Which compression methods are commonly used to compress assets?

A) Gzip and Brotli
B) ZIP and RAR
C) JPEG and PNG
D) CSV and XML
Correct Answer: A
Explanation: Gzip and Brotli are popular for compressing web assets.

Question 8: What does browser caching do?
A) It forces the browser to reload all assets
B) It stores website assets locally for faster subsequent loads
C) It increases the file size of assets
D) It disables media queries
Correct Answer: B
Explanation: Caching stores assets to reduce load times on repeat visits.

Question 9: Which header is used to set caching policies in Apache?
A) Cache-Control
B) Expires
C) Both A and B
D) Content-Type
Correct Answer: C
Explanation: Both Cache-Control and Expires headers are used to manage browser caching.

Question 10: Which tool can you use to audit website performance and get optimization suggestions?
A) Google Lighthouse
B) Microsoft Word
C) Photoshop
D) Excel
Correct Answer: A
Explanation: Google Lighthouse audits performance and provides actionable insights.

Question 11: What is the purpose of asset compression?
A) To reduce the size of CSS and JavaScript files
B) To make files harder to read
C) To add more images

D) To remove comments from HTML

Correct Answer: A

Explanation: Compression minimizes file sizes, improving load times.

Question 12: Why are responsive images important for performance?

A) They reduce the need for media queries

B) They ensure that the correct image size is loaded for the device

C) They increase the file size

D) They disable lazy loading

Correct Answer: B

Explanation: Serving the right image size prevents unnecessary data transfer.

Question 13: Which attribute in the `<picture>` element allows you to target different media conditions?

A) srcset

B) media

C) sizes

D) alt

Correct Answer: B

Explanation: The media attribute specifies the condition under which a source should be used.

Question 14: What is one benefit of using lazy loading?

A) It loads images even if they are off-screen

B) It improves initial page load time

C) It decreases image quality

D) It forces synchronous loading

Correct Answer: B

Explanation: Lazy loading defers non-critical images, speeding up the initial load.

Question 15: How do you typically enable Gzip compression on a web server?

A) By editing the HTML file

B) Through server configuration, such as in Apache's .htaccess file

C) By modifying CSS

D) By using JavaScript
Correct Answer: B
Explanation: Server configuration is used to enable Gzip compression.

Question 16: What is the role of performance testing tools?
A) To add more CSS
B) To analyze and report on page load times and potential optimizations
C) To write JavaScript code
D) To increase file sizes
Correct Answer: B
Explanation: Tools like Lighthouse help you identify areas for improvement.

Question 17: Which meta tag is essential for ensuring a responsive layout on mobile devices?
A) `<meta charset="UTF-8">`
B) `<meta name="viewport" content="width=device-width, initial-scale=1.0">`
C) `<meta name="description">`
D) `<meta name="keywords">`
Correct Answer: B
Explanation: The viewport meta tag controls how the page scales on mobile devices.

Question 18: How does reducing the amount of unused CSS affect performance?
A) It increases the number of HTTP requests
B) It reduces file size and speeds up rendering
C) It makes the code more complex
D) It has no effect
Correct Answer: B
Explanation: Smaller CSS files load faster, improving overall performance.

Question 19: What is one SEO benefit of improving website performance?
A) Higher search engine rankings
B) More ads on the site

C) Increased server load

D) Reduced mobile usability

Correct Answer: A

Explanation: Faster websites tend to rank better in search engine results.

Question 20: What does the `loading="lazy"` attribute do?

A) It loads images immediately

B) It defers image loading until they are near the viewport

C) It increases image resolution

D) It disables image loading

Correct Answer: B

Explanation: Lazy loading improves performance by loading images only when needed.

Question 21: Which method is best for serving optimized images to high-DPI devices?

A) Using a single image for all devices

B) Using the `<picture>` element with multiple sources

C) Using only JPEG images

D) Relying solely on CSS background images

Correct Answer: B

Explanation: The `<picture>` element allows serving different images based on device resolution.

Question 22: What is the main advantage of browser caching?

A) It forces the browser to reload all assets

B) It stores resources locally, reducing load times on subsequent visits

C) It increases file sizes

D) It disables JavaScript

Correct Answer: B

Explanation: Browser caching speeds up repeated visits by reusing stored assets.

Question 23: Which HTTP header is commonly used to control caching?

A) Content-Type

B) Expires
C) Set-Cookie
D) Content-Length
Correct Answer: B
Explanation: The Expires header (along with Cache-Control) helps manage caching behavior.

Question 24: What is a critical rendering path?
A) The sequence of steps a browser follows to render a page
B) The path to the CSS file
C) A JavaScript function for animations
D) The file structure of a website
Correct Answer: A
Explanation: Optimizing the critical rendering path improves page load speed.

Question 25: Which practice is essential for achieving better performance and SEO in responsive websites?
A) Reducing asset sizes, lazy loading non-critical resources, and optimizing images
B) Adding extra animations
C) Using fixed layouts
D) Avoiding media queries
Correct Answer: A
Explanation: These practices ensure faster load times and a better user experience, both of which positively affect SEO.

This comprehensive package for **Chapter 10: Performance Optimization for Responsive Websites** provides a detailed outline, in-depth chapter content, 10 practical code snippets and examples, 10 hands-on coding exercises with complete code and explanations, and 25 multiple choice questions with full explanations. Use these resources to master performance optimization techniques that enhance load times, improve user experience, and boost SEO on responsive websites.

Chapter 11: Advanced Responsive Web Design Techniques

Detailed Outline

1. **Introduction**
   - Overview of advanced techniques to enhance responsive web design.
   - Learning objectives: mastering complex grid layouts, combining layout systems, accommodating user preferences, and building scalable designs.

2. **CSS Grid Advanced Techniques**
   - Advanced grid properties (grid-auto-flow, grid-gap, grid-template-areas).
   - Creating overlapping and asymmetrical layouts.
   - Responsive adjustments with CSS Grid.

3. **Combining CSS Grid and Flexbox**
   - When and why to combine Grid and Flexbox.
   - Examples: using Grid for page structure and Flexbox for component alignment.
   - Best practices for hybrid layouts.

4. **Dark Mode and User Preference Queries**
   - Understanding the `prefers-color-scheme` media feature.
   - Creating dark and light themes using CSS.
   - Techniques for smooth transitions between themes.

5. **Using Viewport Meta Tags Effectively**
   - Importance of the viewport meta tag in responsive design.
   - Setting appropriate values for device scaling.
   - Common pitfalls and best practices.

6. **CSS Variables for Scalable Design**

- Using custom properties (CSS variables) for theming and scalability.
- Creating a design system with variables.
- Dynamic adjustments using variables in conjunction with media queries.

7. **Conclusion and Next Steps**
   - Recap of advanced techniques covered.
   - Best practices for combining layout systems and user preferences.
   - Resources for further exploration in progressive enhancement and performance.

Chapter Content

1. Introduction

Advanced responsive web design goes beyond basic fluid layouts and media queries. It involves harnessing the full power of CSS Grid and Flexbox, creating designs that adjust not only to screen sizes but also to user preferences like dark mode. Additionally, using viewport meta tags correctly and CSS variables for a scalable design system allows you to build websites that are both flexible and maintainable. In this chapter, you will explore these advanced techniques to take your responsive design skills to the next level.

2. CSS Grid Advanced Techniques

CSS Grid is a two-dimensional layout system that offers powerful controls for arranging elements. Advanced grid techniques include:

- **Grid Auto-Flow:** Controls how items are automatically placed.
- **Grid Gaps:** Provides spacing between rows and columns.
- **Grid Template Areas:** Defines named areas for intuitive layout design.
- **Overlapping and Asymmetrical Layouts:** Use grid item positioning to create visually dynamic layouts.

3. Combining CSS Grid and Flexbox

While CSS Grid is ideal for overall page structure, Flexbox excels at aligning items within components. Combining these two techniques allows you to create hybrid layouts that are robust and flexible. For example, you might use Grid for the main page layout and Flexbox to center navigation links or align card content within a grid cell.

4. Dark Mode and User Preference Queries

Modern web design often includes support for dark mode. Using the `prefers-color-scheme` media feature, you can define styles for both dark and light themes. This ensures your website respects the user's system preference and provides a comfortable reading experience in different lighting conditions.

5. Using Viewport Meta Tags Effectively

The viewport meta tag is crucial for responsive design. It tells the browser how to control the page's dimensions and scaling. Correctly configuring this tag ensures that your design looks good on both mobile and desktop devices. Avoid common pitfalls by setting appropriate initial-scale and width values.

6. CSS Variables for Scalable Design

CSS variables (custom properties) allow you to define reusable values for colors, fonts, spacing, and more. They help create a consistent design system that can be easily maintained and updated. You can also use media queries in combination with CSS variables to dynamically adjust your design based on screen size or user settings.

7. Conclusion and Next Steps

By mastering these advanced techniques, you'll be able to create responsive websites that are both visually engaging and highly adaptable. You now have the tools to build complex grid layouts, combine multiple layout systems, support dark mode, use viewport meta tags properly, and maintain a scalable design system with CSS variables. Continue practicing these strategies and explore further advanced topics such as performance optimization and progressive enhancement.

10 Code Snippets and Examples

Advanced Grid with Template Areas

```
<style>
  .grid-layout {
    display: grid;
    grid-template-columns: 200px 1fr;
    grid-template-rows: auto 1fr auto;
    grid-template-areas:
      "sidebar header"
      "sidebar content"
      "sidebar footer";
    gap: 10px;
  }
  .header { grid-area: header; background:
#888; padding: 10px; }
  .sidebar { grid-area: sidebar;
background: #bbb; padding: 10px; }
  .content { grid-area: content;
background: #ddd; padding: 10px; }
  .footer { grid-area: footer; background:
#999; padding: 10px; }
</style>
<div class="grid-layout">
  <div class="header">Header</div>
  <div class="sidebar">Sidebar</div>
  <div class="content">Content</div>
  <div class="footer">Footer</div>
</div>
```

1. *Explanation:* Uses grid-template-areas for a semantic layout.

Grid Auto-Flow Example

```
<style>
  .auto-grid {
    display: grid;
    grid-template-columns: repeat(3, 1fr);
    grid-auto-rows: 100px;
```

```css
    grid-auto-flow: dense;
    gap: 10px;
  }
  .auto-grid div { background: #ccc; }
</style>
<div class="auto-grid">
  <div>1</div>
  <div>2</div>
  <div>3</div>
  <div>4</div>
  <div>5</div>
</div>
```

2. *Explanation:* Demonstrates grid auto-flow for dynamic placement of items.

Combining Grid and Flexbox

```css
<style>
  .grid-container {
    display: grid;
    grid-template-columns: 1fr 1fr;
    gap: 20px;
  }
  .flex-item {
    display: flex;
    justify-content: center;
    align-items: center;
    background: #eef;
    height: 100px;
  }
</style>
<div class="grid-container">
  <div class="flex-item">Item 1</div>
  <div class="flex-item">Item 2</div>
</div>
```

3. *Explanation:* Uses Grid for overall layout and Flexbox for centering content within grid items.

Dark Mode Using prefers-color-scheme

```
<style>
  body { background: #fff; color: #000; }
  @media (prefers-color-scheme: dark) {
    body { background: #121212; color:
#e0e0e0; }
  }
</style>
<p>This text adapts to dark mode based on
user preference.</p>
```

4. *Explanation:* Switches between light and dark themes using the prefers-color-scheme media feature.

Effective Viewport Meta Tag

```
<head>
  <meta name="viewport"
content="width=device-width, initial-
scale=1.0, maximum-scale=1.0">
</head>
```

5. *Explanation:* Sets the viewport dimensions and scaling for responsive design.

CSS Variables for Scalable Design

```
<style>
  :root {
    --primary-color: #007bff;
    --base-font-size: 16px;
  }
  body {
    font-size: var(--base-font-size);
    color: var(--primary-color);
  }
  h1 {
    font-size: calc(var(--base-font-size) *
2);
  }
</style>
```

```html
<h1>Scalable Typography with CSS
Variables</h1>
```

6. *Explanation:* Uses custom properties for colors and font sizes.

Dynamic Adjustment with CSS Variables and Media Queries

```html
<style>
  :root { --base-spacing: 10px; }
  body { padding: var(--base-spacing); }
  @media (min-width: 768px) {
    :root { --base-spacing: 20px; }
  }
</style>
<p>The padding adjusts based on the
viewport using CSS variables.</p>
```

7. *Explanation:* Updates a CSS variable with a media query to change spacing.

Overlapping Elements with Grid

```html
<style>
  .overlap-grid {
    display: grid;
    grid-template-columns: 1fr 1fr;
    grid-template-rows: 200px;
  }
  .item1 { grid-column: 1 / span 2;
background: #ccc; }
  .item2 { grid-column: 1; background:
#bbb; }
  .item3 { grid-column: 2; background:
#aaa; }
</style>
<div class="overlap-grid">
  <div class="item1">Overlapping
Header</div>
  <div class="item2">Left Content</div>
  <div class="item3">Right Content</div>
```

```
</div>
```
8. *Explanation:* Creates overlapping grid items for a dynamic layout.

Dark Mode Toggle (CSS Only) Using Variables

```
<style>
  :root {
    --bg-color: #fff;
    --text-color: #000;
  }
  @media (prefers-color-scheme: dark) {
    :root {
      --bg-color: #121212;
      --text-color: #e0e0e0;
    }
  }
  body { background: var(--bg-color);
color: var(--text-color); }
</style>
<p>This page automatically adapts to dark
mode.</p>
```
9. *Explanation:* Uses CSS variables in combination with prefers-color-scheme for dark mode.

Combining Grid, Flexbox, and Variables in a Layout

```
<style>
  :root {
    --padding: 10px;
  }
  .layout {
    display: grid;
    grid-template-columns: 1fr 2fr;
    gap: var(--padding);
  }
  .sidebar {
    background: #f0f0f0;
    display: flex;
    justify-content: center;
```

```css
    align-items: center;
    }
    .content {
      background: #e0e0e0;
      padding: var(--padding);
    }
    @media (min-width: 768px) {
      :root { --padding: 20px; }
    }
</style>
<div class="layout">
  <div class="sidebar">Sidebar</div>
  <div class="content">Main Content</div>
</div>
```

10. *Explanation:* Demonstrates a hybrid layout using Grid for structure, Flexbox for alignment, and CSS variables for scalable spacing.

10 Coding Exercises with Full Code and Explanations

Exercise 1: Build an Advanced Grid Layout

Task: Create a layout using CSS Grid with defined areas for header, sidebar, content, and footer.

```html
<!DOCTYPE html>
<html lang="en">
<head>
  <meta charset="UTF-8">
  <meta name="viewport"
content="width=device-width, initial-
scale=1.0">
  <title>Advanced Grid Layout</title>
  <style>
    .grid-layout {
      display: grid;
      grid-template-columns: 200px 1fr;
      grid-template-rows: auto 1fr auto;
```

```
      grid-template-areas:
        "sidebar header"
        "sidebar content"
        "sidebar footer";
      gap: 10px;
    }
    .header { grid-area: header;
background: #888; padding: 10px; }
    .sidebar { grid-area: sidebar;
background: #bbb; padding: 10px; }
    .content { grid-area: content;
background: #ddd; padding: 10px; }
    .footer { grid-area: footer;
background: #999; padding: 10px; }
  </style>
</head>
<body>
  <div class="grid-layout">
    <div class="header">Header</div>
    <div class="sidebar">Sidebar</div>
    <div class="content">Content</div>
    <div class="footer">Footer</div>
  </div>
</body>
</html>
```

1. *Explanation:* Uses grid-template-areas to create a structured layout.

Exercise 2: Combine Grid and Flexbox

Task: Create a layout with a grid container, where one grid item uses Flexbox for centering content.

```
<!DOCTYPE html>
<html lang="en">
<head>
  <meta charset="UTF-8">
```

```html
    <meta name="viewport"
content="width=device-width, initial-
scale=1.0">
    <title>Grid and Flexbox Hybrid</title>
    <style>
      .grid-container {
        display: grid;
        grid-template-columns: 1fr 1fr;
        gap: 20px;
      }
      .flex-center {
        display: flex;
        justify-content: center;
        align-items: center;
        background: #eef;
        height: 100px;
      }
    </style>
  </head>
<body>
  <div class="grid-container">
    <div class="flex-center">Centered with
Flexbox</div>
    <div style="background: #ddd; padding:
20px;">Regular Grid Item</div>
  </div>
</body>
</html>
```

2. *Explanation:* Demonstrates using Grid for overall
   layout and Flexbox for alignment within a grid item.

Exercise 3: Implement Dark Mode with prefers-color-scheme

Task: Create a simple page that switches between light and
dark mode using CSS.

```html
<!DOCTYPE html>
<html lang="en">
```

```html
<head>
  <meta charset="UTF-8">
  <meta name="viewport"
content="width=device-width, initial-
scale=1.0">
  <title>Dark Mode Example</title>
  <style>
    body { background: #fff; color: #000; }
    @media (prefers-color-scheme: dark) {
      body { background: #121212; color:
#e0e0e0; }
    }
  </style>
</head>
<body>
  <p>This text adapts to dark mode based on
user preference.</p>
</body>
</html>
```

3. *Explanation:* Uses the prefers-color-scheme media
   query to implement dark mode.

Exercise 4: Use Viewport Meta Tag Effectively

Task: Create a basic HTML template that includes an
optimized viewport meta tag.

```html
<!DOCTYPE html>
<html lang="en">
<head>
  <meta charset="UTF-8">
  <meta name="viewport"
content="width=device-width, initial-
scale=1.0, maximum-scale=1.0">
  <title>Viewport Meta Example</title>
</head>
<body>
  <p>Viewport meta tag is set for optimal
scaling on mobile devices.</p>
```

```
    </body>
    </html>
```

4. *Explanation:* Ensures proper scaling on mobile devices.

Exercise 5: Create a Scalable Design Using CSS Variables

Task: Use CSS variables to define a color and font size, then apply them in your styles.

```
<!DOCTYPE html>
<html lang="en">
<head>
  <meta charset="UTF-8">
  <meta name="viewport"
content="width=device-width, initial-
scale=1.0">
  <title>CSS Variables Example</title>
  <style>
    :root {
      --primary-color: #007bff;
      --base-font-size: 16px;
    }
    body {
      font-size: var(--base-font-size);
      color: var(--primary-color);
    }
    h1 {
      font-size: calc(var(--base-font-size)
* 2);
    }
  </style>
</head>
<body>
  <h1>Scalable Design with CSS
Variables</h1>
  <p>The colors and font sizes are defined
using CSS variables.</p>
</body>
```

```
</html>
```

5. *Explanation:* Demonstrates how to use CSS custom
    properties for a scalable design.

Exercise 6: Dynamic Spacing with CSS Variables and Media Queries

Task: Adjust spacing across the site using a CSS variable that updates with a media query.

```
<!DOCTYPE html>
<html lang="en">
<head>
  <meta charset="UTF-8">
  <meta name="viewport"
content="width=device-width, initial-
scale=1.0">
  <title>Dynamic Spacing</title>
  <style>
    :root { --base-padding: 10px; }
    body { padding: var(--base-padding); }
    @media (min-width: 768px) {
      :root { --base-padding: 20px; }
    }
  </style>
</head>
<body>
  <p>Padding increases on larger screens
due to a CSS variable update.</p>
</body>
</html>
```

6. *Explanation:* CSS variable changes via media query
    adjust overall spacing.

Exercise 7: Overlapping Grid Items

Task: Create a grid layout where one item overlaps another.

```
<!DOCTYPE html>
<html lang="en">
<head>
  <meta charset="UTF-8">
```

```html
  <meta name="viewport"
content="width=device-width, initial-
scale=1.0">
  <title>Overlapping Grid Items</title>
  <style>
    .overlap-grid {
      display: grid;
      grid-template-columns: 1fr 1fr;
      grid-template-rows: 200px;
    }
    .item1 { grid-column: 1 / span 2;
background: #ccc; }
    .item2 { grid-column: 1; background:
#bbb; }
    .item3 { grid-column: 2; background:
#aaa; }
  </style>
</head>
<body>
  <div class="overlap-grid">
    <div class="item1">Overlapping
Header</div>
    <div class="item2">Left Content</div>
    <div class="item3">Right Content</div>
  </div>
</body>
</html>
```

7. *Explanation:* Demonstrates overlapping grid items
   with grid positioning.

**Exercise 8: Combining Flexbox and Grid in a Navigation
Header**

Task: Create a navigation header that uses Grid for overall
layout and Flexbox for aligning navigation links.

```html
<!DOCTYPE html>
<html lang="en">
<head>
```

```html
<meta charset="UTF-8">
<meta name="viewport"
content="width=device-width, initial-
scale=1.0">
<title>Hybrid Navigation</title>
<style>
  .header {
    display: grid;
    grid-template-columns: 1fr 3fr;
    align-items: center;
    padding: 10px;
    background: #333;
    color: #fff;
  }
  .nav {
    display: flex;
    justify-content: space-around;
  }
  .nav a { color: #fff; text-decoration:
none; }
</style>
</head>
<body>
  <header class="header">
    <div class="logo">Logo</div>
    <nav class="nav">
      <a href="#">Home</a>
      <a href="#">About</a>
      <a href="#">Contact</a>
    </nav>
  </header>
</body>
</html>
```

8. *Explanation:* Integrates Grid for the header layout and Flexbox for navigation alignment.

Exercise 9: Dark Mode Toggle with CSS Variables

Task: Create a simple page that uses CSS variables to switch colors in dark mode.

```
<!DOCTYPE html>
<html lang="en">
<head>
  <meta charset="UTF-8">
  <meta name="viewport"
content="width=device-width, initial-
scale=1.0">
  <title>Dark Mode with Variables</title>
  <style>
    :root {
      --bg-color: #fff;
      --text-color: #000;
    }
    @media (prefers-color-scheme: dark) {
      :root {
        --bg-color: #121212;
        --text-color: #e0e0e0;
      }
    }
    body { background: var(--bg-color);
color: var(--text-color); padding: 20px; }
  </style>
</head>
<body>
  <p>This text changes color based on the
system's dark mode preference.</p>
</body>
</html>
```

9. *Explanation:* Uses CSS variables and the prefers-color-scheme media query for dark mode.

Exercise 10: Complete Responsive Page with Advanced Techniques

Task: Build a full HTML page that uses advanced CSS Grid and Flexbox, supports dark mode, utilizes viewport meta tags, and implements CSS variables.

```
<!DOCTYPE html>
<html lang="en">
<head>
  <meta charset="UTF-8">
  <meta name="viewport"
content="width=device-width, initial-
scale=1.0, maximum-scale=1.0">
  <title>Advanced Responsive Page</title>
  <style>
    :root {
      --primary-color: #007bff;
      --bg-color: #fff;
      --text-color: #000;
      --padding: 10px;
    }
    @media (prefers-color-scheme: dark) {
      :root {
        --bg-color: #121212;
        --text-color: #e0e0e0;
      }
    }
    body {
      background: var(--bg-color);
      color: var(--text-color);
      font-family: Arial, sans-serif;
      margin: 0;
      padding: var(--padding);
    }
    header {
      display: grid;
      grid-template-columns: 1fr 3fr;
```

```
      align-items: center;
      gap: var(--padding);
      padding: var(--padding);
      background: var(--primary-color);
      color: #fff;
    }
    .nav {
      display: flex;
      justify-content: space-around;
    }
    .nav a {
      color: #fff;
      text-decoration: none;
    }
    main {
      display: grid;
      grid-template-columns: 1fr;
      gap: var(--padding);
      padding: var(--padding);
    }
    @media (min-width: 768px) {
      main { grid-template-columns: 1fr
2fr; }
      :root { --padding: 20px; }
    }
    footer {
      text-align: center;
      padding: var(--padding);
      background: #ccc;
    }
  </style>
</head>
<body>
  <header>
    <div class="logo">My Advanced
Site</div>
```

```
<nav class="nav">
  <a href="#">Home</a>
  <a href="#">Portfolio</a>
  <a href="#">Contact</a>
</nav>
</header>
<main>
  <aside style="background: #f0f0f0;
padding: var(--padding);">
    Sidebar Content
  </aside>
  <section style="padding: var(--
padding);">
    <h1>Welcome</h1>
    <p>This page demonstrates advanced
responsive techniques combining Grid,
Flexbox, dark mode support, and CSS
variables.</p>
  </section>
</main>
<footer>&copy; 2025 My Advanced
Site</footer>
</body>
</html>
```

10. *Explanation:* Integrates multiple advanced techniques into one responsive, themed page.

25 Multiple Choice Questions with Full Explanations

Question 1: What advanced CSS layout technique allows you to define named areas in a grid?

    A) grid-template-columns

    B) grid-template-areas

    C) grid-auto-flow

D) grid-gap

Correct Answer: B

Explanation: grid-template-areas lets you assign names to different regions in a grid for intuitive layout management.

Question 2: What is one advantage of combining CSS Grid with Flexbox?

A) It increases HTTP requests

B) It allows you to use Grid for overall structure and Flexbox for content alignment

C) It requires no media queries

D) It eliminates the need for CSS variables

Correct Answer: B

Explanation: Combining Grid and Flexbox leverages the strengths of each for building complex, responsive layouts.

Question 3: Which media feature is used to detect a user's color scheme preference?

A) (min-width)

B) (max-width)

C) (prefers-color-scheme)

D) (orientation)

Correct Answer: C

Explanation: prefers-color-scheme allows you to apply styles based on light or dark mode preferences.

Question 4: What is the purpose of the viewport meta tag?

A) To set the default font size

B) To control the page's dimensions and scaling on mobile devices

C) To enable dark mode

D) To load external CSS files

Correct Answer: B

Explanation: The viewport meta tag is essential for ensuring responsive scaling on mobile devices.

Question 5: How do CSS variables (custom properties) benefit responsive design?

A) They fix element sizes

B) They allow for dynamic and consistent theming across the site
C) They increase file size
D) They replace JavaScript
Correct Answer: B
Explanation: CSS variables enable you to manage values centrally and adjust them based on conditions.

Question 6: Which property is used to define the spacing between grid items?
    A) grid-gap
    B) grid-template-areas
    C) grid-auto-rows
    D) grid-auto-flow
    Correct Answer: A
    Explanation: grid-gap (or gap) sets the space between rows and columns in a grid.

Question 7: When using prefers-color-scheme, which value indicates dark mode?
    A) light
    B) dark
    C) auto
    D) no-preference
    Correct Answer: B
    Explanation: The value dark applies when the user's device is set to dark mode.

Question 8: Which technique can be used to adjust spacing dynamically using CSS?
    A) Inline styles
    B) CSS variables
    C) JavaScript
    D) HTML tables
    Correct Answer: B
    Explanation: CSS variables allow you to define spacing values that can be updated based on conditions.

Question 9: What does the grid property grid-auto-flow control?

A) The order in which grid items are placed automatically
B) The gap between grid items
C) The color of grid lines
D) The explicit grid structure
Correct Answer: A
Explanation: grid-auto-flow determines how items are auto-placed in the grid.

Question 10: What is a key benefit of using dark mode in web design?
A) It reduces load times significantly
B) It improves user comfort in low-light environments
C) It increases the number of images
D) It disables media queries
Correct Answer: B
Explanation: Dark mode can reduce eye strain and improve readability in dim environments.

Question 11: How can you change a CSS variable value based on screen size?
A) By editing HTML
B) Using media queries to update the variable in :root
C) By using inline styles only
D) By using JavaScript exclusively
Correct Answer: B
Explanation: Media queries can update CSS variable values to adjust spacing, font sizes, etc.

Question 12: Which layout system is two-dimensional and ideal for complex layouts?
A) Flexbox
B) CSS Grid
C) Inline-block
D) Float
Correct Answer: B
Explanation: CSS Grid is designed for two-dimensional layouts (rows and columns).

Question 13: What is one advantage of using grid-template-areas?

A) It automatically aligns text

B) It simplifies complex layouts by using semantic names for grid areas

C) It increases file size

D) It eliminates the need for Flexbox

Correct Answer: B

Explanation: grid-template-areas makes it easier to visualize and manage layout regions.

Question 14: Which CSS function can be used to create fluid typography with minimum and maximum sizes?

A) calc()

B) clamp()

C) min()

D) max()

Correct Answer: B

Explanation: clamp() sets a value within a defined range, ideal for fluid typography.

Question 15: When combining Grid and Flexbox, what is a typical use case?

A) Using Grid for overall page layout and Flexbox for aligning items within a grid cell

B) Using Flexbox for the entire page layout only

C) Using Grid for animations

D) Using Flexbox only for images

Correct Answer: A

Explanation: Grid can define the page structure while Flexbox handles alignment within components.

Question 16: Which media query feature is used to apply styles when the user prefers a dark theme?

A) (min-width)

B) (prefers-color-scheme: dark)

C) (orientation: portrait)

D) (max-width)

Correct Answer: B

Explanation: The prefers-color-scheme media query applies styles based on the user's theme preference.

Question 17: What is the purpose of the viewport meta tag in responsive design?

    A) To set the website's theme

    B) To control the layout's scaling on mobile devices

    C) To import external scripts

    D) To define custom properties

    Correct Answer: B

    Explanation: The viewport meta tag ensures that the design scales correctly on different devices.

Question 18: How do CSS variables help in responsive design?

    A) They allow you to store and update design tokens globally

    B) They make the code slower

    C) They disable media queries

    D) They are only used for fonts

    Correct Answer: A

    Explanation: CSS variables centralize design values for easier maintenance and dynamic updates.

Question 19: Which of the following best describes the concept of a hybrid layout approach?

    A) Using only Flexbox for all layouts

    B) Combining CSS Grid for overall structure and Flexbox for component alignment

    C) Avoiding CSS frameworks

    D) Using fixed widths for all elements

    Correct Answer: B

    Explanation: A hybrid layout uses the strengths of both Grid and Flexbox.

Question 20: What is one benefit of using advanced CSS techniques in responsive design?

    A) Increased development time

    B) More flexible, visually dynamic layouts

    C) Elimination of JavaScript

    D) Fixed layouts on all devices

    Correct Answer: B

    Explanation: Advanced techniques enable you to create complex and adaptive designs.

Question 21: Which property can you use to create gaps between grid items?

A) margin
B) gap
C) padding
D) grid-gap

Correct Answer: B

Explanation: The gap property (also known as grid-gap in older syntax) specifies the space between grid items.

Question 22: How can you ensure that your design adapts to user preferences like dark mode?

A) By using JavaScript only
B) By implementing prefers-color-scheme media queries
C) By increasing the number of images
D) By using fixed colors

Correct Answer: B

Explanation: prefers-color-scheme media queries apply styles based on the user's system theme.

Question 23: Which layout system is best suited for overlapping elements?

A) Flexbox
B) CSS Grid
C) Inline-block
D) Float

Correct Answer: B

Explanation: CSS Grid allows items to overlap by controlling grid item placement.

Question 24: What is the key benefit of using CSS variables in a responsive design system?

A) They increase code redundancy
B) They enable a centralized, scalable approach to managing design values
C) They require inline styling

D) They are only supported in modern browsers
Correct Answer: B
Explanation: CSS variables allow for centralized control of design tokens, making updates and scalability easier.

Question 25: Which approach is most effective for creating layouts that adjust to both screen size and user preferences?

A) Using fixed layouts with pixel units
B) Combining CSS Grid, Flexbox, media queries, and CSS variables
C) Relying solely on JavaScript for layout changes
D) Using inline styles exclusively

Correct Answer: B
Explanation: A combination of advanced CSS techniques produces highly adaptive and personalized designs.

This comprehensive package for **Chapter 11: Advanced Responsive Web Design Techniques** provides a detailed outline, in-depth chapter content, 10 practical code snippets and examples, 10 hands-on coding exercises with complete code and explanations, and 25 multiple choice questions with detailed explanations. Use these resources to master advanced layout techniques, dark mode integration, dynamic scaling with CSS variables, and best practices for building truly adaptive and responsive websites.

Chapter 12: Building a Complete Responsive Website

Detailed Outline

1. **Introduction**
   - Overview of the project: What you will build and why a complete responsive website is essential.
   - Learning objectives: Planning, structuring, designing, testing, and deploying a website.
2. **Planning a Project**
   - Defining project goals and requirements.
   - Creating a wireframe or mockup.
   - Outlining the content and features (navigation, sections, forms, etc.).
3. **Setting Up an HTML & CSS Structure**
   - Building the basic HTML document with semantic elements.
   - Organizing CSS files (reset, base, layout, components).
   - Including meta tags (viewport) for responsive behavior.
4. **Applying Responsive Design Principles**
   - Using a fluid grid and flexible images.
   - Applying media queries for different breakpoints.
   - Incorporating CSS frameworks if desired (optional).
5. **Adding Navigation, Content Sections, and Forms**
   - Creating a responsive navigation menu (header).
   - Structuring content sections (hero, about, services, etc.) using semantic elements.
   - Building accessible and mobile-friendly forms.

6. **Testing Across Different Screen Sizes**
    - Using browser developer tools and responsive design mode.
    - Testing on physical devices.
    - Debugging layout issues and refining design.
7. **Deploying Your Website Online**
    - Choosing a hosting platform (GitHub Pages, Netlify, Vercel, etc.).
    - Preparing your files for deployment (minification, image optimization).
    - Publishing your website and monitoring performance.
8. **Conclusion and Next Steps**
    - Recap of the entire process.
    - Best practices for maintenance and future updates.
    - Resources for further learning (advanced features, performance, SEO).

Chapter Content

1. Introduction

In this final chapter, you will combine all the skills you've learned to build a complete responsive website. You will plan the project, set up a structured HTML and CSS codebase, and apply responsive design principles to ensure that your website looks great on all devices. Finally, you'll test your site thoroughly and deploy it online for the world to see.

2. Planning a Project

Begin by outlining your website's purpose and requirements. Create wireframes or mockups that define the layout and structure. Decide on the essential components such as a navigation menu, hero section, content areas, and contact forms. This planning phase sets a clear roadmap for your project.

3. Setting Up an HTML & CSS Structure

Start with a basic HTML5 document that includes the necessary meta tags for responsiveness. Organize your CSS into logical sections — such as resets, base styles, layout rules, and component-specific styles — to keep your project maintainable.

4. Applying Responsive Design Principles

Apply a fluid grid system and flexible images to ensure your website adapts to various screen sizes. Use media queries to modify styles at specific breakpoints, ensuring that typography, spacing, and layouts adjust for optimal readability and usability.

5. Adding Navigation, Content Sections, and Forms

Build a responsive navigation bar at the top of your page using semantic elements. Create content sections (like hero banners, about sections, and service areas) and include a well-designed, accessible form for user interactions. Each component should follow responsive design best practices to function across devices.

6. Testing Across Different Screen Sizes

Use browser tools (such as Chrome DevTools) to simulate various devices and screen sizes. Test on actual mobile devices if possible. Identify and fix layout issues, ensuring that your website delivers a consistent and user-friendly experience regardless of device.

7. Deploying Your Website Online

Once your site is complete and thoroughly tested, deploy it online. Choose a hosting service like GitHub Pages, Netlify, or Vercel for simple and free deployment options. Optimize your files (minify CSS/JS, compress images) before deployment to enhance performance.

8. Conclusion and Next Steps

Congratulations on building a complete responsive website! In this chapter, you planned, developed, tested, and deployed your site. As you continue your journey, keep exploring advanced topics such as performance optimization, progressive web apps, and SEO best practices to further enhance your website.

10 Code Snippets and Examples

Basic HTML5 Boilerplate with Responsive Meta Tag

```
<!DOCTYPE html>
<html lang="en">
<head>
  <meta charset="UTF-8">
  <meta name="viewport"
content="width=device-width, initial-
scale=1.0">
  <title>My Responsive Website</title>
  <link rel="stylesheet" href="styles.css">
</head>
<body>
  <!-- Content goes here -->
</body>
</html>
```

1. *Explanation:* Sets up a basic HTML document with the viewport meta tag for responsiveness.

CSS Reset and Base Styles

```
/* styles.css */
* { margin: 0; padding: 0; box-sizing:
border-box; }
body { font-family: Arial, sans-serif;
line-height: 1.6; }
```

2. *Explanation:* Resets default browser styles and establishes a base style for the body.

Fluid Grid Layout Using Flexbox for Header Navigation

```
<header>
  <nav class="nav-container">
    <a href="#">Home</a>
    <a href="#">About</a>
    <a href="#">Services</a>
    <a href="#">Contact</a>
  </nav>
</header>
.nav-container {
```

```css
  display: flex;
  justify-content: space-around;
  background: #333;
  padding: 10px;
}
.nav-container a { color: #fff; text-
decoration: none; }
```

3. *Explanation:* Creates a simple, responsive navigation
   bar using Flexbox.

Responsive Hero Section with Background Image

```html
<section class="hero">
  <h1>Welcome to My Site</h1>
</section>
```

```css
.hero {
  background: url('hero.jpg') center/cover
no-repeat;
  height: 60vh;
  display: flex;
  justify-content: center;
  align-items: center;
  color: #fff;
}
```

4. *Explanation:* Uses a background image that scales
   responsively with viewport height.

Responsive Content Sections Using CSS Grid

```html
<main class="content-grid">
  <section>Section 1</section>
  <section>Section 2</section>
  <section>Section 3</section>
</main>
```

```css
.content-grid {
  display: grid;
  grid-template-columns: 1fr;
  gap: 20px;
  padding: 20px;
}
```

```css
@media (min-width: 768px) {
  .content-grid { grid-template-columns:
repeat(3, 1fr); }
}
```

5. *Explanation:* Adjusts from a single-column layout to a three-column grid on larger screens.

Responsive Contact Form

```html
<form class="contact-form">
  <label for="name">Name:</label>
  <input type="text" id="name" name="name">
  <label for="email">Email:</label>
  <input type="email" id="email"
name="email">
  <label for="message">Message:</label>
  <textarea id="message"
name="message"></textarea>
  <button type="submit">Submit</button>
</form>
```

```css
.contact-form {
  max-width: 500px;
  margin: 20px auto;
  padding: 20px;
  border: 1px solid #ccc;
  background: #f9f9f9;
}
.contact-form input, .contact-form
textarea, .contact-form button {
  width: 100%;
  padding: 10px;
  margin-top: 10px;
}
```

6. *Explanation:* Creates a mobile-friendly, full-width contact form.

Responsive Table with Overflow Scroll

```html
<div class="table-wrapper">
  <table>
```

```html
      <thead>

<tr><th>Name</th><th>Age</th><th>City</th></tr>
      </thead>
      <tbody>
        <tr><td>Alice</td><td>30</td><td>New York</td></tr>
        <tr><td>Bob</td><td>25</td><td>Los Angeles</td></tr>
      </tbody>
    </table>
</div>
```
```css
.table-wrapper {
  overflow-x: auto;
}
table {
  width: 100%;
  border-collapse: collapse;
}
th, td {
  border: 1px solid #ccc;
  padding: 10px;
  text-align: left;
}
```

7. *Explanation:* Wraps a table in a container to allow horizontal scrolling on small screens.

Media Query Example for Adjusting Typography

```css
body { font-size: 16px; }
@media (min-width: 768px) {
  body { font-size: 18px; }
}
```

8. *Explanation:* Increases the base font size on larger screens for better readability.

Using CSS Variables for Consistent Spacing and Colors

```css
:root {
```

```css
  --primary-color: #007bff;
  --base-padding: 10px;
}
body { padding: var(--base-padding); }
header { background: var(--primary-color);
color: #fff; padding: var(--base-padding);
}
```

9. *Explanation:* Sets up CSS custom properties for a consistent theme and spacing.

Complete HTML Structure Example

```html
<!DOCTYPE html>
<html lang="en">
<head>
  <meta charset="UTF-8">
  <meta name="viewport"
content="width=device-width, initial-scale=1.0">
  <title>Complete Responsive
Website</title>
  <link rel="stylesheet" href="styles.css">
</head>
<body>
  <header>
    <nav class="nav-container">
      <a href="#">Home</a>
      <a href="#">About</a>
      <a href="#">Services</a>
      <a href="#">Contact</a>
    </nav>
  </header>
  <section class="hero">
    <h1>Welcome to My Responsive Site</h1>
  </section>
  <main class="content-grid">
    <section>Section 1 Content</section>
    <section>Section 2 Content</section>
```

```html
    <section>Section 3 Content</section>
  </main>
  <section>
    <h2>Contact Us</h2>
    <form class="contact-form">
      <label for="name">Name:</label>
      <input type="text" id="name"
name="name">
      <label for="email">Email:</label>
      <input type="email" id="email"
name="email">
      <label for="message">Message:</label>
      <textarea id="message"
name="message"></textarea>
      <button type="submit">Submit</button>
    </form>
  </section>
  <section class="table-wrapper">
    <table>
      <thead>

<tr><th>Name</th><th>Age</th><th>City</th><
/tr>
      </thead>
      <tbody>

<tr><td>Alice</td><td>30</td><td>New
York</td></tr>
        <tr><td>Bob</td><td>25</td><td>Los
Angeles</td></tr>
      </tbody>
    </table>
  </section>
  <footer>
    <p>&copy; 2025 My Responsive Site</p>
  </footer>
```

```
</body>
</html>
```

    10. *Explanation:* A complete responsive website structure integrating navigation, hero, content sections, a contact form, and a responsive table.

25 Multiple Choice Questions with Full Explanations

Question 1: What is the first step in building a complete responsive website?

    A) Deploying the website
    B) Planning the project and creating a wireframe
    C) Writing custom JavaScript
    D) Choosing a hosting platform
    Correct Answer: B
    Explanation: Planning and wireframing are essential to outline your design and functionality before coding.

Question 2: Which meta tag is crucial for responsive design?

    A) `<meta charset="UTF-8">`
    B) `<meta name="viewport" content="width=device-width, initial-scale=1.0">`
    C) `<meta name="description" content="...">`
    D) `<meta name="keywords" content="...">`
    Correct Answer: B
    Explanation: The viewport meta tag controls scaling and dimensions on mobile devices.

Question 3: What is one benefit of using CSS frameworks in building responsive websites?

    A) They eliminate the need for HTML
    B) They provide prebuilt components and grid systems for rapid development
    C) They automatically generate content

D) They increase file sizes significantly

Correct Answer: B

Explanation: Frameworks speed up development with prebuilt responsive components.

Question 4: In a responsive design, which layout method is ideal for arranging content in a grid?

A) Float-based layout

B) CSS Grid

C) Inline styles

D) Table layout

Correct Answer: B

Explanation: CSS Grid is designed for two-dimensional layouts and is ideal for responsive grids.

Question 5: What is the purpose of using media queries in responsive design?

A) To load different HTML files

B) To apply CSS rules based on screen size and device characteristics

C) To execute JavaScript code

D) To change the content of the page

Correct Answer: B

Explanation: Media queries enable conditional styling for different devices.

Question 6: Which of the following is an essential element for a responsive navigation menu?

A) A fixed-width container

B) A flexible grid or flex container

C) Inline JavaScript only

D) A static image

Correct Answer: B

Explanation: Using flex or grid layouts ensures navigation menus adapt to screen sizes.

Question 7: What is the advantage of using a fluid grid system?

A) It uses fixed pixel values

B) It adapts to various screen sizes using relative units

C) It requires no CSS

D) It makes the website load slower

Correct Answer: B

Explanation: A fluid grid uses relative units (like percentages) to adjust layouts dynamically.

Question 8: Which element is commonly used to create a hero section?

A) `<header>`

B) `<section>`

C) `<article>`

D) `<footer>`

Correct Answer: B

Explanation: A hero section is typically a large, eye-catching section at the top of a page, often created with a `<section>` element.

Question 9: Why is testing across different screen sizes important?

A) To ensure consistent user experience across devices

B) To increase the website's complexity

C) To add more images

D) To decrease mobile usability

Correct Answer: A

Explanation: Testing ensures that your website functions well on all devices.

Question 10: What is the purpose of browser developer tools in responsive design?

A) To write HTML code

B) To simulate different screen sizes and debug issues

C) To host the website

D) To add extra CSS

Correct Answer: B

Explanation: Developer tools allow you to test and debug your responsive layouts.

Question 11: Which tag is used to create a form in HTML?

A) `<form>`

B) `<input>`
C) `<fieldset>`
D) `<section>`
Correct Answer: A
Explanation: The `<form>` tag wraps all form controls and is essential for data input.

Question 12: What role do CSS variables play in responsive design?

A) They store reusable values for colors, spacing, and fonts
B) They replace HTML tags
C) They are only used for animations
D) They disable media queries
Correct Answer: A
Explanation: CSS variables allow for centralized, scalable design adjustments.

Question 13: Which approach is best for designing a website for multiple devices?

A) Fixed layout
B) Responsive design using flexible grids, media queries, and scalable assets
C) Desktop-only design
D) Mobile-only design
Correct Answer: B
Explanation: Responsive design techniques ensure a seamless experience on all devices.

Question 14: What is one key consideration when planning a website project?

A) The color of the hosting provider's logo
B) The wireframe and overall structure
C) The number of images only
D) Ignoring user navigation
Correct Answer: B
Explanation: Planning involves creating wireframes and outlining the structure to guide development.

Question 15: Which of the following is an alternative solution for responsive tables?

A) Overflow scroll and table stacking

B) Fixed table layout

C) Removing all table borders

D) Using inline styles exclusively

Correct Answer: A

Explanation: Overflow scrolling and table stacking are effective ways to handle wide tables on small screens.

Question 16: How do you deploy a website online?

A) By using a hosting platform like GitHub Pages, Netlify, or Vercel

B) By emailing the code to yourself

C) By printing the code

D) By using a text editor only

Correct Answer: A

Explanation: Hosting platforms allow you to publish your website so that it is accessible online.

Question 17: What is the purpose of asset optimization (minification, compression) in website performance?

A) To increase file size

B) To reduce load times by decreasing file sizes

C) To make the code harder to read

D) To disable responsive design

Correct Answer: B

Explanation: Optimized assets reduce bandwidth usage and speed up page loading.

Question 18: Which step is essential before deploying your website?

A) Testing across multiple devices and screen sizes

B) Adding extra animations

C) Removing all media queries

D) Increasing the number of HTTP requests

Correct Answer: A

Explanation: Testing ensures your website functions correctly on all target devices.

Question 19: What is one benefit of using a mobile-first approach?

A) It ignores desktop users

B) It optimizes performance on the most constrained devices

C) It requires more CSS

D) It disables media queries

Correct Answer: B

Explanation: Mobile-first design ensures that performance is optimized for devices with limited resources.

Question 20: How does combining CSS Grid and Flexbox benefit your layout design?

A) It allows you to handle both overall page structure and component-level alignment

B) It forces fixed layouts

C) It eliminates the need for responsive design

D) It makes the design less flexible

Correct Answer: A

Explanation: Grid handles two-dimensional layouts while Flexbox excels at aligning content within individual components.

Question 21: Which of the following is a best practice for optimizing images in a responsive website?

A) Using a single image for all devices

B) Serving different image sizes with srcset or the picture element

C) Always using PNG format

D) Not compressing images

Correct Answer: B

Explanation: Serving appropriately sized images reduces load times and data usage.

Question 22: What is the main advantage of using browser caching?

A) It forces the browser to reload every asset on each visit

B) It stores assets locally, reducing load times on subsequent visits

C) It disables media queries

D) It increases server load

Correct Answer: B

Explanation: Browser caching improves performance by reusing previously downloaded assets.

Question 23: Why is it important to include SEO best practices in a responsive website?

A) To increase website complexity

B) To improve search engine rankings and user experience

C) To disable responsive design

D) To slow down page load times

Correct Answer: B

Explanation: SEO best practices contribute to higher rankings and better user experience, which are both influenced by performance.

Question 24: What does testing a website across different screen sizes help ensure?

A) Consistent functionality and layout on all devices

B) That the website only works on desktops

C) That media queries are not needed

D) That all images are removed

Correct Answer: A

Explanation: Cross-device testing confirms that your website adapts correctly to various screen dimensions.

Question 25: What is the final step in building a complete responsive website before deployment?

A) Adding extra code comments

B) Testing, optimizing, and ensuring compatibility across devices

C) Removing all custom CSS

D) Increasing the website's file size

Correct Answer: B

Explanation: Thorough testing and optimization are essential to ensure a smooth user experience and high performance before going live.

This comprehensive package for **Chapter 12: Building a Complete Responsive Website** provides a detailed outline, in-depth chapter content, 10 code snippets and examples, 10 hands-on coding exercises with full code and explanations, and 25 multiple choice questions with detailed explanations. Use these resources to plan, develop, test, and deploy your responsive website confidently.

Chapter 13: Troubleshooting and Debugging Responsive Issues

Detailed Outline

1. **Introduction**
   - **Purpose:**
     - Understand the importance of troubleshooting in responsive design.
     - Learn to identify common responsive design mistakes.
   - **Learning Objectives:**
     - Debug and resolve layout issues.
     - Enhance your design with best practices for troubleshooting.

2. **Common Responsive Design Mistakes**
   - Overly fixed layouts that don't adapt to small screens.
   - Neglecting to set proper viewport meta tags.
   - Not accounting for different font sizes and spacing.
   - Unoptimized images and tables that break layouts.
   - Poor handling of overflow and layout shifts.

3. **Using Browser Developer Tools for Debugging**
   - Inspecting HTML/CSS in real time.
   - Utilizing responsive design mode (e.g., Chrome DevTools).
   - Analyzing computed styles, box model, and network performance.
   - Debugging JavaScript that affects layout.

4. **How to Test Your Site on Different Devices**
   - Using device emulators and browser tools.
   - Testing on physical devices.
   - Utilizing online testing services (e.g., BrowserStack, Responsinator).

5. **Fixing Layout Shifts and Overflow Issues**
    - Identifying and correcting unintended scroll or overflow.
    - Fixing elements that shift unexpectedly (layout reflows).
    - Using CSS techniques like overflow, clear, and media queries to stabilize layouts.
    - Addressing issues with images, grids, and form elements.
6. **Best Practices for Debugging and Improving Designs**
    - Use a mobile-first mindset when troubleshooting.
    - Document issues and changes.
    - Use version control to track changes.
    - Regularly test after changes.
    - Collaborate and seek feedback from peers.
7. **Conclusion & Next Steps**
    - **Summary of What You've Learned:**
        - Key troubleshooting techniques and common pitfalls.
        - Effective use of developer tools.
        - Strategies for testing and fixing responsive issues.
    - **Where to Go Next:**
        - Expanding into advanced JavaScript interactions.
        - Learning CSS frameworks for more efficient design.
        - Exploring UI/UX design principles.
    - **Recommended Resources and Communities:**
        - Online forums, blogs, and courses on responsive design.
        - Communities like Stack Overflow, CSS-Tricks, and GitHub.
    - **Final Project Challenge:**

- Apply all the troubleshooting skills by auditing a live website, identifying issues, and providing a detailed plan to fix them.

25 Multiple Choice Questions with Full Explanations

Question 1: What is a common mistake in responsive design?

A) Using fluid grids
B) Relying solely on fixed pixel values
C) Using media queries
D) Optimizing images

Correct Answer: B

Explanation: Fixed pixel values often cause layouts to break on smaller screens, making responsiveness difficult.

Question 2: Which meta tag is critical for responsive design?

A) `<meta charset="UTF-8">`
B) `<meta name="viewport" content="width=device-width, initial-scale=1.0">`
C) `<meta name="description" content="...">`
D) `<meta name="keywords" content="...">`

Correct Answer: B

Explanation: The viewport meta tag tells browsers how to control the page's dimensions and scaling on mobile devices.

Question 3: What is one of the most common responsive design mistakes?

A) Using semantic HTML
B) Overloading pages with unnecessary CSS and JavaScript
C) Using relative units

D) Optimizing images
Correct Answer: B
Explanation: Including unnecessary CSS/JS can slow down the site and create issues on various devices.

Question 4: Which tool is most commonly used to inspect and debug responsive layouts?

A) Microsoft Word
B) Chrome DevTools
C) Adobe Photoshop
D) Notepad

Correct Answer: B
Explanation: Chrome DevTools provides features like responsive mode and element inspection, making it ideal for debugging.

Question 5: How can you simulate different device sizes in your browser?

A) Using responsive design mode in developer tools
B) Changing your screen resolution
C) Using a text editor
D) Editing HTML directly

Correct Answer: A
Explanation: Developer tools have built-in responsive design modes to simulate various screen sizes and orientations.

Question 6: What does the overflow property help with in debugging?

A) It sets the background color
B) It manages content that exceeds its container's boundaries
C) It increases font size
D) It fixes broken images

Correct Answer: B
Explanation: The overflow property controls what happens when content exceeds the dimensions of its container.

Question 7: Which technique can help fix layout shifts?

A) Removing media queries
B) Using fixed positioning without care

C) Setting proper height and width values and using CSS transitions

D) Ignoring responsive design

Correct Answer: C

Explanation: Setting explicit dimensions and smooth transitions can reduce unexpected layout shifts.

Question 8: What is a benefit of testing your site on physical devices?

A) Emulators always give perfect results

B) They help you catch real-world issues that emulators might miss

C) They are not necessary if you use Chrome DevTools

D) They increase development time without benefits

Correct Answer: B

Explanation: Physical devices reveal issues like touch interactions and actual performance that emulators might not simulate accurately.

Question 9: Which approach is recommended for diagnosing responsive issues?

A) Guesswork

B) Systematic use of browser developer tools

C) Relying on outdated browsers

D) Only testing on desktop

Correct Answer: B

Explanation: Developer tools allow you to inspect elements, check computed styles, and simulate different devices to diagnose issues.

Question 10: What is a layout shift?

A) When elements reposition unexpectedly during page load

B) When text changes color

C) When images are not optimized

D) When CSS files are not minified

Correct Answer: A

Explanation: Layout shifts occur when page elements move around unexpectedly, often causing poor user experience.

Question 11: Which practice can help reduce layout shifts?

A) Not specifying image dimensions

B) Setting explicit width and height attributes for images

C) Using only inline styles

D) Removing all CSS transitions

Correct Answer: B

Explanation: Specifying image dimensions helps browsers allocate the proper space before the image loads, reducing layout shifts.

Question 12: What is one common cause of overflow issues in responsive design?

A) Using flexible images

B) Fixed-width elements that exceed the viewport

C) Using media queries

D) Optimizing JavaScript

Correct Answer: B

Explanation: Fixed-width elements can extend beyond their container, causing horizontal scrolling or overflow issues.

Question 13: How can you debug JavaScript that affects layout?

A) Using browser console and breakpoints in developer tools

B) Reading the HTML source code

C) Checking server logs

D) Rewriting all JavaScript

Correct Answer: A

Explanation: Browser consoles and breakpoints allow you to step through code and identify issues affecting layout.

Question 14: What does "table stacking" refer to in responsive design?

A) Converting table rows into block elements for better display on small screens

B) Using multiple tables together

C) Creating a table with fixed columns

D) Hiding table headers

Correct Answer: A

Explanation: Table stacking reorganizes table data into a vertical format that's easier to read on narrow screens.

Question 15: Which browser tool can be used to simulate different network speeds?

A) Chrome DevTools Network panel

B) Microsoft Word

C) Adobe Illustrator

D) Notepad

Correct Answer: A

Explanation: The Network panel in Chrome DevTools can throttle network speeds, helping you simulate slow connections.

Question 16: What is a recommended best practice for debugging responsive issues?

A) Only test on desktop

B) Use version control and document your changes

C) Avoid using media queries

D) Always use fixed units

Correct Answer: B

Explanation: Documenting changes and using version control ensures that you can track and revert changes when necessary.

Question 17: What is one tool you can use for performance testing of responsive websites?

A) Google Lighthouse

B) Microsoft Excel

C) Adobe Photoshop

D) Notepad++

Correct Answer: A

Explanation: Google Lighthouse audits performance, accessibility, SEO, and more, offering actionable insights.

Question 18: Why is it important to test a responsive website on multiple devices?

A) To ensure consistency in layout and functionality across various screen sizes
B) To increase page complexity
C) To reduce the need for CSS
D) To show more ads
Correct Answer: A
Explanation: Testing on multiple devices ensures that the site functions and appears as intended for all users.

Question 19: Which of the following is a best practice for troubleshooting layout issues?
A) Ignoring the box model
B) Using the element inspector to review computed styles and dimensions
C) Deleting all custom CSS
D) Disabling media queries
Correct Answer: B
Explanation: The element inspector helps you understand how CSS is affecting layout and identify issues.

Question 20: What is a final project challenge suggested in this chapter?
A) Building a static website with fixed dimensions
B) Auditing a live website for responsive issues and creating a detailed fix plan
C) Removing all CSS and JavaScript
D) Ignoring performance metrics
Correct Answer: B
Explanation: The final challenge is to apply your debugging skills to a live project, identify issues, and propose solutions.

Question 21: Which common responsive mistake often leads to horizontal scrolling?
A) Using max-width: 100% on images
B) Fixed-width elements that exceed the viewport
C) Using flexible layouts

D) Applying media queries

Correct Answer: B

Explanation: Fixed-width elements can cause overflow, resulting in unwanted horizontal scrolling.

Question 22: What does the term "layout shift" refer to?

A) A planned design change

B) Unexpected movement of elements during page load

C) A change in color scheme

D) The use of media queries

Correct Answer: B

Explanation: Layout shifts occur when elements move unexpectedly, often due to delayed resource loading.

Question 23: Which of the following is an example of a responsive design mistake?

A) Using relative units for fonts

B) Not setting a viewport meta tag

C) Testing on multiple devices

D) Applying overflow: auto to a container

Correct Answer: B

Explanation: Omitting the viewport meta tag prevents proper scaling on mobile devices.

Question 24: What role does version control play in debugging responsive issues?

A) It tracks changes and allows you to revert problematic updates

B) It automatically fixes layout issues

C) It increases file size

D) It disables responsive design

Correct Answer: A

Explanation: Version control is essential for tracking changes and troubleshooting issues by reverting to previous versions if necessary.

Question 25: What should be your final step after troubleshooting and debugging your responsive website?

A) Deploy the website without further testing

B) Document the fixes, test on multiple devices, and then deploy

C) Remove all media queries

D) Increase the number of images

Correct Answer: B

Explanation: Comprehensive testing and documentation ensure that all issues have been resolved before deploying the site.

This comprehensive package for **Chapter 13: Troubleshooting and Debugging Responsive Issues** includes a detailed outline to guide your learning and 25 multiple-choice questions with full explanations. Use these resources to master the techniques for identifying, diagnosing, and fixing responsive design issues, and to plan your next steps in web development.

Chapter 14: Conclusion and Final Assessment

Congratulations on reaching the end of your journey through responsive web design! In this final chapter, we'll review the key concepts covered throughout the book, discuss best practices and next steps, and present a final assessment to test your mastery of the material. This chapter is designed to help you reflect on what you've learned and to challenge you with 50 multiple choice questions. Each question is accompanied by a detailed explanation to reinforce your understanding and help you identify areas for further study.

Chapter Overview

Throughout this book, you have learned how to build modern, responsive websites using HTML5 and CSS3. Here's a brief recap of what we covered:

- **Introduction to Responsive Web Design:**
  We defined responsive web design (RWD) and discussed its importance in today's mobile-first world. You learned how the web evolved and the core technologies (HTML5 and CSS3) that power responsive sites.

- **HTML5 and CSS3 Fundamentals:**
  We explored the structure of an HTML document, learned about semantic elements, and mastered the basics of CSS syntax, selectors, and the box model.

- **Responsive Design Principles:**
  You discovered how fluid grids, flexible images, and media queries form the backbone of responsive design. We also examined techniques for creating responsive typography and images.

- **Navigation, Forms, and Tables:**
  We built responsive navigation menus (including hamburger menus), designed mobile-friendly forms with accessibility in mind, and learned methods to make tables adapt to various screen sizes.

415

- **CSS Frameworks:**
  An overview of popular frameworks like Bootstrap and Tailwind CSS showed you how to rapidly prototype and build responsive websites while still offering the possibility to customize designs.
- **Performance Optimization:**
  We discussed strategies for reducing unnecessary CSS/JS, optimizing images, lazy loading, asset compression, browser caching, and SEO best practices to boost your site's performance.
- **Advanced Responsive Techniques:**
  You learned advanced CSS Grid and Flexbox techniques, combined layout systems for robust designs, and explored dark mode implementation, viewport meta tag usage, and CSS variables for scalable design.
- **Troubleshooting and Debugging:**
  We provided guidance on identifying common responsive issues, using browser developer tools, testing on various devices, and applying best practices for debugging and improving your designs.
- **Building a Complete Responsive Website:**
  You received an end-to-end walkthrough of planning, developing, testing, and deploying a responsive website—preparing you for real-world projects.

Next Steps

Now that you've built a strong foundation in responsive web design, here are a few suggestions for further exploration:

- **Advanced JavaScript:** Enhance interactivity and dynamic content.
- **CSS Frameworks and UI/UX:** Explore more on Bootstrap, Tailwind CSS, and advanced UI/UX design.
- **Performance Optimization:** Continue refining your optimization skills to create lightning-fast websites.

- **Community Engagement:** Join communities like Stack Overflow, CSS-Tricks, and GitHub to share your work and learn from others.

For your final project challenge, consider auditing a live website, identifying responsive issues, and creating a detailed plan for improvements. This will consolidate your learning and prepare you for professional work.

Final Assessment: 50 Multiple Choice Questions

Below are 50 multiple choice questions covering all topics from this book. Each question includes a detailed explanation of the correct answer to help you review and solidify your understanding.

What is Responsive Web Design (RWD)?

    A) Designing websites for desktops only

    B) Creating websites that adapt to various screen sizes and devices

    C) A technique to make websites load faster

    D) Using only fixed-width layouts

Correct Answer: B

Explanation: RWD ensures that a website's layout and content adjust fluidly to different screen sizes, providing an optimal user experience on all devices.*

Why is Responsive Web Design important?

    A) It makes the website look the same on all devices

    B) It enhances user experience and improves SEO

    C) It reduces server load exclusively

    D) It is required for desktop browsers only

Correct Answer: B

Explanation: Responsive design improves usability on mobile devices and is a key factor in search engine rankings.*

Which HTML5 element is used to denote the main content of a document?

    A) `<header>`

    B) `<footer>`

    C) `<main>`

D) `<section>`

Correct Answer: C

Explanation: The `<main>` element is specifically designed to contain the primary content of a page.*

What is the purpose of the viewport meta tag?

    A) To specify the character encoding

    B) To control the page's dimensions and scaling on mobile devices

    C) To link external stylesheets

    D) To set default browser settings

Correct Answer: B

Explanation: The viewport meta tag tells the browser how to adjust the page's dimensions and scaling for different devices.*

Which unit is considered relative in CSS?

    A) px

    B) em

    C) pt

    D) cm

Correct Answer: B

Explanation: The "em" unit is relative to the font-size of its parent, making it ideal for scalable designs.*

What does the CSS property `box-sizing: border-box;` do?

    A) Excludes padding and border from the element's width

    B) Includes padding and border in the element's total width and height

    C) Sets a fixed width for the element

    D) Hides the border

Correct Answer: B

Explanation: This property includes padding and border in the element's dimensions, simplifying layout calculations.*

Which CSS layout module is primarily used for one-dimensional layouts?

    A) CSS Grid

    B) Flexbox

    C) Table layout

D) Float

Correct Answer: B

Explanation: Flexbox is designed for one-dimensional layouts, either in a row or column.*

What is the key feature of CSS Grid?

    A) It only works on mobile devices

    B) It is used for two-dimensional layouts, managing rows and columns

    C) It replaces Flexbox completely

    D) It is an outdated technique

Correct Answer: B

Explanation: CSS Grid is ideal for creating complex two-dimensional layouts.*

Which of the following is an example of a media query?

    A) `@media (max-width: 600px) { ... }`

    B) `@viewport (max-width: 600px) { ... }`

    C) `@responsive (600px) { ... }`

    D) `@screen (600px) { ... }`

Correct Answer: A

Explanation: The correct syntax for a media query uses `@media` with a condition, such as `(max-width: 600px)`.*

Which attribute allows an image to be lazy loaded?

    A) `loading="lazy"`

    B) `srcset="lazy"`

    C) `data-lazy="true"`

    D) `lazyload="on"`

Correct Answer: A

Explanation: The `loading="lazy"` attribute defers the loading of the image until it is close to entering the viewport.*

What does the `srcset` attribute do in an `<img>` tag?

    A) Specifies alternative text

    B) Provides multiple image sources for different resolutions

    C) Sets the image width

    D) Styles the image border

Correct Answer: B

Explanation: The `srcset` attribute allows the browser to choose the most appropriate image based on device resolution and viewport size.*

Which element is used to serve different images based on device characteristics?

    A) `<picture>`
    B) `<img>`
    C) `<source>`
    D) `<figure>`

Correct Answer: A

Explanation: The `<picture>` element lets you specify different image sources using `<source>` elements, each with media conditions.*

What is one of the primary benefits of a mobile-first approach?

    A) It creates fixed layouts
    B) It optimizes performance on devices with limited resources
    C) It disables media queries
    D) It eliminates the need for CSS

Correct Answer: B

Explanation: Mobile-first design ensures that the website is optimized for smaller screens and less powerful devices.*

Which browser tool is most effective for debugging responsive issues?

    A) Chrome DevTools
    B) Microsoft Paint
    C) Adobe Acrobat
    D) Notepad

Correct Answer: A

Explanation: Chrome DevTools offers features like responsive mode, element inspection, and network performance analysis.*

What is a common cause of layout shifts in responsive design?

    A) Specifying explicit image dimensions
    B) Delayed loading of fonts and images

C) Using relative units for spacing

D) Including a viewport meta tag

Correct Answer: B

Explanation: Delayed resource loading, such as fonts and images, can cause unexpected layout shifts during page load.*

Which property can help control overflow issues in layouts?

A) `overflow: hidden;`

B) `display: none;`

C) `visibility: collapse;`

D) `position: relative;`

Correct Answer: A

Explanation: The `overflow` property controls how content that exceeds an element's dimensions is handled, preventing unwanted scrolling.*

Which of the following is a best practice for debugging responsive issues?

A) Only testing on desktop

B) Using both device emulators and physical devices for testing

C) Ignoring performance metrics

D) Relying solely on screenshots

Correct Answer: B

Explanation: Testing on both emulators and real devices helps catch issues that may not be apparent in a single testing environment.*

Which HTTP header is commonly used to control browser caching?

A) Cache-Control

B) Content-Type

C) Set-Cookie

D) Content-Length

Correct Answer: A

Explanation: The Cache-Control header instructs the browser how to cache resources, improving load times on subsequent visits.*

Which tool can help you measure website performance and identify optimization opportunities?

    A) Google Lighthouse

    B) Adobe Illustrator

    C) Microsoft Word

    D) Slack

Correct Answer: A

Explanation: Google Lighthouse audits performance, accessibility, SEO, and more, providing actionable recommendations.*

What is the main purpose of asset compression (e.g., Gzip, Brotli)?

    A) To improve code readability

    B) To reduce file sizes and improve load times

    C) To add extra features

    D) To increase the number of HTTP requests

Correct Answer: B

Explanation: Compressing assets decreases file sizes, which speeds up page loading.*

Which of the following is a key factor in SEO for responsive websites?

    A) The number of images

    B) Page load speed

    C) The use of Flash

    D) Fixed layouts

Correct Answer: B

Explanation: Faster load times improve user experience and are a significant ranking factor for search engines.*

Which practice helps reduce unnecessary CSS and JavaScript?

    A) Keeping all code in a single file

    B) Using tools like PurgeCSS or UnCSS

    C) Adding more comments

    D) Duplicating code across files

Correct Answer: B

Explanation: Tools like PurgeCSS remove unused styles, reducing file sizes and improving performance.*

What does lazy loading do?

A) Loads all images immediately
B) Defers loading of off-screen images until needed
C) Increases image resolution
D) Disables CSS

Correct Answer: B

Explanation: Lazy loading delays the loading of images until they are about to be viewed, improving initial load time.*

What is the purpose of using responsive design testing tools like BrowserStack?

A) To write CSS code
B) To simulate your website on multiple devices and browsers
C) To edit HTML files
D) To deploy your website

Correct Answer: B

Explanation: These tools help you test your responsive design across various devices and browsers.*

Which method can be used to fix horizontal scrolling issues on mobile?

A) Using fixed widths for all elements
B) Setting max-width: 100% on images and containers
C) Removing all media queries
D) Using inline styles exclusively

Correct Answer: B

Explanation: Ensuring elements don't exceed their container's width prevents unwanted horizontal scrolling.*

What is a common cause of layout overflow?

A) Using relative units for dimensions
B) Fixed-width elements exceeding the viewport width
C) Using the box-sizing property
D) Setting width: 100% on images

Correct Answer: B

Explanation: Fixed-width elements can force the layout to exceed the viewport, causing overflow issues.*

Which CSS property can help maintain the aspect ratio of an image?

>A) width: auto;
>
>B) height: auto;
>
>C) max-width: 100%;
>
>D) All of the above

Correct Answer: D

Explanation: Combining these properties ensures that images scale proportionally with their container.*

What does the term "critical rendering path" refer to?

>A) The steps a browser takes to render a webpage
>
>B) The path to the website's CSS file
>
>C) A type of CSS selector
>
>D) A JavaScript function

Correct Answer: A

Explanation: It refers to the sequence of steps the browser follows to convert HTML, CSS, and JavaScript into pixels on the screen.*

Which of the following is a best practice when debugging responsive websites?

>A) Only testing on desktop
>
>B) Using both developer tools and physical device testing
>
>C) Ignoring error messages
>
>D) Relying solely on screenshots

Correct Answer: B

Explanation: Combining tools and real-device testing provides a more comprehensive understanding of issues.*

Which attribute is used to describe an image for accessibility?

>A) src
>
>B) alt
>
>C) title
>
>D) href

Correct Answer: B

Explanation: The alt attribute provides alternative text that is important for screen readers and accessibility.*

Which layout system is most effective for creating a multi-column design?

 A) Flexbox
 B) CSS Grid
 C) Float-based layouts
 D) Inline-block

Correct Answer: B

Explanation: CSS Grid is designed to handle two-dimensional layouts, making it ideal for multi-column designs.*

What does the term "mobile-first" imply?

 A) Designing exclusively for mobile devices
 B) Building the base design for mobile and enhancing for larger screens
 C) Creating separate websites for mobile and desktop
 D) Using fixed layouts

Correct Answer: B

Explanation: Mobile-first means starting with the smallest screen and progressively enhancing the design for larger devices.*

Which of the following is a tool for performance testing of responsive websites?

 A) Google Lighthouse
 B) Adobe Photoshop
 C) Microsoft Word
 D) Notepad++

Correct Answer: A

Explanation: Google Lighthouse audits performance, accessibility, and SEO, providing actionable feedback.*

How does using CSS variables improve maintainability?

 A) They increase code duplication
 B) They allow centralized management of design values
 C) They require inline styles
 D) They disable media queries

Correct Answer: B

Explanation: CSS variables let you manage colors, spacing, and fonts in one place, making updates easier.*

Which tool can simulate different network speeds to test performance?

    A) Chrome DevTools Network panel

    B) Adobe Illustrator

    C) Microsoft Excel

    D) Slack

Correct Answer: A

Explanation: The Network panel in Chrome DevTools can throttle network speeds, simulating slow connections.*

What is a key benefit of using lazy loading for images?

    A) It increases initial load time

    B) It defers the loading of images not immediately in view

    C) It makes images appear immediately

    D) It removes the need for alt text

Correct Answer: B

Explanation: Lazy loading reduces the initial load time by loading images only when needed.*

Which technique is used to serve images of different resolutions?

    A) Using a single image

    B) Using srcset and the picture element

    C) Using inline CSS

    D) Using JavaScript only

Correct Answer: B

Explanation: srcset and the picture element allow the browser to select the best image based on device resolution.*

What is the purpose of asset compression (e.g., Gzip, Brotli)?

    A) To increase file size

    B) To reduce file size and speed up loading times

    C) To add animations

    D) To convert CSS to JavaScript

Correct Answer: B

Explanation: Compression minimizes file sizes, which reduces download times and improves performance.*

How can browser caching improve website performance?

    A) By forcing all assets to reload on every visit

    B) By storing resources locally to reduce repeated downloads

    C) By increasing the number of HTTP requests

    D) By disabling media queries

Correct Answer: B

Explanation: Caching allows frequently used resources to be stored locally, reducing load times on subsequent visits.*

Which HTTP header is used to control browser caching?

    A) Content-Type

    B) Cache-Control

    C) Set-Cookie

    D) Content-Length

Correct Answer: B

Explanation: Cache-Control headers instruct the browser on how long to cache resources.*

What is a common responsive design mistake?

    A) Using flexible units

    B) Using fixed-width elements that exceed the viewport

    C) Implementing media queries

    D) Optimizing images

Correct Answer: B

Explanation: Fixed-width elements can cause overflow and horizontal scrolling on small screens.*

Which approach should you take when planning a responsive website?

    A) Ignore mobile devices

    B) Create wireframes and define content hierarchy for all devices

    C) Design only for desktops

    D) Use only inline styles

Correct Answer: B

Explanation: Proper planning and wireframing ensure that your design meets the needs of users on every device.*

Which of the following is a benefit of testing on real devices?

    A) Emulators always catch every issue

    B) Real devices can reveal touch interaction and performance issues

    C) It is unnecessary if you use Chrome DevTools

    D) It slows down development

Correct Answer: B

Explanation: Physical testing provides insights that emulators might miss, such as actual performance and touch behavior.*

What does "overflow: auto;" do when applied to a container?

    A) Hides overflowing content

    B) Adds a scrollbar if the content exceeds the container's bounds

    C) Forces content to expand

    D) Removes the content

Correct Answer: B

Explanation: Overflow auto allows scrolling if the content overflows the container.*

Which element is used to wrap a responsive table for horizontal scrolling?

    A) `<div>` with overflow-x: auto

    B) `<span>`

    C) `<header>`

    D) `<footer>`

Correct Answer: A

Explanation: Wrapping a table in a `<div>` with overflow-x: auto enables horizontal scrolling on small screens.*

What is the benefit of minifying CSS and JavaScript?

    A) It makes the code more readable

    B) It reduces file sizes and speeds up load times

    C) It increases the file size

    D) It adds extra comments

Correct Answer: B

Explanation: Minification removes unnecessary whitespace and comments, reducing file sizes for faster loading.*

Which of the following is a best practice for debugging responsive issues?

    A) Only checking on one device

    B) Using browser developer tools to inspect elements and test different screen sizes

    C) Avoiding CSS variables

    D) Removing all media queries

Correct Answer: B

Explanation: Developer tools help you inspect CSS, simulate devices, and identify responsive issues.*

Which of these is an effective tool for version control during development?

    A) Git

    B) FTP

    C) Email

    D) Notepad

Correct Answer: A

Explanation: Git tracks changes, allowing you to revert problematic updates and collaborate efficiently.*

What is the purpose of a final project challenge in a learning resource?

    A) To increase the workload

    B) To apply all learned skills in a real-world scenario

    C) To skip testing

    D) To focus only on theory

Correct Answer: B

Explanation: The final project challenge consolidates your knowledge and prepares you for professional work.*

What should be your final step before deploying your responsive website?

    A) Skipping browser tests

    B) Comprehensive testing, optimization, and documentation

    C) Removing all CSS

    D) Ignoring feedback

Correct Answer: B

Explanation: Thorough testing and optimization ensure your website is fully functional and performant across all devices before launch.*

Conclusion

In this final chapter, we reviewed the most common responsive design challenges and explored effective troubleshooting and debugging strategies. You've learned how to use browser developer tools, test your site on multiple devices, fix layout shifts and overflow issues, and apply best practices for continuous improvement. The 50 multiple choice questions provided in this chapter are designed to reinforce your learning, identify areas for further review, and ensure you're well-prepared for real-world projects.

As you move forward, continue to refine your skills, explore advanced topics, and engage with the web development community. Whether you decide to dive deeper into JavaScript, experiment with CSS frameworks, or focus on UI/UX design, your journey into responsive web design has only just begun.

Thank you for joining this adventure.

About the Author

Laurence Lars Svekis is a distinguished web developer, educator, and best-selling author, renowned for his expertise in HTML, CSS, and modern web design. With over two decades of experience in front-end development, Laurence has dedicated his career to teaching and empowering aspiring web designers through hands-on exercises, practical projects, and in-depth learning resources.

Specializing in HTML and CSS, Laurence has helped thousands of students master the fundamentals of web page structure, styling, and responsive design. His teaching approach focuses on clear explanations, real-world applications, and step-by-step coding exercises, making complex web development concepts easy to grasp. From semantic HTML and accessible web design to advanced CSS techniques like Flexbox, Grid, and animations, Laurence provides learners with the tools they need to create professional, visually appealing websites. With over one million students worldwide, his courses, books, and live workshops have become a go-to resource for beginners and experienced developers alike. His interactive teaching style, enriched with coding challenges and design projects, ensures that learners gain practical skills to build stunning, functional websites.

Beyond teaching, Laurence is an active member of the web design community, contributing to educational resources, open-source projects, and industry discussions. His passion for innovation and accessibility in web design continues to inspire thousands to pursue their goals in creating and enhancing the digital web.

To explore more of Laurence's work, access additional learning materials, and connect with him, visit BaseScripts.com.

www.ingramcontent.com/pod-product-compliance
Lightning Source LLC
LaVergne TN
LVHW051220050326
832903LV00028B/2180